Perfec

SCOTLAND

Travel with Insider Tips

www.marco-polo.com

Contents

 TOP 10   4

That Scotland Feeling   6

For chapters: See inside front cover

Not to be missed!
Our TOP 10 hits – from the absolute No. 1 to No. 10 –
help you plan your tour of the most important sights.

⭐1 SKYE & OUTER HEBRIDES ► 150

Solitary mountains, rugged cliffs, dark lochs and broad white beaches make each of the Western Isles (pictured left) a unique Highlands experience.

⭐2 NEW TOWN ► 52

The Georgian New Town looks like it was cast in a huge mould. This is where Edinburgh's glittering new age began – and it still sparkles for those who like to stroll or shop.

⭐3 EDINBURGH CASTLE ► 55

Enthroned on the edge of a rock wall at the top of the medieval Royal Mile, this king of all castles towers over the town of seven volcanic hills.

⭐4 THE ROAD TO THE ISLES ► 155

From Ben Nevis to the islands, the roads and railway lines meander through glistening glens and past magnificent lochs – an awe-inspiring trip you will want to do again.

⭐5 CAIRNGORMS ► 158

This breathtakingly beautiful national park in the Highlands boasts the famous Caledonian Pines, and from early summer the heather blooms in its wistful lilac hues.

⭐6 GLEN COE ► 162

A clan massacre gave this valley a bad reputation, but it makes a very civilised impression today. Dark mountains line either side, and there is no better place to experience the mystic of the Highlands.

⭐7 KELVINGROVE MUSEUM & ART GALLERY ► 78

The Victorian sandstone castle in Glasgow offers a wonderfully whimsical potpourri of art, armaments, mummies and animal figures, and even includes a Spitfire.

⭐8 BURNS COUNTRY ► 106

Between Dumfries and Ayr, Scotland's national poet Robert Burns seems to have penned romantic or humorous verse about every stream, grove and arch.

⭐9 SCOTTISH PARLIAMENT ► 61

The initial scepticism about the integration of modern architecture in medieval Edinburgh turned into pride when the Scots inaugurated their spectacular parliament in 2004.

⭐10 MERCHANT CITY ► 81

Glasgow's oldest warehouse district testifies to the pomp and circumstance of the old merchants. Today, the opulent buildings are home to restaurants, bars and shops.

THAT
SCOTLAND

Find out what makes Scotland tick, experience its unique flair – just like the Scots themselves.

SCULPTURE AND NATURE

Enjoy a fascinating 4mi (6km) walk along the western bank of **Glenkiln Reservoir** (✚ 206 A2; www.walking englishman.com/scotland01.htm). Sadly the famous **sculptures by Jacob Epstein, Henry Moore and Auguste Rodin** were removed a couple of years ago after the theft of Henry Moore's *Standing Figure*.

TRAINSPOTTING

Why bother driving along narrow country roads, worried about who is about to zoom around the corner ahead of you, when you can travel in comfort in the train watching the spectacular countryside flashing past the window. Remote stops, such as **Corrour Station** in Rannoch Moor on the **West Highland Line** (✚ 209 F2; www.corrour-station-house-restaurant.co.uk) will tempt you to disembark and explore. And what's to stop you leaving out a train to spend a few hours in the only building – once the station, now a restaurant – or to take a walk along the moors to the youth hostel perched on its own on the banks of **Loch Ossian**?

WHISKY ON THE ISLES

A distillery tour is a must! At **Highland Park** in Kirkwall on Mainland (✚ 215 D4; www.highlandpark. co.uk), an abundance of sensory joys await you. Colour: pale gold. Nose: warm, florid, heather, smoky fragrance, very aromatic. Body: smooth, strong, rounded. Taste: slightly salty, leaves, pine nuts. Aroma development: nuts, honey, cinnamon, dry ginger. Afterglow: spicy, very dry, oak tone, smoky and warm.

AS FAR AS YOUR FEET WILL TAKE YOU

Walking is the best way to really see the Highlands. The 94mi (152km)-long **West Highland Way** (► 128) from Glasgow to Fort William offers the ultimate walking experience. Accommodation is in rustic hotels far out in the country-side. Many people have their luggage driven from hotel to hotel. The stretch between Rowardennan and Inverarnan is via the tiny Ardlui ferry over **Loch Lomond**, which you summon by hoisting an orange ball.

FEELING

A view of the treasure chamber in the Highland Park's distillery

That Scotland Feeling

DREAM FLIGHTS

Scotland has dream beaches. And Scotland has dream flights. Twice a day a Twin Otter lands on the Hebrides island of **Barra** (➕ 208 A3) – on a sandy beach, which is only big enough for the manoeuvre at low tide. Shell collectors duck when they hear the flight coming from Glasgow. Scotland has the only scheduled flight worldwide that is dependent on the tide – and the shortest at that: it takes two minutes to make the trip between the Orkney Islands **Westray** and **Papa Westray** (➕ 215 D5).

ISLAND HOPPING

When the sun shines, this boat trip exudes Caribbean flair. The small Hebrides islands of **Rum, Muck and Eigg** are each totally individual in form and lifestyle. The small Sealife Cruise from Arisaig to the panorama route **Road to the Isles** (➤ 155; www.arisaig.co.uk) offers an opportunity to stay for a few hours on Eigg or Rum, before the boat comes by again. If you are lucky, you will see the **dolphins** on their turquoise tour.

UNDER PEAT WITH A VIEW

What could be nicer than sitting comfortably in a luxuriously furnished cottage with a turf room as you watch a storm, torrential rain or even a magnificent sunset? That is possible in two places, one on the island of **Harris** (➤ 151) and the other on **South Uist**. The accommodation is built to blend into the hillside in the style of Viking houses, (www.stay-hebrides.com, www.hebhide.co.uk).

HIGHLANDS RELOADED

A private wildlife park is planned here, in which elk, boars, bears and even wolves will live. You can already visit the **Alladale Wilderness Reserve** (➕ 214 A1, near Ardgay; www.alladale.com). On a guided tour, experience the vision of millionaire Paul Lister to restore the natural ecosystem. Awaiting you: beautiful mountain landscape, a romantic manor house, luxurious lodges and hundreds of thousands of newly planted trees.

Stone house on the Alladale Estate

The Magazine

WILD at Heart

Scotland's awe-inspiring wild places – its mountains, moors, lochs and islands – are shared between the indigenous wildlife and a seasonal population of walkers, climbers, cyclists and kayakers.

Side By Side

You don't have to venture into the Highlands to catch a glimpse of Scotland's most identifiable creatures. Since 2004, visitors to Glentress Forest and Kailzie Gardens in the Tweed Valley, near Peebles, have been able to watch live video of ospreys in their eyries at two viewing centres. The osprey has been one of Scottish wildlife's success stories: all but wiped out 100 years ago, breeding pairs gradually returned to fish the lochs and rivers of Scotland. What's remarkable is that the ospreys share the Tweed Valley with not only anglers but also an ever-increasing number of cyclists. It's a perfect example of man and wildlife thriving side by side.

Similarly, when you're pedalling through the conifer forests of the Borders, watch out for another creature that has found a refuge in Scotland: the red squirrel. Scotland has the highest population of these endearing native mammals in the UK.

Otters and red squirrels are on the increase in Scotland

In Scotland, there are about 700,000 red and roe deer. They provide natural wildlife but also endanger young plants. North of the Borders, Britain's largest land mammal, the red deer, patrols the open hillsides of the Highlands and islands. Thanks to Scotland's new access laws introduced in 2003 – you can venture almost anywhere so long as you act responsibly – there is a good chance of hill walkers in the Highlands encountering these magnificent creatures. The stags are at their most visible and vocal during the annual red deer rut in October.

> ## "Red deer patrol the open hillsides of the Highlands and islands"

Rarer Species

The Isle of Skye is famed as a sea-kayaking destination. Paddlers have more chance than other visitors of espying otters, red deer, wildcats, eagles and the like (www.skyakadventures.com).

A very rare and extremely threatened species is the wildcat, of which just 35 known pure-bred specimens were known to be in existence in 2012. Optimistic estimates put the number at about 400, which are mainly resident in the western Cairngorms National Park. It is thought that there are about 3,500 crossbreeds.

The largest feathered predator in Scotland is the golden eagle. Their 2m (6.5ft) wingspan and soaring flight are unmistakeable, and they have a smaller head and longer tail than the sea eagle. If you want to catch sight of one of the approximately 400 pairs, then lie quietly for a while on the grass in the mountains or by the sea.

Red deer and golden eagles can be found in Cairngorms National Park

SCOTTISH
Cuisine

**When the Scots used to live on root vegetables, oats and fish,
they were as fit as a fiddle. However, during the Industrial
Revolution, sugar imports made Glasgow rich and its inhabitants addicted; the result was Europe's unhealthiest diet.
Now liberating themselves from deep fried junk food, the
Scots are returning to their roots in all senses. And it is not
just 17 Michelin stars that prove it.**

A Bountiful Natural Larder

Scotland has long boasted world-class ingredients, and the rising interest
in fine dining and increasingly prominent chefs, such as Scot Martin Wishart,
have brought the nation's ingredients to the fore, with delicacies coming
from the field, the orchard, the farmyard and the sea.

Aberdeen Angus beef is world renowned, and some savvy Scots de-
clare Buccleuch Beef to be even finer. Lamb from all over the country is
considered to be excellent, with that from the rolling hills of the Borders
being particularly highly regarded. Recently, more and more Scots have
shown an interest in local seafood, which, in the past, has often been
spirited off to the restaurant tables of Madrid and Paris. Shellfish is world
class, with plump lobster, oysters and langoustines all thriving in the
cold, nutrient-rich local waters. The country's rivers are alive with the
hallowed wild salmon, but more sustainable salmon is grown in farms in
the ubiquitous sea lochs.

Scottish cheese has also come to the fore in recent years, muscling
French rivals off the top of the selection on menus in the country's fine-
dining restaurants. The finest cheddar is perhaps the powerful Mull Cheddar,
while first-class blue cheeses include Lanark, Strathdon and Dunsyre Blue,
which is best enjoyed accompanied by a smoky Islay malt whisky.

You can also acquire a taste for Scottish specialities by planning your trip
 along the Food Trail. Culinary highlights are offered by the manufacturers
and shops along the Seafood Trail and the Scottish Cheese Trail (www.
visitscotland.com/see-do/itineraries/food-drink/).

Insider Tip

Scottish cheese and pancakes are two typical foods that are seeing a renaissance

Scottish Brands

Famous names include Loch Fyne Oysters, the haggis producer Macsweens; Mackies, the award-winning, all-Scottish-dairy ice cream makers; and MacLeod's of Stornoway, famed for its rich black pudding. Arbroath Smokies (smoked haddock) has been registered as a Protected Geographical Indication under the EU's Protected Food Name Scheme – and new regional brands are continuously appearing throughout the country.

THE RISE OF THE SCOTTISH CHEF

No longer purveyors of all things deep fried, Scottish chefs have really come to the fore in recent years with a confidence in their cooking styles:

- **Gordon Ramsay**: Scotland's über chef may no longer live in Scotland, but his influence is still keenly felt.
- **Tom Kitchin**: The representative of the exciting new breed of chef, really bringing local produce and seasonality to the fore at his Michelin-starred Kitchin restaurant in Edinburgh.
- **Martin Wishart**: Committed Francophile Wishart's landmark Edinburgh restaurant won its Michelin star in 2001, with his new operation at Cameron House, on the edge of Loch Lomond, also doing well.
- **Andrew Fairlie**: Perthshire boy Fairlie has come a long way to run a double Michelin-starred restaurant in the region's grand Gleneagles Hotel (▶ 141). He is arguably the finest chef working in Scotland today.

GLASGOW
STYLE

True Glasgow Style, a fusion of Art Nouveau and the Arts and Crafts Movement, is hard to define. It's the confidence that built this magnificent city, it's the imaginative adaptations of old buildings for new uses and it's the daring architecture of the late 20th century.

Glasgow Style, as defined by art historians, peaked at the time of the 1901 Glasgow exhibition, when Art Nouveau was sweeping through Europe. Fused with the Arts and Crafts Movement, it was the style associated with architect and designer Charles Rennie Mackintosh (1868–1928) and his contemporaries at the Glasgow School of Art, under the dynamic leadership of Francis Newbery (1855–1946).

An Architectural Legacy

Mackintosh attended evening classes at the School of Art when he became an apprentice architect. He was an outstanding student, attracting attention not only for his architecture but also for his drawing and painting. Influenced by the romanticism of the pre-Raphaelites

From left to right: Charing Cross; the former Luma Light Factory

14

The Magazine

and the simplicity of Japanese design, he and his friends Herbert McNair (1868–1955) and Margaret (1865–1933) and Frances MacDonald (1873–1921) became known as "the Four", gaining a reputation for their striking designs using stylised natural forms.

The Mackintosh Trail

Mackintosh design is everywhere in Glasgow. An essential stop is the Glasgow School of Art. Widely considered his greatest work, this building illustrates the beauty of Mackintosh's creations. Combining traditional Scottish baronial style with fluid metalwork and carved stone, he designed a complete Art Nouveau building, including furnishings. Badly damaged during a fire in 2014, the building is currently being restored (▶92). Queen's Cross Church, an engaging collage of Gothic and Art Nouveau, is so appealing that the Charles Rennie Mackintosh Society (CRMS) have made it their headquarters. The Hunterian Art Gallery at Glasgow University meanwhile houses the Mackintosh House, a breathtaking reconstruction of his home, complete with the furnishings he designed for it. More MacKintosh furnishings are on display at The Kelvingrove Museum & Art Gallery (▶78–80), while the Willow Tearooms (▶91, 98) offer a more relaxing way to see his work. Finish by taking the train to Helensburgh and Hill House, designed for the publisher Blackie and now restored, or by visiting the amazing House for an Art Lover at Bellahouston Park (▶93), designed in collaboration with his wife Margaret MacDonald. Mackintosh and his wife moved to London in 1915, but little of his subsequent work compares with his Glasgow legacy.

Grassroots Style

Despite the abundance of Mackintosh design in the city, Glasgow Style is more than Mackintosh. It's also the tenement house in which most Glaswegians of the 19th and early 20th century grew up, and where the workers from the shipyard and heavy-engineering plants of industrial Glasgow lived. Although the solid sandstone, terraced tenement houses were overcrowded and unsanitary, it was here that the friendliness and warmth that is Glasgow was nurtured. Many of the houses that survived the architectural ravages of the 1960s and 1970s have now been impressively cleaned and renovated.

Glasgow Style houses a gallery of modern art in a grand classical building (▶91) and decorates the pediment with primary colours and mirrors, or wears Versace with thrift-shop finds. It is the Barras (▶90) and the Golden Z, Glasgow's shopping heartland. It is two centuries of wonderful architecture: the 18th-century Trades Hall, designed by Robert Adam (▶83); the 19th-century Egyptian Halls warehouse, designed by influential Glasgow architect Alexander (Greek) Thompson; the 19th-century

Templeton's Carpet Factory (► 185), whose elaborate edifice is reminiscent of the Doge's Palace in Venice. The most eye-catching postmodern buildings are the Clyde Auditorium (1997), affectionately known as "the Armadillo", and Zaha Hadid's Riverside Transport Museum (2011).

More importantly, Glasgow Style is about the people, the wit and panache that has reinvented the city as the City of Culture and the City of Architecture and Design. And underlying it all is a humorous audacity that punctures pomposity with a wee touch of the ridiculous.

From top to bottom: Glasgow School of Art Centre; Riverside Museum; Mackintosh design at the House for an Art Lover

From
STICKS and STONES

The modern sport of golf, watched by millions each year, has come a long way from the ancient Scottish game of gowf, developed over the centuries from the simple delight people took in whacking a stone with a stick.

Stick and ball games like hockey, hurling and shinty evolved in other countries, but Scotland gave the world golf. Scotland is the game's spiritual and historical home, and its spectacular courses attract golfers from around the globe.

The game was popular from the start – too popular it would seem. In 1475 (the earliest mention of golf) it was prohibited by the Scottish Parliament on Sundays because it interfered with archery practice.

In 1754 a handful of players founded a small club that they called The Society of St Andrew's Golfers. King William IV became their patron in the early 19th century and they became The Royal and Ancient Golf Club. The R&A is the world authority on the sport, and it administers the rules and runs the British Open Championship. That small private golf club still operates, but today it has around 2,500 members worldwide.

The Gutta Percha Ball

Until the mid-19th century, golf balls, traditionally made from feathers, were expensive, unpredictable and often lasted just one round, making golf more a game of chance than of skill. Then, in 1848, James Patterson produced an experimental ball made from gutta percha (a tough coagulated latex), which had been used as packing on a parcel that he had been sent. Suddenly, cheap, mass-produced, controllable balls were viable. They were also strong enough to be hit by materials harder than wood, and so iron clubs were developed.

Old Tom

Tom Morris Sr, four times winner of the British Open between 1861 and 1867, was largely responsible for the layout of modern courses. "Old Tom" was greenkeeper and golf professional on the Old Course at St Andrews for 40 years. He pioneered the change from 22 to 18 holes and designed championship courses at Muirfield, Carnoustie and the first purpose-built "modern" course at Prestwick.

How to Book a Round

Most of Scotland's 500-plus golf courses, including the championship ones, are open to the public. You can usually book by phoning the club, although for top courses you may need to reserve a year in advance. Rules on admission vary from club to club, so check for any restrictions when booking. VisitScotland.com also produces a free *Guide to Golf in Scotland* with details of more than 300 courses (tel: 0845 225 5121).

Mary, Queen of Scots often played golf at St Andrews

TOP TEN GOLF COURSES

- **St Andrews** – www.standrews.org.uk
- **Turnberry Ailsa** – www.turnberry.co.uk
- **Royal Troon** – www.royaltroon.co.uk
- **Royal Dornoch** – www.royaldornoch.com
- **Muirfield** – www.muirfield.org.uk
- **Carnoustie** – www.carnoustiegolflinks.co.uk
- **North Berwick** – www.northberwickgolfclub.com
- **Machrihanish** – www.machgolf.com
- **Nairn** – www.nairngolfclub.co.uk
- **Turnberry Kintyre** – www.turnberry.co.uk

MUSIC
and MOVEMENT

Celtic music developed among the people of the Celtic fringe – remnants of the Celtic tribes of Europe now confined to its western extremities, such as Wales, Ireland, Galicia in Spain, Brittany in France, Cornwall and the Isle of Man in England, and, of course, Scotland.

Each country's traditional music is distinctive, yet a common thread runs through their dance tunes, airs, songs and ballads. Celtic immigrants to North America took their music with them and it was absorbed into a new society. Now their descendants are bringing it back across the Atlantic. Innovative musicians are fusing ancient tunes with jazz, rock and pop, and bagpipes play alongside synthesizers. Singers collect old songs and teach them to children to ensure that the Celtic tradition continues to thrive.

Curious? Then contact The Traditional Music and Song Association (TMSA) in Edinburgh for details about concerts, ceilidhs, folk clubs and pub sessions. Call 0131 555 2224 or log on to the TMSA's listings section at www.tmsa.org.uk.

Celtic Connections

The brilliant two-week Celtic Connections Festival (www.celticconnections. com) lights up the dark days of a Glaswegian January. It's a wonderful introduction to Celtic music, with singers and musicians from across the globe, vibrant musicians playing Celtic music to a rock beat or Beethoven in reel time. There are huge concerts and small, intimate, late-night venues, ceilidhs and pub sessions where anyone can join in, children's events involving local schools, and fascinating lectures and discussions.

The success of Celtic Connections has sent people in search of traditional music in other pubs and festivals. By the Clyde. the long-established Scotia Bar and the reopened Clutha Vaults (both in Stockwell Street), are hang-outs for musicians and poets. Rock'n Roll till your heart's content can be found in King Tut's (Vincent Street) and Barrowland Ballroom

Above: Folk concert in Sandy Bell pub in Edinburgh; right: Fiddler Chris Stout

(Gallow Gate), jazz in Avant Garde (Merchant City). In Edinburgh, check out the variations on a Celtic theme in Sandy Bell's (Forrest Road), Royal Oak (Infirmary Street) and The Tass (High Street/Royal Mile). See ► 72 for all three venues.

TOP MUSICIANS

Aly Bain and Phil Cunningham: Shetland's famous fiddler and accordion virtuosi
Battlefield Band: long-established Glasgow band
Shooglenifty: one of the brightest stars of the new wave of progressive Celtic music that blends an eclectic array of musical styles
Bùrach: Edinburgh folk-rock band led by Sandy Brechin
Capercaillie: popular band fusing trad and modern Gaelic sounds
Hidden Orchestra: Famous mix of hip-hop, electronica, jazz, ambience
Dougie McLean: Perthshire-based singer-songwriter and composer
Back of the Moon: award-winning traditional band with a line up of pipes, fiddle and vocals underpinned by guitar and piano
Chris Stout: superb fiddler, who also fronts Shetland band Fiddler's Bid
Eddi Reader: formerly front woman of Fairground Attraction, now singing Burns' songs to a wider audience

LITERARY
Scotland

With a rich oral tradition of songs and stories and a fertile
Gaelic vernacular, Scottish writing has deep roots. You can hear
a distinctly Scottish voice in authors as diverse as Robert
Burns and Irvine Welsh *(Trainspotting)*, writers separated by
two centuries but equally committed to their Scotland.

Sketch In Verse

Robert "Rabbie" Burns (1759–1796) is fondly regarded as Scotland's
national poet. Born into a farming family, Burns stunned Scotland with
an inspired ability to compose song lyrics and poems that resonated from
the highest to the lowest walks of life. His *Auld Lang Syne* is still sung on
New Year's Eve and his rural poems are among the most touching of any
Scottish writer. Burns was a man of passion: he loved women and drink.

Burns' fortunes could not have differed more greatly from those of
Sir Walter Scott (1771–1832), perhaps Scotland's most prolific novelist
and poet. While both were celebrated by the Scottish literati, immersed
themselves in Scottish folklore and shaped Scottish literature, Burns died
in relative poverty at the young age of 37 while Scott was knighted and
joined the Establishment, becoming Laird of Abbotsford.

> "Scott's *Waverley* developed the genre of the historical novel"

Unbiased Eyes?

The publication of Scott's historical novel *Waverley* in 1814
developed the genre in Britain, paving the way for many great writers and
their memorable characters. The Waverley Novels, devoured by an eager
public, presented a romantic view of the Highlands and moorlands, but
didn't shy away from urban concerns: Scott's depiction of Edinburgh's
Tolbooth prison was unflinching. His life was almost as dramatic as his
novels, and towards the end he was writing proliferously in order to pay
off his mountain of debts. Posthumously, his works inspired many operas
and films. Scotland's Highland mystical appeal and the tourism it has
encouraged ultimately has a lot to thank him for.

Historical *Peter Pan* illustration

Tales of Derring-do

Scottish writers have also created fantasies, such as the immortal *Peter Pan* by James Matthew Barrie (1880–1937), while *The Raiders* and *The Grey Man* by S R Crockett (1859–1914) are fast-paced adventures in the tradition of Robert Louis Stevenson's *Kidnapped* and *Treasure Island*.

Stevenson (1850–1894) was born in Edinburgh but began his writing career with accounts of his travels in Europe and America. While in America he married Fanny Osbourne and began writing *Treasure Island* for her young son. Stevenson continued writing a mixture of essays, romance novels and poems until ill health forced him to seek a warmer climate; he settled in Polynesia where he died prematurely.

The Magazine

Novelist Ian Rankin, creator of Inspector Rebus

In the 20th century, John Buchan (1875–1940) continued the Scottish vein of adventure stories with *The Thirty-Nine Steps* (1915), the first popular spy novel of the 20th century.

Modern Success Stories

In the 19th century, Edinburgh-born Sir Arthur Conan Doyle (1859–1930) established the detective story as a genre of popular fiction. He modelled the character of his detective, Sherlock Holmes, on one of his professors at Edinburgh University, who was a pioneer in the field of forensic science.

The character of Detective Inspector John Rebus, created by novelist Ian Rankin (born 1960) is a maverick with a drink problem. He was constantly assigned to obscure and peripheral cases, but somehow he always

INSPECTOR REBUS TOURS

Deep in the **Oxford Bar** you might spot a lone drinker with a pint of beer and a whisky chaser. He's middle-aged, with a face raddled from years of drinking and smoking. He's the archetype of Ian Rankin's fictional detective, Inspector Rebus, and fans of the character are flocking to Edinburgh to visit places mentioned in the novels. Colin Brown of **Rebustours** (www.rebustours.com) will guide you on **The Body Politic Tour**, around the Royal Mile, on the theme of politics and corruption, or the New Town, **Old Crimes Tour**, which starts and finishes in the Oxford and takes in the Georgian squares and streets of the New Town. Advance booking is essential on all the tours.

J K Rowling, author of the internationally acclaimed *Harry Potter* series

ended up solving the big headline case by unorthodox means before the recent retirement.

The latest literary star to emerge from Scotland is J K Rowling. Her most famous character, the schoolboy wizard Harry Potter, first took the world by storm in 1997. He came to life in an Edinburgh café where Rowling wrote over a cup of coffee because she couldn't afford to heat her flat. He has now featured in a series of seven books that have been translated into at least 67 languages and sold hundreds of millions of copies worldwide. With her books dominating the bestseller lists and dramatisations dominating the headlines, Rowling helped her city to become the first UNESCO City of Literature in 2004, further cementing Scotland's literary pre-eminence.

LITERARY PUB TOURS

In Edinburgh you can visit the favourite taverns of Scottish writers past and present. Evening tours start from the Beehive Inn in the Grassmarket and are hosted by the fictional characters Clart and McBrain, who argue passionately about the importance of pubs and drinking to the creativity of Scotland's writers, while they lead you through Edinburgh's closes, wynds and narrow streets. En route, you'll hear the stories and see the places behind the creation of Dr Jekyll and Mr Hyde, pass the nocturnal haunts of Robert Louis Stevenson and discover the bawdy poetry of Robert Burns (tel: 0800 169 7410; www. edinburghliterarypubtour.co.uk). Glasgow offers similar tours.

EDINBURGH
Celebrates

Edinburgh Festival, the city's annual, month-long cultural extravaganza, attracts visitors from around the globe.

It's Tuesday afternoon and the Royal Mile is closed to traffic. The motorists are exasperated but the assembled multitude thronging the steep cobbled street is oblivious to their angst. Outside St Giles Cathedral (►64) a lone piper dressed in traditional tartan belts out a folk-rock version of some ancient Scottish reels. Beside him a native of Gambia in national costume lays down a deep rhythmic African beat. They've only just met, but the assembled crowd would swear they've been playing together for years. Farther down the street a top-hatted flame-thrower spews fire high into the air. On the next corner a woman dressed like the Tin Man from the Wizard of Oz does a robot mime. It's like Mardi Gras meets medieval street fair, but it's Edinburgh in August so it must be Festival time.

Cultural Extravaganza

This cultural extravaganza, one of the world's largest, attracts thousands of visitors to Edinburgh each year and for a month you can overdose on the arts, whether you're into classical music, jazz, opera, theatre or comedy, with performances by renowned musicians or actors in every major venue in Edinburgh. Over the years, the Festival has mutated into a many-headed event – there are now several festivals taking place simultaneously. There's the grand old Edinburgh International Festival, several spin-off festivals of film and literature, and the edgy, avant-garde or just plain ridiculous Fringe.

The Fringe

While the EIF makes a sober and serious appraisal of the arts, its chaotic younger sibling, the Fringe, grabs the headlines. Best known for its prestigious annual comedy award, the Fringe is a barometer of comic talent – you can see who's on the way up and whose days are numbered. Past winners of the comedy award include Dylan Moran, Al Murray and Steve Coogan, who all moved from stage to television. The Fringe has also seen names as famous as Monty Python, Emma Thompson and Stephen Fry.

However, arguably, it is the more obscure acts that make the Fringe so exciting. Every possible performance space is pressed into service and you can witness a stand-up comedian or a play of surprising brilliance in the most unlikely of venues. The headline acts, however, prefer the principal venues of the Pleasance, the Gilded Balloon and the Assembly Rooms – it's best to book ahead as tickets for these shows are snapped up quickly.

> "You can see acts of surprising brilliance in the most unlikely of venues"

To experience just how much yarn-spinning is part of Gaelic DNA, you should visit the Scottish Story Telling Centre (John Knox House, Royal Mile, with Café). The International Story Telling Festival takes place in the last week of October and topics also cover current global issues such as the environment, ageing populations and the fate of refugees.

Left: the spectacular firework finale; right: The Military Tattoo performs on the Castle Esplanade throughout the entire festival

FESTIVAL CONTACTS

Edinburgh International Festival: The Hub, Castlehill, Edinburgh EH1 2NE; tel: 0131 473 2000; www.eif.co.uk

The Fringe: The Fringe Office, 180 High Street, Edinburgh EH1 1QS; tel: 0131 226 0026; www.edfringe.com

Military Tattoo: 32 Market Street, Edinburgh EH1 1QB; tel: 0131 225 1188; www.edintattoo.co.uk

Edinburgh International Film Festival: 88 Lothian Road, Edinburgh EH3 9BZ; Tel. 0131 228 40 51; www.edfilmfest.org.uk

Scottish Story Telling Centre: 43-45 High Street, Edinburgh EH1 1SR; Tel. 0131 556 95 79; www.tracscotland.org/scottish-storytelling-centre

FREEDOM'S SWORD

For centuries Scotland's identity has been moulded by its relationship with England. Scotland was self-governing from the 14th century until 1707, a right the people had valiantly fought for against their more powerful English neighbours, and the Scots strong sense of identity has been fiercely defended ever since.

A Question of Succession

Scotland's victory at Bannockburn in 1314 (▶ 133) brought to an end the long Scottish Wars of Independence. It was unhappy chance more than 30 years earlier that precipitated Scotland's loss of independence, and the country's subsequent struggle to regain the right to govern itself. In 1286, Alexander III, King of Scots, suffered a tragic death when he fell from his horse and tumbled over a cliff. As all the King's children had died before him, arrangements were made for his three-year-old granddaughter, Margaret, to succeed him. In poor health, she died on the boat journey from Norway to her new realm. With no obvious monarch in waiting, the guardians appointed to run the country in Margaret's infancy asked King Edward I of England to adjudicate on the many claimants to the throne. But Edward asserted his own claim to the country, making the contenders swear an oath of fealty to him.

It eventually came down to a decision between Robert Bruce (1220–1295; grandfather of Robert the Bruce, 1274–1329) and John Balliol (c.1250–1313). Edward chose Balliol, who was little more than the King's puppet. When Balliol began to show some resistance to Edward's wishes, Edward simply removed him and, in 1296, invaded Scotland, carrying off the potent symbol of Scottish monarchy, the Stone of Destiny, on which all Scottish monarchs had been crowned (▶ 56). With Scotland under English domination, one man emerged who was to become the country's greatest hero – Sir William Wallace.

Braveheart routed the English at Stirling Bridge

Braveheart

Sir William Wallace (c.1270–1305), popularly known as Braveheart, was a shadowy figure about whom little is known before he routed the English at Stirling Bridge in 1297. He continued to wage an outstanding guerrilla war against them and his actions found favour with the Scots nobility, who knighted him and appointed him Guardian of Scotland. He was eventually captured after the second English invasion and taken to London, where he was tried for treason and brutally hung, drawn and quartered.

Robert the Bruce

Meanwhile, Robert the Bruce (grandson of Robert Bruce) was advancing his claim to the Scottish throne. After murdering one of Balliol's leading supporters, the Red Comyn, he seized the castle and the town and advanced through the southwest. He was crowned king at Scone and, despite mixed fortunes, he finally won a decisive victory against the English at Bannockburn in 1314. But it was not until the Treaty of Northampton was signed in 1328 that Scotland was acknowledged as "independent of England for all time".

An Uneasy Union

But this was not to be: almost 400 years later it was not war that ended Scotland's independence but economics and, some would argue, greed. The English, embroiled in a major war in Europe (The War of the Spanish

The Magazine

Succession 1701–14), wanted the union of the two countries for reasons of national security. Scotland's economy was in a disastrous situation, and union would allow the Scots free trade and access to a huge market. The Act of Union of 1707 was almost universally unpopular but was pushed through in the face of heavy opposition by the 31 Parliamentary Commissioners, ably assisted by huge amounts of English money for the purpose of buying support. Robert Burns later declared in song, "We were bought and sold for English gold", describing the commissioners as "a Parcel of Rogues in a Nation". Although Scotland prospered from the Union, shifting political control

Alex Salmond, First Minister of Scotland from 2007 to 2014

to London was seen by many as being taken over. However, despite the political union, Scotland's legal system has remained separate.

20th-century Politics

Scotland's voting patterns in the 1980s and 1990s differed considerably from those of southern England. Scots consistently voted for the Labour party but were ruled by the Conservative party of the London-based government Conservative policies, especially those under Margaret Thatcher (1979–90), proved unpopular in Scotland and in the 1997 election no Conservative members for Scotland were voted into the Westminster Parliament.

Many Scots felt a need to reinforce their national identity, and the Scottish National Party (SNP) began to make inroads into traditional

> "The issue of Scottish independence remains as prickly as ever"

Labour support. Labour pursued a policy of devolution, promising the Scots their own parliament but stopping short of full control. Policies such as immigration and defence would still be under Westminster's control. When Labour under Tony Blair won in the election in 1997, the Scottish referendum that followed produced an overwhelming majority in favour of devolution.

The Chamber at the Scottish Parliament

In an historic moment, the veteran Scottish Nationalist Winnie Ewing, as the oldest MSP, declared on 12 May, 1999, "The Scottish Parliament, which adjourned on 25 March, 1707, is hereby reconvened".

Together, Apart

Since then, the SNP has been the country's main governing power, and as of 2011 it has even held the majority of the 129 seats. First Minister Alex Salmond used this political clout, to channel the devolution policies introduced by Tony Blair – such as self-determination in areas like health, education and law relating to Wales, Northern Ireland and Scotland – towards the dream of complete independence. The referendum on this issue in 2014 resulted in 55.3 percent against and 44.7 percent in favour of Scottish independence, mainly because the older generation voted against leaving the United Kingdom. At the last minute, in a great panic, Westminster promised far-reaching independent rule for Scotland. The Scots were now very involved in the political debate, and the SNP won 56 of the 59 Scottish constituencies in the House of Commons. Another factor that is currently stirring up this pivotal question in British politics is why Scots are allowed to have a say in Westminster but the English do not have any part in the decisions in Scotland. Nicola Sturgeon, the charismatic successor to Alex Salmond, seems even more suited to eventually uniting Scottish opinion for the SNP and continuing the fight for an independent Scotland. England is watching developments nervously.

ANGELS' SHARE
THE MISSING MALT

The whisky that evaporates from the barrels over many years of maturing is known as "the angels' share". Whether or not you believe in angels, the prospect of a wee dram waiting for you is certainly a cheering thought.

From the Gaelic *uisge beatha*, meaning "water of life", whisky is credited with many medicinal and magical properties. It isn't really a cure; it's just that once you've had a few drams, you feel no pain.

Changing Habits

Whisky wasn't always Scotland's national drink. In the 17th and 18th centuries claret was the favoured tipple, imported from Bordeaux to the port of Leith in huge barrels. Robert Burns testified to the copious quantities drunk in his song "Gae bring tae me a pint o' wine". It was the tax on wine that popularised whisky as an alternative, and many of today's famous distilleries were built on the sites of old illegal stills.

FIVE POPULAR MALTS

- The Macallan, Craigellachie
- Glenmorangie, Tain
- Talisker, Carbost
- Balvenie, Dufftown
- Laphroaig, Islay

Types of Whisky

Whisky comes in three types: blended, grain and single malt. **Blended whisky** is a mixture of grain whisky and malt whisky. The malt in the blends determines their quality. Aficionados can differentiate between different blends, but to ordinary drinkers they taste similar and are often mixed with soft drinks, so special flavours tend to be lost.

Single malts (from a single distillery), on the other hand, have their own distinctive aromas and flavours, just like fine wines, and here it's the variations of malt, peat, water and cask that give each malt its taste signature. Such whisky is drunk pure or with a splash of water, and it is regarded as sacrilege to use such a fine dram in a cocktail. The centre of whisky production is the Speyside district in the northeast, followed by the Islay region. The Islay malts, in particular, have a delicious, smoky smoothness that is imparted from the peat drying together with the peaty water. Much of the barley is malted and dried with peat smoke and, after distilling, the drink is aged in casks for many years. Wealthy connoisseurs are willing to pay thousands of pounds for a rare malt.

You can have a great time comparing different brands in places like the Scotch Whisky Heritage Centre (➤ 64) on Edinburgh's Royal Mile or in one of the many well-stocked hotel bars. Just make sure to leave your car behind, then quietly raise your glass to the hovering angels before draining it dry.

Insider Tip

Great SCOTS

For a small country, Scotland can boast an impressive list of people who have made their mark on the world, from medical research centres to the glitzy boulevards of Hollywood.

From left to right: James McAvoy, Andy Murray and Sir Alexander Fleming

An Inventive People

It has been claimed that Scotland has produced more inventors and pioneers per capita than any country in the world and it is hard to disagree. Alexander Fleming brought the world antibiotics, Paraffin Young pioneered oil production, while tarmac was the brainchild of John McAdam and John Boyd Dunlop developed rubber tyres. Then, of course, Alexander Graham Bell invented the telephone and John Logie Baird invented television. And who could forget Dolly the cloned Sheep – another controversial, Scottish first?

Famous Faces

Hollywood has always been fond of Scottish brogues and of none more so than that of Sir Sean Connery, everyone's favourite Bond. Then there is the more cerebral Brian Cox and the ubiquitous trio of Ewan Macgregor, Robert Carlyle and James McAvoy, with a celluloid heritage that stretches back to such legends as David Niven and Gordon Jackson.

Sporting Legends

Scots will tell tragic stories of sporting near-misses suffered by their national rugby and football teams, but there have also been many Scottish sporting success stories. Golfers Sam Torrance and Sandy Lyle have made their mark, Stephen Hendry is a seven-time world snooker champion, and Andrew Murray has been a global tennis sensation and the first British player to win Wimbledon in 77 years (2013). Multi-Olympic gold medallist Sir Chris Hoy has also led the field on the cycling track.

Finding Your Feet

First Two Hours

Scotland is well-connected, with direct international flights from many parts of the world to its main airports. It has strong connections with the rest of the UK and, increasingly, Europe. Urban areas are well organised with integrated public transport, though hiring a car is advised for visiting more remote areas.

Arriving By Air

Scotland has three main airports: Edinburgh (code EDI), Glasgow International (GLA) and Glasgow Prestwick International (PIK), and all have a choice of onward transport. Public transport is generally reliable. Edinburgh and Glasgow International have tourist information offices.

Edinburgh Airport

- Scotland's **main airport** (tel: 0870 040 0007; www.edinburghairport.com) is 6mi (9.6km) west of Edinburgh.
- **Taxis** are available from a rank in front of the terminal. With fares of around £20 to the city centre, cabs are good value for groups of up to four people travelling together.
- **Lothian Buses** (tel: 0131 555 6363; www.flybybus.com) runs Airlink coach transfers to Waverley railway station adjacent to Princes Street, via the smaller Haymarket Station. Services run every 10 minutes during peak hours, and 15 minutes at off-peak times (£4.50). The journey takes 25 minutes, or around 45 minutes during the rush hour. There are tram lines (www.edinburghtrams.com; £5) to Princes Street and York Place
- If you're **driving**, take the A8 east and follow the city centre signs. It is a 30-minute drive to the city centre, but takes longer in peak periods.

Glasgow International Airport

- Glasgow Airport (tel: 0844 481 5555; www.glasgowairport.com) is in **Paisley**, 8mi (13km) west of Glasgow city centre.
- **Paisley Gilmour Street** railway station is 2mi (3km) from the airport.
- **Taxis** are available from the front of the terminal building for transfers to central Glasgow (£20) or to nearby Paisley (£4.50).
- **Arriva** (tel: 0344 800 4411; www.arrivabus.co.uk) .com) and **First** (tel: 0141 423 6600; www.firstgroup.com) shuttle buses run to Glasgow city centre every 10–15 minutes during peak times and every 30 minutes in the evening (£6.50). Local buses also run to Paisley Station every ten minutes (£2.50).
- **Drivers** should take the M8 west and follow signs for the city centre. Glasgow airport is about 30 minutes' drive from the city centre.

Glasgow Prestwick International

- **Prestwick** airport (tel: 0871 223 0700; www.glasgowprestwick.com) is 31mi (50km) from Glasgow city centre, about a 45-minute drive.
- **Trains** run every 20 minutes to Glasgow Central Station and take 50 minutes (£5.80).
- The **X77** express shuttle bus runs into Glasgow every 30–60 minutes and takes 50 minutes (££). The **X99** (££) runs early morning and late at night.
- To **drive** from Prestwick airport, take the M77 north following the signs for Glasgow. Expect delays at peak times.

Arriving By Train

Waverley Railway Station
- Situated at **Waverley Bridge**, Edinburgh. Exit via the Waverley Steps to reach Princes Street.
- **Virgin Trains** (tel: 0871 977 4223; www.virgintrains.co.uk) operate east-coast mainline services from **London King's Cross** station. Services arrive hourly and a good four hours.
- **National Rail Enquiry Service**, tel: 0345 748 4950

Glasgow Central Station
- Situated at **Argyle Street,** Central Station is the terminal for East Coast mainline trains from **London Euston** (average journey time 5–6 hours). Trains to towns in the immediate vicinity of Glasgow also leave from here.
- It is a ten-minute walk through the city centre to **Queen Street Station**, from which services leave for the rest of Scotland.

Arriving by Bus

St Andrew Square Bus Station
- Situated in **Clyde Street**, Edinburgh, the heart of the New Town and five minutes' walk from Princes Street, along which principal city buses run.
- **National Express Coaches** (tel: 0871 781 8181; www.nationalexpress.com) arrive here from England and Wales. **Scottish Citylink** (tel: 0871 266 3333; www.citylink.co.uk) covers all of Scotland.

Buchanan Street Bus Station
- Situated in **Killermont Street**, Glasgow, about ten minutes' walk from Central Station or George Square (tel: 0141 333 3708).
- Well served by the **National Express** and **Scottish Citylink** network covering most destinations in Britain.

Tourist Information Offices
The tourist offices in Edinburgh and Glasgow provide a good service, including help with hotel reservations. Both have outlets at the airports. The central number for most local tourist information centres is 0845 225 5121.

Edinburgh
✉ 3 Princes Street, above Waverley Shopping Centre
☎ 0845 225 5121; www.edinburgh.org
🕐 Apr and Oct Mon–Sat 9–6, Sun 10–6; May–Jun and Sep Mon–Sat 9–7, Sun 10–7; Jul–Aug Mon–Sat 9–8, Sun 10–8; Nov–Mar Mon–Sat 9–5, Sun 10–5

Glasgow
✉ 10 Sauchiehall Street
☎ 0845 859 10 06; www.peoplemakeglasgow.com; www.seeglasgow.com
🕐 Mon–Sat 9–6, Sun 10–5, Sun (Oct–March noon–4).

Visit Scotland
ℹ Information pertaining to typical travel questions, providing the addresses and telephone numbers of 75 tourist information centres can be found at www.visitscotland.com/travel/information/centres
☎ 0131 472 2222

Getting Around

The public transport network is fairly extensive in Scotland's main towns and cities, but a car is more convenient in rural and remote areas where bus and train services are often infrequent.

Rail Passes

- **Freedom of Scotland Travelpass** Available for 4 or 8 days, it is valid on all rail services within Scotland, as well as those to/from Carlisle and Berwick-Upon-Tweed, all Caledonian MacBrayne ferries within Scotland, some Scottish Citylink bus connections and some services operated by Stagecoach, First and Bowman Coaches (from £134).
- **Strathclyde Passenger Transport** (tel: 0141 332 6811; www.spt.co.uk). Zonecards and Daytripper tickets allow unlimited travel within western Scotland and Glasgow underground, bus services and the Gourock Kilcreggan Ferry.
- For all public transport enquiries within Scotland call Traveline Scotland, tel: 0871 200 2233; www.travelinescotland.com). Open 24/7.

Trains

- For rail information, use **National Rail Enquiries** (tel: 03457 748 4950; www.nationalrail.co.uk).
- **Scotrail** (tel: 0344 811 0141; www.scotrail.co.uk) operates most rail services within Scotland.
- Since 2015, **Borders** provides a connection between Edinburgh's Waverley Station and Tweedbank in the Borders, sometimes under steam! (www.borders railway.co.uk)
- **Virgin** (tel: 0871 977 4223; www.virgintrains.co.uk) also operates services on the main intercity routes and to the rest of the UK.

Buses

- **Scottish Citylink** covers most of Scotland and also the rest of the UK (tel: 0871 266 3333; www.citylink.co.uk).
- Numerous small **local companies** link areas not covered by the main operators. Information and timetables are available from tourist offices.
- The **Royal Mail Postbus** service, which operates in the Highlands, Islands and remote rural areas, carries passengers in addition to the mail (tel: 08457 740 740; www.royalmail.com/you-home/your-community/postbus/routefinder).

Ferry Services

- **Caledonian MacBrayne** (CalMac) has an extensive car-ferry service covering the main island destinations on the west coast of Scotland, including Arran, the Hebrides, Skye and the smaller islands. Its website has full details and timetables (tel: 01475 650 397; www.calmac.co.uk).
- **Northlink Ferries** operates overnight ferries from Aberdeen to Orkney and Shetland (tel: 01856 885 500; www.northlinkferries.co.uk). It also operates the service between Scrabster and Stromness.

Internal Air Travel

- **Loganair** flies from Glasgow and Edinburgh to parts of the Highlands and Islands, including the Western Isles, Orkney and Shetland. Flight times average 90 minutes. This is the quickest way to reach these destinations but it is expensive (tel: 01856 873 457 Orkney; tel. 0371 700 2000; www.loganair.co.uk).

- The 10 main **regional airports** are Campbeltown, Islay, Tiree, Barra, Benbecula, Stornoway (Lewis), Sumburgh (Shetland), Kirkwall (Orkney), Wick and Inverness. These are all operated by Highlands and Islands Airports Ltd (HIAL, tel: 01667 462 445; www.hial.co.uk).
- Flights may be delayed or cancelled in **poor weather**.

Taxis

- In cities and larger towns the standard **black hackney cabs** ("London" cabs) are licensed, have meters and should display a tariff.
- **Taxi ranks** are usually found near stations and larger hotels and in the main shopping centres. Raise your arm to hail a cab in the street when its light is showing.
- **Minicabs and private hires** are also licensed and may have a meter. If not, agree a price before you get in. To hire a minicab, phone one of the numbers in the Yellow Pages or telephone directory. They are not allowed to pick up fares in the street, but some ignore this rule.

Driving

Driving in Scotland, particularly outside Glasgow and Edinburgh, is enjoyable and by far the best way to see the country. Roads are generally in good condition, but the farther north you go the narrower they become.

- If you bring your **own car** you'll need its registration documents (and a letter of authorisation) and valid insurance for the UK.
- Drive on the **left**.
- Drivers and all passengers must wear **seat belts**.
- **Speed limits** are 30mph (48kph) in towns, 60mph (96kph) on other roads and 70mph (113kph) on motorways and dual-carriageways, unless signs indicate otherwise.
- The **legal alcohol limit** for drivers is 80mg alcohol per 100ml blood (blood alcohol content 0.08). Drivers may be breathalysed if stopped by police in an accident. Transgressors may be locked up, brought to court, fined and banned from driving. The best policy is not to drink when driving.
- **Fuel prices** vary but are much higher in the Highlands and Islands. Best prices are at supermarket filling stations. There are some 24-hour stations on motorways and in large urban areas, but filling stations are few and far between in rural areas. Most filling stations are self-service.
- You'll find **emergency telephones** along motorways. The Automobile Association (AA; tel. 0800 887 766; www.theAA.com) operates a 24-hour breakdown service for members and for members of other organisations with reciprocal agreements.

Car Rental

- Most major car rental companies have facilities at airports and in major towns. Advance reservations can save money and avoid lengthy waits.
- Car rental is usually available to over-21s only, and you'll need a full driving licence or international permit and a major credit card.

Avis tel: 0808 284 0014; www.avis.co.uk
Budget tel: 0808 284 4444; www.budget.co.uk
Europcar tel: 0871 384 1087; www.europcar.co.uk
Hertz tel: 0207 026 0077; www.hertz.co.uk
Arnold Clark tel: 0141 237 4374; www.arnoldclarkrental.com

Accommodation

Standards of accommodation are generally high throughout the country, and wherever you stay the Scottish people are warm and hospitable (as long as you don't call them "Scotch").

Hotels

- **Rates** are normally quoted per person and include VAT (value added tax). Luxury hotels can cost over £200 per night and the average price in Edinburgh or Glasgow is about £90–160 for two people, including breakfast. Elsewhere, expect to pay £60–90.
- Scotland is noted for its **country-house hotels**, most of which were built in the 19th century by rich industrialists to indulge their sporting passions. Often remote and set in vast estates – fishing (and occasionally shooting) can be included in the costly price – these places enable you to experience the pampered world of the super rich. Other grand houses stand beside world-famous golf courses and give you the chance to play a course that would otherwise be out of bounds.
- Although most genuine **castles** are privately owned, a few have been converted into hotels. Resplendent in granite and castellation, often complete with turrets and towers, such hotels have an intimate yet refined atmosphere and, although prices are high, comfort and luxury are second to none.

Other Accommodation

- For traditional Scottish hospitality and a chance to rub shoulders with local people, a **bed and breakfast** (B&B) is the best option. Most of Scotland's B&Bs and guest houses are family homes, and even inexpensive B&Bs usually have good facilities. The hosts are usually a wonderful source of information (www.visitscotland.com/accommodation/bandbs-guesthouses).
- **Guest houses** are more like small hotels than ordinary family homes (even though many have resident proprietors) and offer simple accommodation at reasonable prices.
- **Coaching inns** were once integral to Scottish life, when they were staging posts for weary horses and travellers. These attractive historic buildings exist in nearly every town. Traditional décor is standard, and there's usually a restaurant serving regional, home-cooked food.

Booking Accommodation

- It's always wise to book ahead as major cities, especially Edinburgh and Glasgow, are busy all year. Elsewhere, many attractions and a lot of the accommodation closes from October until Easter.
- May to August is the **peak season**, so any visit off-season in early spring or late autumn may avoid the crowds and bring discounted accommodation.
- Anyone wishing to organise a spontaneous trip – ideal in Scotland – only needs internet access and a telephone to be able to select a regional room in a B&B or hotel: www.visitscotland.com/accommodation/. Country B&B's that are fully booked are usually quite willing to recommend accommodation nearby so that you will soon find something that meets your requirements.
- In mid- to top-range hotels, **breakfast** may not be included in the price of the room, and it may turn out to be an expensive and disappointing

option. It is often better value, and more fun, to find a local café instead. Breakfast in smaller hotels and bed and breakfasts is usually very good. Expect large portions of traditional Scottish fare such as bacon, eggs, sausages, tomatoes, mushrooms, black pudding and kippers (smoked herring), as well as simple toast and marmalade for those watching their figure.

Camping and Caravanning

■ Despite the damp climate, camping and caravanning is popular with both locals and visitors. It is possible to "wild camp" by pitching a tent away from recognised campsites (though it is wise, and polite, to ask the landowner for permission first).

■ Roads that are unsuitable for towing caravans are usually marked clearly. However, take care when towing a caravan along a single-track road as it is an offence to hold up a following vehicle.

■ Although welcome at dedicated sites, caravans are not permitted to park overnight in lay-bys (rest-stop) or other car parks. Barriers may be placed across entrances to prevent this from occurring.

■ Scotland has more than 400 official, licensed camping and caravan sites. Listings and directions can be provided by local tourist offices and on the website: www.scottishcamping.com.

Youth Hostels

■ If you're on a tight budget but don't want to camp out, backpacking and youth hostels provide cheap alternative accommodation. The simple lodgings are usually in the form of dormitories, which will also give you an opportunity to meet fellow travellers. Washing and cleaning facilities are also provided, although at some hostels you will be expected to clean up after yourself.

■ The **Scottish Youth Hostel Association** (tel: 0845 293 7373; www.syha. org.uk) offers an extensive network of properties, some of which occupy buildings such as croft houses, converted churches and schools.

Information Sources

■ *AA Bed & Breakfast Guide* and *Hotel Guide* – annual publications with comprehensive sections devoted to Scotland (www.theAA.com).

■ *Scotland Bed-and-Breakfast* and *Hotels and Guest Houses* – directories of more than 1,700 B&Bs and more than 1,500 hotels and guest houses, published by VisitScotland (www.scotlandsbestbandbs.co.uk).

■ **Visitors with disabilities** who fond of travelling do not need to make great compromises if they plan ahead and request the help of VisitScotland (tel. 0845 859 1006; www.visitscotland.com/accommodation/accessible).

■ **Self-catering properties are generally available on a week-by-week basis** (www.visitscotland.com/accommodation/self-catering).

■ More **unusual, historic and architecturally attractive accommodation** is offered by the National Trust for Scotland (tel: 0844 493 2108 (from UK) or +44 (0)131 23 9331 (from outside UK); www.ntsholidays.com) and the Forestry Commission (tel: 0845 130 8223; www.forestholidays.co.uk).

Accommodation Prices

Expect to pay per standard double room per night, including breakfast:

£ under £85	££ £85–£125	£££ over £125

Food and Drink

Scottish cuisine is far better than its reputation, with everything from traditional Scottish classics to the latest culinary innovations on offer. The secret is good-quality local produce, with the best menus featuring such delights as Aberdeen Angus beef, salmon, venison and lamb, an array of fresh vegetables and a bewildering selection of cheeses.

Scottish Cuisine

■ The best-known Scottish delicacy is **haggis** – sheep's offal mixed with beef suet and lightly toasted oatmeal, and then boiled in the synthetic skin. With a rich, spicy flavour it tastes better than its description might imply. Haggis is traditionally served with **"neeps"** (turnips) and **"tatties"** (potatoes). You'll find it in butchers' and supermarkets everywhere, but the best-known haggis makers are **Charles MacSween & Son** of Edinburgh (www.macswee.co.uk).

■ Local cooking is widely available, either in its traditional form or with a spin, such the haggis in filo pastry parcels covered in a rich plum sauce found in Edinburgh's Stac Polly restaurants (www.stacpolly.com).

■ **Traditional Scottish dishes** to look out for include:
Scotch broth (hotch-potch) – a light, thin soup of mutton or beef, pearl barley and vegetables.
Cock-a-leekie soup – chicken, leeks, rice and prunes.
Cullen skink – a soup made from smoked (finnan) haddock, milk and mashed potatoes.
Forfar bridies – a pie of flaked pastry filled with minced beef and suet.
Scotch pies – similar to bridies but with a delicious watercrust pastry, found in fish and chip shops along with other deep-fried delicacies like black and white puddings.

■ **Scottish cheeses** – these are among the finest in Europe and range from hard, cheddar-like varieties to soft, creamy types flavoured with herbs, oatmeal or garlic. They are eaten with oatcakes – oatmeal biscuits baked on a griddle. Edinburgh cheesemonger **Iain Mellis** (www.mellischeese.net) stocks a great range.

Informal Eating

You will often find a cosy café in the most remote corner that offers homemade soup and cake at least, one example being the Skoon Art Café in Geocrab in the east of the Isle of Harris www.explorescotland.net/holiday-in-scotland/restaurants). In the towns, too, it is worth trying out meals in the cafés and bistros, for example in Edinburgh's Valvona & Crolla (➤ 70).

High Tea

Traditional Scottish high tea is still served in some hotels, tearooms and cafés. Unlike English high tea, it often includes fish and chips or cold meat in addition to sandwiches. Also expect local specialities such as Dundee fruit cake, shortbread and scones or Scotch pancakes served with butter and jam.
Great places for High Tea include:
■ **Café Gandolfi**, Glasgow (➤ 98)
■ **The Gleneagles Hotel**, Auchterarder (➤ 141)
■ **Kailzie Gardens Restaurant**, Peebles (➤ 120)

Eating Out

- **Breakfast** is served from about 7:30 to 10:30am; **lunch**, noon to 2:30; high **tea** or early dinner, 4:30 to 6:30pm; **dinner**, from about 6:30 to 9pm. Last orders are often taken 45 minutes before closing.
- Some prices include a 10 per cent **service charge**, otherwise tipping is discretionary and can be anything from 10 to 15 per cent.
- Many places offer good value early-evening or pre-theatre **menus**. In top restaurants, lunch may be a comparatively inexpensive option.
- **Dress codes** are increasingly relaxed and very few restaurants insist on a jacket and tie; smart casual is usually acceptable.

Drinking

- There are three basic types of whisky (➤ 32). When you drink a "dram" (glass) of malt whisky, add nothing to it but water – Scots see anything else as an insult.
- **Beer** is not known by the English term "bitter", but "lager", "ale" and "stout" cause no problems.
- There's been a revival of small, traditional **breweries**, including Belhaven of Dunbar, Traquair of Innerleithen, Sulwath Brewery (Castle Douglas, ➤ 122), Broughton Ales of Biggar (Ballindalloch) and Edinburgh's Caledonian, producer of the Golden Promise organic ale.
- The **minimum age** for buying alcohol is 18.
- It is generally prohibited to drink alcohol, or even to carry opened bottles, in the street, and the drink will be confiscated by police if you are caught.
- Irn-Bru, the Scottish soda drink, is something of an acquired taste. Tea and coffee are also generally available in pubs and bars.

Useful Publications

- The **Taste of Scotland** website provides information about restaurants serving high-quality traditional cuisine. It also includes a restaurant directory of the best places to eat and stay (www.taste-of-scotland.com).
- The AA *Restaurant Guide* and *Pub Guide* are available via www.theAA.com.

Restaurant Prices

Expect to pay per three-course meal per person, excluding drinks:

£ under £20	££ £20–£30	£££ over £30

Shopping

Shopping opportunities are abundant in Scotland, not only in modern city malls but tucked away in individual craft and specialist shops, and in smaller towns and villages. Traditional favourites such as tartan scarves, woollens, Celtic brooches, silverware and glassware make ideal gifts. Souvenirs range from cheap and tacky Loch Ness monsters to classy cashmere and silverware (including quaichs, Scotland's traditional two-handled drinking cup).

Tartans, Tweeds and Knitwear

Good purchases are traditional kilts, jackets, skirts, suits and sweaters, es-pecially if hand-made, and durable high-quality goods are widely available. Edinburgh's **Royal Mile** and **Princes Street** are two of the best places to browse, and bargain hunters can't beat the **mill factory shops** in the Borders.

Finding Your Feet

Crafts and Jewellery

- You'll find a vast array of arts, crafts and kitsch everywhere from high street shops to country craft stores, but the **House of Bruar**, just off the A9 north of Pitlochry, and the **National Trust for Scotland** (NTS) gift shops are the best places for Scottish crafts. Gift ideas include Scottish crystal glasses, vases and bowls. There are small, traditional potteries all over Scotland, including the **Lighthouse Pottery** at Portpatrick and the **Borgh Pottery** on Lewis.

- Also popular and widely available is **pewter and silver jewellery**, crafted to traditional Celtic designs copied from ancient illuminated books and manuscripts. Antiques shops and second-hand shops are good for unusual Victorian jewellery, but also look out for the work of new young designers in the trendy shops of Edinburgh and Glasgow.

Food and Drink

- **Scotch whisky** makes an excellent gift and what you don't drink while you're here you can take home. It's available everywhere, but it's more fun to try before you buy at a distillery (➤ 178).

- Food also makes great souvenirs, but, if you are not a UK resident, check your home country's food import regulations first. Good buys include **smoked salmon** and **Loch Fyne kippers**, or try **oatcakes**, **shortbread** and **Dundee cake** in traditional tartan presentation tins. An option for those with strong teeth is **Edinburgh rock**, a hard, sugary treat available at sweet shops and souvenir shops throughout Edinburgh and beyond.

Entertainment

The Scottish entertainment scene includes everything from incomprehensible avant-garde theatre to traditional Scottish shows. Tourist information packs in hotels and guest houses usually include listings. In Edinburgh or Glasgow buy a copy of *The List* magazine, published every two weeks. It's the best guide to what's on, and covers cinema, theatre, clubs, concerts, the arts and readings by local and visiting authors. The *Herald*, one of Scotland's quality newspapers, publishes national listings in its Saturday supplement.

Theatre, Music and Dance

- Scotland has a strong tradition of theatre, and modern and classical productions, musicals and pantomimes are staged throughout the year. Venues include the **Dundee Rep**, **Pitlochry Festival Theatre**, **Tron** and the **Citizens** in Glasgow, the **Traverse** in Edinburgh or the **Theatre Royal**, Dumfries, Scotland's oldest working theatre.

- Opera, classical concerts and most other forms of music are available in abundance in the main cities. Try Glasgow's **Royal Concert Hall** for a varied programme or the **Queens Hall**, Edinburgh, which is also home to the Scottish Chamber Orchestra.

- For classical dance lovers, the acclaimed **Scottish National Ballet** is the main company.

Pubs and Clubs

- The pub scene has changed greatly over the years and most bars now serve food as well as drink. If music is featured, it's usually free when playing in the main bar, and there is something to suit all tastes, from traditional Scottish to jazz.

- During the week, pubs are open from 11–11 and till 1am on Friday and Saturdays, and pubs with special licences stay open until 2am and longer. On Sundays, pubs do not open until midday and are only allowed to serve alcohol from 12:30 pm. In places like the Isles of Lewis and Harris, Sunday remains a day of rest and pubs are closed.
- The best pubs, in which you can find live music:
  The Ceilidh Place, Ullapool (tel. 0185 461 2103; www.theceilidhplace.com)
  The Taybank, Dunkeld (tel. 0135 072 7340; www.thetaybank.com)
  The Famous Bein Inn, Glenfarg (tel. 0157 783 0216; www.beininn.com)
  The Royal Oak, Edinburgh (tel. 0131 557 2976)
  Hootananny, Inverness (tel. 0146 323 3651; www.hootananny.com)
- Clubs offer a wide range of events, from ceilidh (pronounced "kay-lee" – traditional folk dance) to hip parties, with the best choices in the main cities. For the most up-to-date and full club listings check out *The List* magazine's website (www.list.co.uk).

Outdoor Activities

- **Golf** is one of Scotland's major attractions and many visitors come to play on its world-class courses (► 18). With more than 500 courses to choose from, you can get full details from an excellent searchable website: golf.visitscotland.com. You can also get a list of local courses from area tourist offices.
- Scotland is ideal for **hiking and climbing**, with challenging peaks in the Highlands, gentle hill walks in the Lowlands and a series of waymarked, long-distance paths, including the West Highland Way (► 128) and the Southern Upland Way.
- Most tourist information offices have books, leaflets and maps covering walks in their area. For general books on **walking** in Scotland, maps, clothing and safety equipment, try Graham Tiso's shops in Edinburgh (Rose Street), Glasgow (Buchanan Street) and other main towns and cities, or buy online at www.tiso.com.
- For practical information and locations of walks and trails check http://walking.visitscotland.com/see-do/activities/walking.
- **Safety note:** Scottish hills and mountains can be lethal even in summer. Before undertaking any walks or climbs, make sure you are skilled and fit enough to complete them, with adequate footwear and outdoor clothing for the terrain and the necessary safety equipment.
- There's some excellent **fishing** to be had, whether by fly in the lochs and famous salmon rivers, beach casting from spots round the coastline or sea fishing from purpose-built boats. Great information can be gained online from www.fishpal.com/Scotland, or contact the area tourist offices for details on close seasons, local fishing spots and where to get permits. Many hotels also offer fishing for guests.

Spectator Sports

- **Football** (soccer) is a passion for the average Scot. The season runs from around August to May and most league matches are held on Saturday afternoons, with some Sunday and midweek evening games. Most large towns have at least one league team, and local rivalry, such as between Rangers and Celtic in Glasgow, can be intense. Catching a Scotland game at Hampden Park (► 94) can be a mind-blowing experience with the legendary Tartan Army in full force.
- **Rugby union** is almost an obsession in the Scottish Borders towns, but for an unforgettable experience catch an international match at Edinburgh's

Finding Your Feet

Murrayfield stadium, particularly during the Six Nations Championship (www.scottishrugby.com), especially if Scotland is playing England for the Calcutta Cup. The post-match atmosphere in pubs is amazing.

■ **Shinty**, the national sport of the Gaels, originated 2,000 years ago with the ancient Celtic people. Played by teams of 12 with a ball and stick, it has been described as a "warlike version of hockey". Details of fixtures can be found on the Camanachd Association website (www.shinty.com).

Festivals

Festivals and gatherings of all descriptions, from highland games to cultural events, take place in most Scottish towns and villages. There is rarely a time of year when there is not a festival to visit.

■ **The Edinburgh International Festival** in August is the best known and attended of Scotland's festivals of performing arts (▶ 26).

■ The **Traditional Music and Song Association** (TMSA) at 95 St Leonard's Street, Edinburgh, produces a comprehensive calendar of events (tel: 0131 555 2224; www.tmsa.org.uk).

Other Festivals and Village Galas

■ **Up Helly Aa**, Lerwick, Shetland, last Tuesday in January (www.uphellyaa. org) – Viking Fire Festival with no allowances for the weather (▶ 171).

■ **Inverness Music Festival**, last week in February (www.invernessmusic festival.org) – covers all music, from classical to traditional.

■ **International Science Festival**, Edinburgh, beginning of April (www. sciencefestival.co.uk).

■ **Glasgow Art Fair**, mid-April (www.glasgowartfair.com) – art from selected galleries displayed in marquees in George Square.

■ **Beltane Fire Festival**, Edinburgh, evening of 30 April (www.beltane.org) – a celebration of the start of the ancient pagan summer, on Calton Hill. Some smaller towns hold similar events around this time.

■ **Shetland Folk Festival**, end April/May (www.shetlandfolkfestival.com) – four days of lively folk music, with top Scottish and international performers.

■ **Spirit of Speyside Whisky Festival**, early May (www.spiritofspeyside.com) – four days of whisky-flavoured fun, from vintage tastings to distillery tours.

■ **Royal Highland Show**, June (www.royalhighlandshow.org) – Scotland's biggest agricultural show at Edinburgh's Ingliston showground.

■ **T in the Park**, Balado, Fife, second weekend in June (www.tinthepark. com) – mega rock festival attracting big name bands as well as big crowds. A campsite is provided for those staying for the whole weekend. Book early as it generally sells out.

■ **St Magnus Festival**, Orkney, third week in June (www.stmagnusfestival. com) – superb arts festival.

■ **World Pipe Band Championships**, Glasgow, mid-August (www.theworlds. co.uk) – a sea of tartan invades Glasgow Green.

■ **Cowal Highland Gathering**, Dunoon, last weekend in August (www.cowal gathering.com) – the world's largest Highland Games.

■ **Braemar Gathering**, Aberdeenshire, early September (www.braemar gathering.org) – quintessential Highland Games, including caber tossing, tug o' war and pipe bands.

■ **Royal National Mod**, changing locations, second week in October (www. acgmod.org) – festival and competitions for all areas of Gaelic culture.

■ **Hogmanay**, 31 December to 1 January – New Year's celebrations occur throughout Scotland, but Edinburgh's Princes Street is *the* venue for this massive outdoor party (www.edinburghshogmanay.com). Book early.

Edinburgh

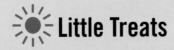 **Little Treats**

Heavenly Music

How enchanting: two carved angels play
the bagpipes in the Thistle Chapel of **St Giles
Cathedral** (➤ 64).

Heart of Midlothian

Don't be surprised if you see somebody
spitting on the heart-shaped mosaic in
the granite pavement near **St Giles Cathedral**
(➤ 64) – it is supposed to bring luck.

Idolised Novelist

Towering opposite the Jenners department
store on Princes Street (➤ 52) is a **memorial
to Walter Scott**: 287 steps lead up to the
panoramic view at the top.

Getting Your Bearings

Edinburgh is one of the most beautiful and well-preserved historic cities in Europe. Set among the volcanic plugs of Castle Rock, Arthur's Seat and Calton Hill, the medieval Old Town and the Georgian New Town provide contrasting historical insights. The narrow closes, steep winding alleys and tall tenements of the Old Town recall the overcrowded conditions of "Auld Reekie" (Old Smokey) in the Middle Ages, and it's easy to imagine the black smog from a thousand chimneys that gave old Edinburgh its nickname. Go from here to the light, airy squares of the New Town, with spacious avenues, elegant terraces and spruce gardens, to see how things were different for the wealthy citizens who moved to these streets.

Despite the hills, Edinburgh is best explored on foot. Wherever you turn there's a breathtaking view, and in summer there's greenery everywhere, from the great open space of Princes Street Gardens to the enclosed gardens of the **New Town** or the tiny hidden corners in the **Old Town**. The architecture of the 1970s made few inroads in Edinburgh, with the notable exception of Princes Street. Viewing them from the gardens, try to picture these buildings before they were encased in unlovely concrete boxes. The **castle** dominates the city, of course, peeping over the tenements, silhouetted in the sunset or towering over Princes Street.

There's always a buzz about Edinburgh, with plenty of cafés and pubs in the **Royal Mile**, excellent restaurants and a lively nightlife around **Grassmarket** and **Cowgate**. In August the city explodes into life, with the **Edinburgh International Festival** attracting thousands of visitors to its colourful mixture of events (➤ 26).

Each year in August, during the annual festival, the esplanade in front of Edinburgh Castle becomes the stage for the Edinburgh Military Tattoo

Getting Your Bearings

Scotland Street in the New Town

Map labels

Royal Yacht *Britannia* **19**

Broughton Street

London Road

Leith Walk

York Place

Gardens

Leith St.

Queen Street

Calton Hill

w Town

Waterloo Place

Regent Road

Abbeyhill

Palace of Holyroodhouse **18**

Street

Gardens

Waverley Station

North Bridge

Canongate

Royal Mile

Scottish Parliament

9

Street

St Giles Cathedral **14**

Royal High Street

Mile Street

Museum of Childhood **16**

Our Dynamic Earth **17**

Holyrood Road

otch Whisky Experience **12**

George IV Bridge

Underground Edinburgh **15**

Cow-gate

Pleasance

13 Grassmarket

11 National Museum of Scotland

Potter Row

Nicolson Street

Holyrood Park

Lauriston Pl.

0 — 400 m
0 — 400 yd

The Perfect Day

Edinburgh's unique mix of medieval Old Town and carefully planned Georgian New Town earned it a place on UNESCO's list of World Heritage Sites some time ago. If you're not quite sure where to begin your travels, this itinerary recommends a practical and enjoyable day in Edinburgh, taking in some of the best places to see. For more information see the main entries (➤ 52–66).

🕘 9:30am

Start the day by exploring ⭐Edinburgh Castle (pictured left, ➤ 55) for an hour and a half.

🕚 11:00am

Head down Castlehill and pop into the **12** Scotch Whisky Experience (➤ 64), then cross over Johnston Terrace and walk along Upper Bow to Victoria Terrace. Take the steps down into Victoria Street, which is lined with small shops selling whisky, Scottish designer fashion and books. At the end of the street is the piazza-style **13** Grassmarket (➤ 64), where executions used to take place, but where life now bustles around a famous second-hand shop (Armstrongs), a milliner (Fabhatrix) and the pub restaurants.

🕛 Noon

From the Grassmarket head up Candlemaker Row. At the top on the left look out for the statue of the Skye terrier **Greyfriars Bobby**, who guarded his master's grave for 14 years and is the only dog to have been awarded the freedom of the city. Cross the road to the modern **11** National Museum of Scotland (➤ 62). Allow a couple of hours for a visit, including lunch in the Tower Restaurant (➤ 63) with a great view over the castle.

🕑 2:15pm

From the museum, head along George IV Bridge. At the Royal Mile turn right into the High Street for a quick look at splendid **14 St Giles Cathedral** (pictured right, ▶ 64) and the famous Thistle Chapel. There is a fabulous view of the city from the roof of the cathedral. On your way down the Mile, stop off to visit the timbered house that belonged to John Knox and eavesdrop on the enacted arguments between the Presbyterian church reformer and the Catholic Queen Mary. At the bottom of Royal Mile, you come to the modern ⭐**Scottish Parliament** (▶ 61), after which the royal palace Holyrood House offers a stark architectural contrast.

🕔 5:30pm

After crossing Calton Road you walk past the volcanic lookout hill Calton Hill and on towards the Georgian **New Town** (▶ 52) and **St. Andrew Square**, the crown at the head of the George Street shopping mile. Take the time to visit one of the cafés as you stroll along the boulevard; admire the linear structures and windows along George Street and the more formal contrast offered by **Charlotte Square**, seat of the First Minister of the Scottish government (no. 6).

🕢 7:30pm

Wander along Rose Street, a narrow street that runs parallel to George Street and is lined with shops and restaurants, until you reach Hanover Street, where **Henderson's** (no. 94, tel. 0131 225 2131; www.hendersons ofedinburgh.co.uk) serves fantastic vegetarian dishes. Try Haggis made without meat.

🕘 9:00pm

In summer, it is still light at this time. Take an after-dinner walk down Hanover Street to **Princes Street Gardens**, from where you can view two of Edinburgh's volcanic hills: Castle Hill on the right and Calton Hill on the left. Turn left and head towards the ornate Gothic **Scott Monument** on Calton Hill. At Waverley Station and a clock tower that is reminiscent of Big Ben, the route continues uphill until you reach the **top**. There is a whole array of monuments to be seen, one particularly eye-catching example being the National Monument built in the style of a Greek temple. Enjoy the romantic setting as the sun goes down over the skyline of the Old Town.

Edinburgh

⭐ New Town

Stray into the quiet Georgian streets of Edinburgh's New Town and even the parked cars cannot break the spell of a time warp of 200 years. It richly deserves its status as a World Heritage Site and even in its day would have been an outstanding collection of buildings. You can quite easily wander for hours around the cobbled grid of parallel avenues, backstreet mews, private gardens and curving terraces.

The area was a pioneering venture in town planning, prompted by the desire of Edinburgh's wealthy merchants to escape the medieval squalor of the Old Town, where rich and poor lived cheek by jowl. The young architect James Craig won the competition to design the New Town in 1767, with a simple grid design of three parallel streets with a square at each end. Central to the design is the broad avenue of **George Street,** while below, **Princes Street** looks out over the Old Town and the castle, and **Queen Street** enjoys uninterrupted views to the Forth and Fife.

View from Calton Hill (➤ 60) of Princes Street and the Balmoral Hotel

Shop front in Dundas Street

Between the broad main streets, narrower **Rose Street** and **Thistle Street** provided service access, and this part became known as the First New Town while development continued around it. The New Town now encompasses the **series of crescents** arching west as far as Haymarket Station, the terraces of Dean village and the quiet streets below Queen Street Gardens. Linking these are the magnificent sweeping curves of Moray Place, Ainslie Place and Randolph Crescent, with their neoclassical façades.

Charlotte Square and Around

Other famous architects and engineers also contributed to the New Town. The elegant north side of **Charlotte Square** by Scottish architect Robert Adam (1728–92) is considered a masterpiece, while, further north, artist Alexander Nasmyth (1758–1840) designed the **Pump Room** on the Water of Leith, and Dean Bridge was the work of Thomas Telford (1757–1834).

At No 28 Charlotte Square, arguably the UK's finest Georgian square, you'll find the headquarters of the **National Trust for Scotland**. There are exhibitions, information and a restaurant, as well as a Georgian drawing room with original furniture. For a better idea of the elegant life lived here, visit the **Georgian House** at No 7, where the domestic life of Edinburgh's 18th-century gentry is faithfully re-created, from the china and furniture to the wine cellar and kitchen. The light, airy rooms and the open vistas of the square contrast with the tiny windows, low ceilings and cramped conditions of the Old Town – as you'll see if you visit **Gladstone's Land**, a 17th-century merchant's house in the Royal Mile. The official residence of the First Minister of the Scottish Parliament is next door to the Georgian House at No 6, **Bute House**.

Near Charlotte Square on the other side of Queen Street, **Moray Place** was certainly the grandest of the New Town

developments. Walk round to absorb the scale of the huge classical-pillared frontages surrounding the central garden. Robert Louis Stevenson, author of *Treasure Island*, lived at **17 Heriot Row**, overlooking Queen Street Gardens – still one of Edinburgh's best addresses. Many original features remain, including fan lights, lampposts and boot scrapers at the doors. At the bottom of India Street, with its tall tenements stepping down the hill, the two crescents of **Royal Circus**, designed by William Playfair (1789–1857), are restrained and simple compared with the scale of Moray Place. **St Stephen's Church** in Howe Street is another Playfair building. Its distinctive classical frontage can be seen clearly down the length of the street.

Georgian jewel in the heart of the First New Town: Charlotte Square

TAKING A BREAK

Have lunch or tea in the revamped **Roxburghe Hotel** (38 Charlotte Square). It's easy to miss because, in keeping with the architecture of the square, there's no obvious hotel sign.

🕂 200 C3 ▣ 23

Georgian House
🕂 200 A3 ✉ 7 Charlotte Square
☎ 0844 4 93 2117; www.nts.org.uk/Property/Georgian-House
🕐 March 11–4, April–June, Sep–Oct 10–5, July–Aug 10–6, Nov 11–3 💷 £6

INSIDER INFO

Children tired of constant sightseeing can be pacified with a visit to the beautifully located 🐧 **Edinburgh Zoo** on the hilly ground west of New Town. Besides the koalas and giant pandas, the penguin parade that takes place every day – a voluntary stroll by inquisitive penguins along the "parade route" lined with visitors – at 2:15pm has been a hit since it started over 60 years ago (Corstorphine Road, tel. 0131 334 9171; www.edinburghzoo.org.uk, April–Sep daily 9–6, Oct and March 9–5, Nov–Feb 9–4:30, entrance fee £18, children under 15 £13.50).

★ Edinburgh Castle

Around a million people visit the castle every year, and if you only have time to see one attraction in Scotland, make it this one. Perched high on a 442ft (135m)-high craggy outcrop, the 800-year-old castle has served as a royal palace, a military garrison and a battleground. This great sheer rock face dominates the view from every direction as you approach Edinburgh, and it must have looked awesome to tired and footsore infantry marching from England. Yet the castle is not as impregnable as it looks, and has often changed hands over the centuries.

The castle dominates the city from almost every angle

The Crown Room

Once through the gate, keep climbing the curving cobbled road up to **Crown Square**, then work your way down. The entrance to the Crown Room, housing the ancient Honours of Scotland – the oldest crown jewels in Europe – is in the corner of the square and you may have to queue. After a short trip through Scottish history through a series of

Edinburgh

tableaux, the Crown Room itself is undoubtedly the highlight. The **crown**, made for King James V, is richly decorated with pearls, precious gems and ermine, and incorporates the gold crown of Robert the Bruce. It has been frequently repaired over the years, but remains an important national treasure. The fine **gold sceptre** topped with a sparkling crystal orb is decorated with religious icons. It was originally given to James IV by Pope Alexander VI in the 15th century, whilst the sword, with its elaborately decorated two-handed hilt and scabbard, was a present from Pope Julius II.

The Stone of Destiny
Next to these glittering icons lies an equally potent but surprisingly mundane symbol of Scottish sovereignty – the Stone of Destiny or **Stone of Scone**. Weighing 208kg

A statue of Robert the Bruce at the Gatehouse greets visitors to the castle

(32 stone), the coarse pink sandstone block with iron rings attached to each end was the coronation stone on which the kings of Scotland were inaugurated for more than 400 years. Edward I of England had it transferred to London in 1296, where it became the coronation stone of England and, later, the United Kingdom and was kept in Westminster Abbey. It was temporarily "repossessed" by four Scottish students at Christmas 1950, but it was not until 1996 that it was formally returned to Scotland.

The Royal Apartments
Also on public view are the Royal Apartments, particularly the chamber where Mary, Queen of Scots gave birth to the future James VI, later to become James I, King of England. The rooms have been refurbished and sensitively restored to their original 16th-century splendour, including beautifully carved wood panelling, replica wall coverings and ornate fireplaces.

The stained-glass window in the small 12th-century chapel shows its namesake Saint Margaret of Scotland

Around Crown Square
On the south side of Crown Square, the **Great Hall**, with its massive wooden vaulted ceiling, once housed the Scottish Parliament, and is still used for receptions and state functions by the First Minister of Scotland.

On the north side of the square, the **Scottish National War Memorial** is a tribute to the dead of all wars. Behind it stands Edinburgh's oldest building, the tiny 12th-century **St Margaret's Chapel**, which provided respite to marauding soldiers for 800 years. Beside it stands the great 15th-century siege gun **Mons Meg**, along with the enormous stone cannonballs it could fire over a distance of 2.5mi (4km). Known as the Muckle Murderer, it was used at the Battle of Flodden in 1513.

From Crown Square, descend to the chilling corridors of the vaults in the **Prisons of War exhibition**, which are built into the solid rock. They have been used variously as stores, bakeries and prison cells. Look for the graffiti left by French prisoners incarcerated here in the 18th and 19th centuries.

TAKING A BREAK
Stop at the **Scotch Whisky Experience** by the castle for something to eat, a coffee or one of their range of whiskies.

➕ 200 B3
✉ Top of the Royal Mile
☎ 0131 225 9846; www.edinburghcastle.gov.uk
🕐 Apr–Sep daily 9:30–6; Oct–Mar 9:30–5
🚇 Waverley 💷 £16.50 including tour

Landmark of the City

According to legend, the Picts built a first fort on the volcanic rock in the 5th century. The oldest parts of the castle complex today date from the 12th century. Edinburgh Castle is one of the country's top tourist attractions and dominates the capital's skyline.

❶ Esplanade: More than 200,000 visitors come to the Edinburgh Military Tattoo music festival every year in August. Queen Elizabeth II awarded it the title of "Royal Edinburgh Tattoo" in 2010.

❷ Gatehouse: Two bronze statues at the main entrance commemorate Scotland's national heroes: Robert the Bruce (left) und William Wallace (right).

❸ Half Moon Battery: James Douglas, 4th Earl of Morton, had the Half Moon Battery built from the ruins of the medieval David's Tower destroyed during The Lang Siege that ended in 1573. Completed in 1588, the Battery's 18-pound canons were added in 1810 during the Napoleon wars.

❹❺ Portcullis Gate in Argyle Tower: The Royal Coat of Arms of Scotland and a Scottish crown adorn the portcullis, which is where the castles tours start.

❻ St Margaret's Chapel: Margaret who was declared a saint in 1250 was the second wife of King Malcolm III. In 1130, David I built this little chapel in her honour – it is the city's oldest preserved building.

❼ Water Tower: The water supply for the castle inhabitants

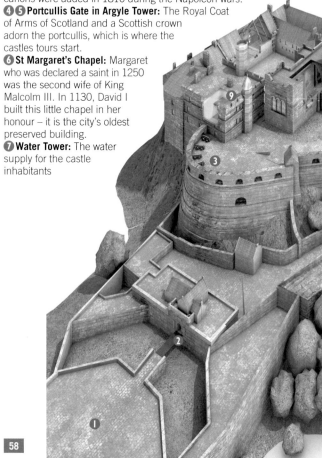

8 Scottish National War Memorial: Memorial to the people killed during the two World Wars.

9 Royal Palace: The royal palace with the Crown Room.

10 Mons Meg: This bombard cast in 1449 in Mons was in military use for almost 100 years. In 1558, it fired the gun salute to mark the marriage of Mary, Queen of Scots.

11 National War Museum: Located in the former hospital

12 Redcoat Café: Ideal for a relaxing break and to recharge the batteries

13 One o'clock Gun: During the week, on the Mills Mount Battery, the One o'clock Gun is fired at precisely 1pm. It is a tradition dating back to the time when ships in the Firth of Forth set their chronometers by it.

View of the Armoury
Room at Edinburgh Castle

Edinburgh

INSIDER INFO

Insider Tip

- Get your picture taken astride the cannons on the Argyle Battery.
- Try to be at **Mills Mount Battery** at 1pm for the firing of the gun. This was originally for the benefit of ships in the Firth of Forth, but now Edinburgh folk just check their watches by it. On **Calton Hill**, on the other side of Waverley Station, look for **Nelson's Monument**, a strange telescope-shaped feature with a suspended ball at the top. Watch for the ball dropping when the One o'Clock Gun fires.
- Even if you're short of time, don't be so keen to see inside the castle that you miss the **panoramic views** of the town and surrounding countryside. The best view-point is from the battlements in front of St Margaret's Chapel, where the formal plan of the New Town is laid out before you with the Firth of Forth and the Lomond Hills of Fife beyond.
- Just below the battlements of the Argyle Battery is the tiny and always beautifully kept **Pets' Cemetery**, the resting place of soldiers' pets. Just as you enter the Esplanade, look out for a small iron wall-fountain known as the **Witches' Well**, where women found guilty of witchcraft were once burned at the stake.

In More Depth West of Crown Square in an 18th-century barracks is the **Scottish National War Museum**, with a comprehensive display of uniforms and weaponry. Unless you're particularly interested in military history, you could give this a miss, but try to see the model ship, the *Great George*, which was made by French prisoners of war.

⭐Scottish Parliament

To create a grand, modern structure in a city as reserved as Edinburgh was always going to be controversial and expensive, but since the Scottish Parliament opened its doors in 2004 its critics have gradually fallen silent. As the extravagances of its cost fade from memory, there is a growing sense of pride that the seat of Scottish democracy should be seen as innovative and refreshingly different.

The new Scottish Parliament cost the Scottish taxpayer about £430,000,000

Designed by the Catalan architect Enric Miralles, the building of concrete, glass, steel, granite, oak and sycamore, is both functional and fascinating, as is immediately obvious from the eye-catching exterior. The steel roofs look like upturned boats, the oriels like residential and fortified towers. For the outline of the windows, Miralles took his inspiration from Henry Raeburn's portrait of the Reverend Walker skating on Duddingston Loch. The wall that fronts onto the Canongate is well worth seeing. Designed by Sora Smithson, it is inset with evocative and witty quotes, from psalms to song lyrics and snatches of poetry about how the Scots see themselves. Inside, **join a tour** to admire the architectural concept of Miralles, notably in the light and airy **Garden Lobby**, and in the soaring roof of the **Main Chamber**.

Insider Tip

➕ 201 E3
✉ Canongate, at the foot of the Royal Mile
☎ 0131 348 5200; www.scottish.parliament.uk
🕐 Tue–Thu 9–6:30 and when parliament is in recess April–Sep 10–5; Oct–March 10–4
🍴 Café (£) 🎫 Free entrance and tour

INSIDER INFO

- Advance **reservations** for tours is essential.
- Access to the Main Hall and a peep inside the Chamber (on non-business days) will **cost you nothing**; the **public entrance** is round a corner, opposite the Palace of Holyroodhouse. Be prepared and allow time for **airport-style security checks** when you go in.
- On the Scottish Parliament's home page you will find **Information brochures** in PDF format that you can download: www.scottish.parliament.uk/visitandlearn/leaflets-and-guides.aspx.

Edinburgh

⑪ National Museum of Scotland

Opened in 1998, the National Museum of Scotland, housed in a large sandstone structure described as "the finest Scottish building of the 20th century", complements the adjoining Victorian Royal Museum of Scotland. It tells the story of the country from its geological formation to the end of the second millennium. More than 10,000 of the nation's treasures and countless everyday objects are displayed over several floors.

A good starting point on **Level 0** is at the abstract human figures sculpted in bronze by Sir Eduardo Paolozzi (born 1924), displaying the rings, necklaces and amulets of shadowy early generations. In the "**Dead and Sometimes Buried**" section is a skeleton lying in its burial position on a bed of flat stones in a reconstructed Viking grave.

On **Level 1** you'll find one of the museum's most important objects – **the Monymusk Reliquary**, a tiny eighth-century casket that once held a relic of St Columba. Revered and treasured as a holy shrine, it was carried to the army of Robert the Bruce before the Battle of Bannockburn in 1314. Here too are the Lewis chess pieces, intricately carved in ivory by invading Vikings, discovered in the 19th century. The gruesome but compelling **Maiden**, Scotland's guillotine, used for public executions in the Grassmarket from the 16th century, is also here. A multimedia display demonstrates its workings, complete with chilling sound effects.

On **Level 2** visitors travel on a journey through Scotland's past from 900 through to 1707. Highlights include ancient weapons and some used in the Jacobite Uprisings.

The entrance to **Level 3** takes you under the royal arms into the United Kingdom. The full story of the bitterly contested succession is told in **The Jacobite Challenge** exhibit. Jewellery, portraits and glassware inscribed with the image of Bonnie Prince Charlie (Charles Stuart, 1720–88) testify to the cult that grew in the years after his defeat at the Battle of Culloden in 1746. Pride of place goes to his personal items, especially the silver travelling canteen that he abandoned at Culloden along with his sword and *targe* (shield).

Levels 4 and 5 move to an age of machinery and factories, when Scotland became one of the most industrialised countries in Europe. The Victorian

---

🔍 FOR LITTLE EXPLORERS

The **Discovery Centre** on Level 3 is a hands-on zone where children can touch the exhibits, reconstruct ancient pottery, dress in period clothes and explore the **Animal World**.

The spectacular architecture of the museum is an attraction in its own right

steam locomotive *Ellesmere* dominates the railway engineering display, and you can learn all about whisky distilling around the huge copper still.

TAKING A BREAK

The café in the adjacent Royal Museum of Scotland building is great for a quick coffee or a light lunch. For a bigger bite, the **Tower Restaurant,** overlooking Edinburgh Castle, is one of the city's top eating places (➤ 70).

🔲 201 D2 ✉ Chambers Street
☎ 0131 225 7534; www.nms.ac.uk ⏰ Daily 10–5
🍴 Café in Royal Museum (£), Tower Restaurant (££)
🚌 14, 7, 8, 87 from Princes Street (east end);
21, 33, 30, 3, 31, 36, 69 from west end 🚉 Waverley
🎫 Free; may charge for some temporary exhibitions

INSIDER INFO

- The **gift shop**, shared with the Royal Museum next door, is a great place for high-quality souvenirs and books, from pocket-money toys to designer scarves and glassware.
- The **roof terrace** on Level 7 has breathtaking views over Edinburgh, the Firth of Forth and the Pentland Hills.

At Your Leisure

One of the city's most popular attractions

12 🔔 Scotch Whisky Experience

This popular attraction, just below Edinburgh Castle, is a great way to discover the secrets of the national liquor – and, unlike the distillery tours, this can be enjoyed by young children as well. Tours set off every 15 minutes and last around one hour, taking in a short film introduction, a gentle barrel-ride through history, a legendary "ghost" and a talk through the manufacturing process. Adults get a free tasting at the end, and there's juice for the kids.

➕ 200 C3 ✉ 354 Castlehill, The Royal Mile
☎ 0131 220 0441;
www.scotchwhiskyexperience.co.uk
🕐 Daily 10–6 💷 From £14

13 Grassmarket

Grassmarket, with the castle looming over it, has been a focal point and market-place for the town for more than 500 years. Public executions were carried out here on the infamous Maiden (▶ 62), the last taking place in 1697. It was here, too, that the notorious 19th-century body snatchers (William) Burke and (William) Hare sought victims for their grizzly trade in cadavers. The area is now a lively nightspot, its streets swarming with revellers wandering from packed pubs to the latest nightclubs. By day you can visit idiosyncratic shops such as Mr Wood's Fossils, and Armstrong's, a fabulous second-hand clothes shop, or just relax with a cup of coffee at one of the pavement tables.

➕ 200 C2 ✉ Grassmarket

14 St Giles Cathedral

Dating from 1120, and featuring the 15th-century Crown Spire, St Giles has been at the centre of Edinburgh's turbulent past. A fine building, also known as the High Kirk of Edinburgh, it is the Mother Church of Presbyterianism and is famed for its superb stained glass and grand organ. The small Thistle Chapel is dedicated to Scotland's highest award for chivalry. Look out for the carved angels playing the bagpipes. St Giles, a seventh-century hermit, is the city's patron saint.

➕ 195 D3 ✉ Royal Mile
☎ 0131 225 9442; www.stgilescathedral.org.uk
🕐 May–Sep Mon–Fri 9–7, Sat 9–5, Sun 1–5;
Oct–May Mon–Sat 9–5, Sun 1–5
💷 Free

15 Underground Edinburgh

The modern streets of Edinburgh conceal a maze of ancient streets below, as any new buildings simply used the existing streets and tenements as their foundations. Several guided tours explore these streets, but the most interesting centres are on **Mary King's Close** just off the Royal Mile. This area suffered particularly badly from the plague, which frequently swept through the polluted streets of the Old Town, and the entire close was sealed for a period in around 1645. Excavations have allowed a lively insight into life in the multi-storey tenements, including details of some of the actual inhabitants who

lived here into the 20th century. There are lots of walking tours of Edinburgh, based around a number of themes – look for details on boards around the Mercat Cross, near St Giles Cathedral.

➕ 200 C3
✉ 2 Warriston's Close ☎ 0845 070 6244; www.realmarykingsclose.com
🕐 Mar–Oct daily 10–9, Sun–Thu 10–5; tours every 20 mins, book ahead 💷 £13.95

16 🚼 Museum of Childhood

A real highlight awaits kids and their parents in the Royal Mile. The collection includes tin soldiers, Barbie dolls and a whole hotch-potch of other children's toys arranged according to different eras. It also offers adults a nice outing, during which they can bring the toys to life for their offspring with their own childhood stories.

➕ 201 D3
✉ 42 High Street ☎ 0131 529 41 42; www.edinburghmuseums.org.uk
🕐 Mon–Sat 10–5, Sun noon– 5 💷 Free

17 🚼 Our Dynamic Earth

Housed in a futuristic dome close to the Royal Mile, this exhibition explores the geography and geology of the world through interactive screens and displays. Children of all ages will love it. Highlights are the floor pad to stamp out your own earthquake, the time machine with wide-screen effects and trembling floors, the enormous curved block of ice to touch and the realistic model of a tropical rain forest to explore.

➕ 201 E3 ✉ 112 Holyrood Road
☎ 0131 550 7800; www.dynamicearth.co.uk
🕐 Apr–Jun, Sep–Oct daily 10–5:30; Jul–Aug 10–6; Nov–Mar 10–5
🍴 Restaurant (£) 🚌 35, 64 💷 £12.50

18 Palace of Holyroodhouse

At the end of the Royal Mile, be-hind elegant wrought-iron gates, is the Queen's official residence in Scotland. Built for James IV in 1498, it was extensively renovated in the 1670s. The palace is normally open to the public and the tour includes Mary, Queen of Scots' apartments. Holyroodhouse sits within the vast **Royal Park**, where you can take a gentle stroll by the pond to watch the swans, climb the hill paths to the top of **Arthur's Seat** or cycle through to nearby Duddingston to

Palace of Holyroodhouse

enjoy a drink in the quaint Sheep's Heid Inn.

➕ 201 E3 ✉ Canongate
☎ 0131 556 5100; www.royalcollection.org.uk
🕐 Apr–Oct daily 9:30–6; Nov–Mar 9:30–4:30
(Palace may occasionally close at other times)
🚌 35 🚆 Waverley 💷 £11.60

🔟9 Royal Yacht *Britannia*

Now docked at the **Port of Leith**, the Royal Yacht *Britannia* is a magnet for royalists but has a much wider appeal. A tour gives a fascinating insight into the private lives of the British royal family, who often took holidays on board. Countless royal couples, including the Prince and Princess of Wales, honeymooned here. You can peep into the bedrooms of the Queen and her family, as well as her office, and also walk through the informal lounge. In complete contrast are the state rooms and formal dining room where politicians, diplomats and world leaders were entertained. Don't miss the engine – a gleaming antique but still in perfect working order.

➕ 201, off E5
✉ Ocean Terminal Shopping Centre, Leith
☎ 0131 555 5566;
www.royalyachtbritannia.co.uk
🕐 Jan–Mar and Nov–Dec 10–3:30;
Apr–Jun and Oct 10–4; Jul–Sep 9:30–4:30
🍴 Cafés in shopping centre
🚌 Bus from Waverley Station 💷 £14

FOUR GREAT VIEWPOINTS

Calton Hill From here you get a superb view along Princes Street to the castle (above), particularly impressive as the sun sets over the city. There are also fine views of the New Town, the Port of Leith, the River Forth and the Kingdom of Fife.

The Camera Obscura On the Royal Mile just down from the castle, this is a great place from which to spy on the shoppers in Princes Street. Using a Victorian lens and mirror, an image of the surrounding city is projected onto a table in front of you. There are also good views from the roof.

Salisbury Crags These rocky crags in Holyrood Park, just in front of Arthur's Seat, offer panoramic views of the city, particularly the Old Town and the countryside to the south.

Tower Restaurant, National Museum of Scotland The restaurant is on the seventh floor of the museum, and you can enjoy fabulous views over the city's rooftops as you dine in style.

Insider Tip

Where to...
Stay

Prices
Expect to pay per standard double room per night, including breakfast:
£ under £70   ££ £70–£100   £££ over £100

Balmoral £££

The clock in this endearingly imposing classic Edwardian building is two minutes fast (except at Hogmanay) to ensure that no one misses their train at Waverley Station next door. The Balmoral is expensive, central and offers every facility, ranging from an indoor swimming pool and gym to a health spa. Bedrooms are luxurious, some with superb views over the city. Afternoon tea in the Palm Court is a must, and there's acclaimed cooking at the Number One Restaurant. There is also a less formal brasserie.

➕ 200 C3 ✉ 1 Princes Street
☎ 0131 556 2414; www.roccofortehotels.com/hotels-and-resorts/the-balmoral-hotel/

Best Western Bruntsfield ££–£££

This smart stone-fronted hotel overlooks a golf course. There are 73 well-equipped and comfortable bedrooms in a variety of sizes and styles, and a bright conservatory restaurant, where hearty traditional breakfasts and imaginative dinners are served. There's also a lively pub.

➕ 200 B1 ✉ 69/74 Bruntsfield Place
☎ 0131 229 1393; www.thebruntsfield.co.uk

The Bonham £££

Occupying an elegant and discreet Georgian town house in a fine West End crescent on the edge of the New Town, the Bonham is one of Edinburgh's smartest hotels. It's a converted university residence, but you'd never know. All of the 48 bedrooms are imaginatively designed and equipped with splendid bathrooms. Its striking, brasserie-style restaurant offers adventurous dishes.

➕ 200, off A2 ✉ 35 Drumsheugh Gardens
☎ 0131 226 6050; http://thebonham.com

Carlton Hotel ££–£££

This large hotel is in a prime position between Princes Street and the Royal Mile. The bedrooms are traditionally styled but well-equipped. There is also a leisure centre and nightclub. The Bridge restaurant is a contemporary setting in which to enjoy fine Scottish produce.

➕ 201 D3 ✉ 19 North Bridge
☎ 0131 472 3000; www.thehotelcollection.co.uk/hotels/carlton-hotel-edinburgh

Dunstane House Hotel ££

There's a very comfortable, intimate, country house feel to this privately run hotel, in a magnificent crow-stepped Victorian villa between Murrayfield sports stadium and the Haymarket railway station, on the airport side of the city. There are just 16 bedrooms, including four family rooms, and also a top-class restaurant, which often serves fish from the proprietor's native Orkney islands.

➕ 200 A2 ✉ 4 Westcoates, Haymarket ☎ 0131 337 6169; www.dunstane-hotel-edinburgh.co.uk

Grassmarket Hotel £–££

Offering modern, minimalistic room design as well as functional accessories such as iPod-Docks, this inexpensive accommodation is located in the middle of the Old Town and pub scene. Tip: early bird booking is available on the website.

➕ 200 C3 ✉ 94–96 Grassmarket ☎ 0131 22 00 22 99; www.grassmarkethotel.co.uk

Edinburgh

The Howard £££

The austere exterior conceals a hotel of comfort and discreet luxury, created from three linked town houses in the New Town. The Edwardian drawing room is filled with sumptuous furnishings and ornate chandeliers. The bedrooms are furnished with antiques, while the bathrooms have shower cubicles or old-fashioned, free-standing tubs. The highly regarded Atholl Dining Room is adorned with hand-painted murals from the 1800s.

⊞ 194 B5 ✉ 34 Great King Street
☎ 0131 557 3500; www.thehoward.com

Hotel Ibis ££

The opening of the new Scottish Parliament initiated a veritable hotel building boom in Edinburgh – Ibis was one of the first new hotels. The converted warehouse offers 99 practical en suite rooms that are reasonably priced in a pleasant location not far from the Royal Mile.

⊞ 201 D3 ✉ 6 Hunter Square
☎ 0131 240 70 00; www.accorhotels.com

Malmaison ££–£££

This upbeat designer hotel is part of an acclaimed and rapidly expanding chain. It occupies a fine period building that was formerly a seaman's mission, next to Leith dock gates. The bedrooms are minimalist, but manage the right degree of comfort, and facilities such as CD players are standard. The brasserie and all-day café are also fashionable.

⊞ 201, off E5 ✉ 1 Tower Place
☎ 0131 468 5000; www.malmaison.com

Sheraton Grand Hotel & Spa £££

This striking, modern building forms part of an evolving development known as Exchange Square. Attention to small details extends to the hotel's own, specially commissioned tartan. The best bedrooms have castle views, and all rooms are comfortable, well proportioned and pleasantly styled. A leisure centre with swimming pool and gym adds to the attractions. The conservatory-style Terrace Restaurant overlooks the square, Usher Hall and the historic castle beyond, while the Grillroom is elegant and discreet.

⊞ 200 B2 ✉ 1 Festival Square
☎ 0131 229 9131; www.sheraton.com

The Sun Inn ££–£££

This recently revamped inn on the outskirts of Edinburgh is a perfect wee escape from the bustle of the town centre. The rooms upstairs are best. The suite, is worth the extra as it boasts a bespoke copper bathtub and Egyptian cotton linen. Downstairs the open-plan bar and bistro areas work really well. Staff are friendly and the cooking is excellent, drawing on Borders lamb and Scottish seafood to conjure up one of those menus from which it is hard to select.

⊞ 206 C4 ✉ Lothianbridge, Dalkeith ☎ 0131 663 2456; www.thesuninnedinburgh.co.uk

Ten Hill Place ££–£££

Mention this hotel to many citizens of Edinburgh and they won't have a clue where it is. Ten Hill Place, however, is a great value and stylish base for a weekend in the capital. It is located close to the Festival Theatre. Top-floor rooms boast sweeping views of Arthur's Seat and all the way down to the Firth of Forth.

⊞ 201 D2 ✉ 10 Hill Place
☎ 0131 622 2080; www.tenhillplace.com

Hotel Twenty ££

Housed in a Georgian building, this B&B hotel boasts a spectacular location on the north side of the green Calton Hill. The owners have renovated the interior with meticulous care – with red as the dominant colour. The small rooms are attractive, the breakfast good and the food in the adjoining Thai restaurant is authentic and delicious.

⊞ 201 E4 ✉ 20 Leopold Place, London Road
☎ 0131 556 35 56; www.hoteltwenty.co.uk

Where to…
Eat and Drink

Prices
Expect to pay per three-course meal per person, excluding drinks:
£ under £20   **££** £20–£30   **£££** over £30

RESTAURANTS

David Bann ££
Scottish cuisine that does not include meat and even includes a choice for vegans? Yes, it is possible, and is actually of a very high quality. Homemade pasta variations, Thai-style fritters, Scottish blue cheese gratin: David Bann serves international vegetarian cuisine. Everything is very tasty, even the "Kelpie Ale" brewed with seaweed.
➕ 201 D3 ✉ 56–58 St Mary's Street
☎ 0131 556 58 88; www.davidbann.com
🕒 Lunch and dinner daily

The Grain Store ££
For years, high above the Old Town looking down on Victoria Street, chef Carlo Coxon has been serving well seasoned Scottish-European cuisine made of mainly local products. Halibut, venison and black pudding are served in a romantic atmosphere surrounded by old stone walls and beneath a vaulted ceiling: kitsch-free Old Town, accompanied by the photo art of co-owner Paul MacPhail. An insider lunch tip!
➕ 200 C3 ✉ 30 Victoria Street ☎ 0131 225 76 35; www.grainstore-restaurant.co.uk
🕒 Lunch and dinner daily

Henderson's £
A vegetarian icon of the New Town, consisting of a restaurant, bistro, bakery and deli shop – buy here and sit down in the Queen Street Gardens. *Insider Tip*
➕ 200 C4 ✉ 94 Hanover Street ☎ 0131 225 21 31; www.hendersonsofedinburgh.co.uk
🕒 Mon–Sat 8am–10/11pm

Kalpna £–££
This vegetarian Indian restaurant is one of the best in the country. Freshly ground spices give the dishes a special note.
➕ 201 D2 ✉ 2–3 St Patrick's Square
☎ 0131 667 9890; www.kalpnarestaurant.com
🕒 Lunch and dinner daily

The Kitchin £££
For foodies, the Michelin-starred Kitchin is a must-visit restaurant on Leith's revitalised waterfront and worth the trip and the expense. Award-winning chef Tom Kitchin's philosophy is: "from nature to plate". Using Scottish produce and a modern approach to flavours, he sends out dishes such as Ayrshire pork loin with aubergine compote. Desserts are a particular strength.
➕ 201, off F5 ✉ 78 Commercial Quay, Leith
☎ 0131 555 1755; www.thekitchin.com
🕒 Lunch and dinner Tue–Sat

The Outsider ££
The Outsider's stylish candlelit interior and views of Edinburgh Castle might lead you to expect a hefty bill at the end of your meal. But the hearty dishes – often inspired by rustic British and French classics – are keenly priced. Lunches especially are a bargain: ham hock and marrow-fat pea ragout, chicken liver risotto with caramelised onions, walnuts and brandy. Service is friendly and the wine list is inventive. Make reservations in advance.
➕ 200 C2
✉ 15–16 George IV Bridge ☎ 0131 226 3131; www.theoutsiderrestaurant.com
🕒 Daily noon–11

Edinburgh

Plumed Horse £££

Tony Borthwick's fine dining temple is one of the best in Scotland, even if it has lost its Michelin star. The trim restaurant is the perfect setting for some seriously grand and innovative cooking, with local produce coming through strongly. its four-course lunch menu is well worth trying.

➕ 201, off F5
✉ 50–54 Henderson Street, Leith
☎ 0131 554 5556; www.plumedhorse.co.uk
🕐 Lunch and dinner Tue–Sat

Restaurant Martin Wishart £££

Confident cooking from a chef who has worked with some of the greats. The Michelin-starred menu is small but ranges from classic French to Mexican-infused innovations. Set by the water in Leith, it's a bright, intimate place ideal for a special occasion.

➕ 201, off F5 ✉ 54 The Shore, Leith
☎ 0131 553 3557; www.martin-wishart.co.uk
🕐 Lunch and dinner Tue–Sat

Tower Restaurant & Terrace ££

Take the lift to the National Museum of Scotland, to try this sophisticated brasserie-style restaurant, which offers a superb view of the castle. Dishes are modern British, with great beef served at the grill.

➕ 201 D2 ✉ National Museum of Scotland, Chambers Street
☎ 0131 225 3003; www.tower-restaurant.com
🕐 Lunch and dinner daily

The Witchery by the Castle £££

The atmosphere of this restaurant, set in a 16th-century building, is indeed bewitching. Both dining-rooms are candlelit, adorned with gilded heraldic ceilings, tapestries, and leather and wood panels. Expect confident, innovative modern cooking.

➕ 200 C3 ✉ Castlehill, Royal Mile
☎ 0131 225 5613; www.thewitchery.com
🕐 Lunch and dinner daily

The Elephant House £

This is the spot where J K Rowling started penning her classic Harry Potter novels and the café's owners are not shy of reminding you of the fact. But you can see why she chose this warm and welcoming friendly spot with its first-class coffee, decent cakes and sandwiches, and good views.

➕ 200 C2 ✉ 21 George IV Bridge
☎ 0131 220 5355; www.elephanthouse.biz
🕐 Mon–Fri 8–11, Sat–Sun 9–11

Valvona & Crolla Caffè-Bar £–££

The Continis import produce from Italy for sale in their delicatessen, and to supplement the prime Scottish beef, west-coast seafood and organic vegetables that appear on the menu of their bright caffè-bar. Food is served until 5pm and queues can build up.

➕ 201 D4 ✉ 19 Elm Row, Leith Walk ☎ 0131 556 6066; www.valvonacrolla.co.uk 🕐 Mon–Thu 8:30–5:30, Fri–Sat 8–6, Sun 10:30–4:30

The Bow Bar £

This blue-painted pub is the best in the city for whisky, with more than 290 to choose from and usually several on special offer. Wood panelling and old brewery mirrors inside.

➕ 200 C3 ✉ 80 The West Bow, Victoria Street
☎ 0131 226 7667
🕐 Mon–Sat 12–11:30, Sun 12:30–11

Café Royal ££

This bustling pub has a Victorian-baroque elegance, summed up by its showy central bar counter. There's also a stylish, if expensive, restaurant and oyster bar that offers elegant fish and game dishes à la carte, plus caviar, lobster and Champagne.

➕ 200 C3 ✉ 19 West Register Street
☎ 0131 556 1884; www.caferoyal.org.uk
🕐 Mon–Wed 11–11, Thu 11am–midnight, Fri–Sat 11am–1am, Sun 12:30–11

Where to...
Shop

SHOPPING HOURS

Shopping hours are 9am to 6pm, with late opening until 8 or 9pm on Thursdays. Many shops open on Sunday afternoons, especially in the summer. The main shopping areas are **Princes** and **George Streets** in the New Town and the **Royal Mile** and **Grassmarket** in the Old Town.

DEPARTMENT STORES

Often called the Scottish Harrods, **Jenners** (founded in 1838) on Princes Street is worth a visit if only to wander round the old-fashioned tiered wooden balconies, take tea and stock up on Scottish fare. It has been joined by **Harvey Nichols** in St Andrew Square.

SCOTTISH SOUVENIRS

Gift shops abound on the Royal Mile, selling everything from whisky to cashmere. **Scottish Gems** (24 High Street) offers Celtic jewellery; **Geoffrey** (Tailor) (57–61 High Street; tel: 0131 557 0256) is the place for kilts, off-the-peg or bespoke; and for tartan, there's the **Tartan Weaving Mill and Exhibition** at the top of the Royal Mile, with a contemporary take on offer at **Anta** (17 George Street; tel: 0131 225 9096).

GROCERIES

Valvona & Crolla (19 Elm Row; tel: 0131 556 6066), at the top of Leith Walk, sells cooking oils, olives, bread and pasta. **Iain Mellis Cheesemonger** (30a Victoria Street; tel. 0131 226 62 15) and **Demijohn**

(32 Victoria Street; tel. 0131 225 32 65) have a delicatessen, whisky, oil and vinegar. For whisky galore, try the **Scotch Whisky Heritage Experience** (354 Castlehill; tel: 0131 220 0441), **Royal Mile Whiskies** (379 High Street; tel: 0131 225 3383) opposite St Giles Cathedral and **William Cadenhead** (172 Canongate; tel: 0131 556 5864), or **The Scotch Malt Whisky Society** (87 Giles Street, Leith; tel: 0131 554 3451; 28 Queen Street; tel: 0131 220 2044) for rare malts.

BOOKS

Edinburgh is a splendid city for bookworms. Places to head for include the excellent **Old Town Bookshop** (8 Victoria Street; tel: 0131 225 9237), **James Thin** (53 South Bridge; tel: 0131 622 8222) and **Waterstone's** (13–14 Princes Street; tel: 0131 556 3034; 128 Princes Street; tel: 0131 226 2666; 83 George Street; tel: 0131 225 3436). There are antiquarian bookshops along the Westport from the Grassmarket. Particularly tempting is **Edinburgh Books** (145–147 Westport; tel: 0131 229 4431).

THE QUIRKY AND UNUSUAL

Edinburgh has a fine selection of individual and offbeat shops. Try **Mr Wood's Fossils** (5 Cowgatehead; tel: 0131 220 1344) in the Grassmarket or **Wm Armstrong and Son** (81–83 Grassmarket; tel: 0131 220 5557), the capital's coolest second-hand clothes shop. In Victoria Street look out for handcrafted jewellery at **Clarkson**'s (87 West Bow; tel: 0131 225 8141). And at Westport, **Godiva Boutique** (No 9; tel: 0131 221 9212), is an award-winning independent clothing boutique. For other memorable shops wander down **Cockburn Street** from the Royal Mile or along **Rose Street**, between George Street and Princes Street.

Where to...
Go Out

THEATRES & CONCERT HALLS

The **Royal Lyceum** (Grindlay Street; tel: 0131 248 4848) stages plays and comedies; in contrast, the **Traverse Theatre** (10 Cambridge Street; tel: 0131 228 1404) is known for experimental performances; the **Playhouse** (18–22 Greenside Place; tel: 0844 447 1660) and the **King's Theatre** (2 Lewen Street; tel: 0131 529 6000) both offer lightweight or musical entertainment.

The **Festival Theatre** (13/29 Nicholson Street; tel: 0131 529 6000) and **Usher Hall** (Lothian Road; tel: 0131 228 1155) are prestigious concert venues; the **Queen's Hall** (85–89 Clerk Street; tel: 0131 668 2019) offers a more intimate setting.

CINEMAS

Independent cinemas include the **Dominion** (18 Newbattle Terrace; tel: 0131 447 4771) in Morningside and the **Cameo** (38 Home Street; tel: 0871 704 2052) in the West End. The **Filmhouse** (88 Lothian Road; tel: 0131 228 2688) shows less commercial and art house films.

BEST PUBS

Starting at the **Ensign Ewart** (521 Lawnmarket; tel: 0131 225 7440) at the castle end of the Royal Mile, you can pub crawl to **Jenny Ha's** (68 Cannongate; tel: 0131 556 2101) near Holyrood.

Don't miss **Deacon Brodie's** (435 Lawnmarket; tel: 0131 225 6531) on the corner of George IV Bridge, the interior of the **Café Royal Circle Bar** (19 West Register Street; tel: 0131 556 1884) or the whisky selection in the old-fashioned **Bow Bar** (▶ 70). **The Tass** (1 High Street; tel: 0131 556 6338) has real ale, cheap food and folk music. The **World's End** (4 High Street; tel: 0131 556 3628) is famous for food. In Old Town, **Sandy Bell's** (25 Forrest Road; tel: 0131 225 2751) is very atmospheric. The tiny bar of the **Royal Oak** (1 Infirmary Street; tel: 0131 557 2976; www.royal-oak-folk.com) attracts interesting characters, has a selection of fine malts and cask ales and nightly music downstairs.

Bannerman's (212 Cowgate; tel: 0131 556 3254) is a cosy collection of vaulted rooms with live rock, soul and jazz. In the New Town, **Mather's Bar** (1 Queensferry Street; tel: 0131 225 3549) has a Victorian interior, while the **Oxford Bar** (8 Young Street; tel: 0131 539 7119) is the fictitious Inspector Rebus' local (▶ 24).

NIGHTLIFE

Youngsters gravitate towards the **Grassmarket**, along the **Cowgate, Lothian Road** and in the **West End**.

The sophisticated and trendy hang out around **George Street** in café-bars such as the **Opal Lounge** (No 51A; tel: 0131 226 2275) or **Tigerlily** (No 125; tel: 0131 225 5005). At 11pm these bars turn into nightclubs and are open until the small hours. Fashions change regularly so consult *The List* (see below) before going out.

The List, published fortnightly and available from newsagents, is the best guide to what's on. There are detailed listings carried daily in the *Edinburgh Evening News*, the weekend section of the *Scotsman* and in *Scotland on Sunday*. The *Scotsman's* website (www.scotsman.com) also lists events for the week ahead.

Glasgow

 Little Treats

The Noble Elephant
Even so many years after his death, this
stuffed pachyderm in Kelvingrove Museum
(►78) still looks very dignified.

Victorian Nirvana
The tombstones in the **Necropolis** next to
the cathedral show just how affluent, proud
and important Glasgow used to be (►91).

Rummage to Your Heart's Content
Forget the time as you wander around
The Barras (►90) – exploring all the market's
curiosities and kitsch.

Getting Your Bearings

From its Victorian position as second city of the British Empire to UK City of Architecture and Design at the end of the 20th century and Scotland with Style in the new millennium, Glasgow is continually reinventing itself while preserving its past. The rejuvenation treatment it received prior to hosting the Commonwealth Games in 2014 has done nothing to detract from this reputation. At its heart is the River Clyde, with the remnants of a once mighty shipbuilding industry. Close by, in the Merchant City, the refurbished mansions of the Industrial Revolution barons and the opulent Victorian public buildings recall the city's prosperous trading past. Nowadays trendy bars, pavement cafés and restaurants buzz with Glasgow's stylish young as they take a break from shopping in the "Golden Z", the best three shopping streets in Britain outside London.

If your shopping style is more flea market than upmarket, **The Barras**, Glasgow's famous market in the East End, is the place to rummage and enjoy the noisy sales pitches of the stallholders. **The West End**, with parks and museums around the university, is more refined. But, wherever you go in this friendliest of cities, you'll never be alone – sit on a park bench at Kelvingrove, in Glasgow Green or George Square and people-watch.

Glasgow has an excellent public transport system, so buy a **Discovery Ticket** for the local rail network and Glasgow's Underground, the famous "Clockwork Orange".

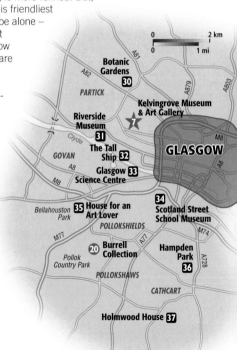

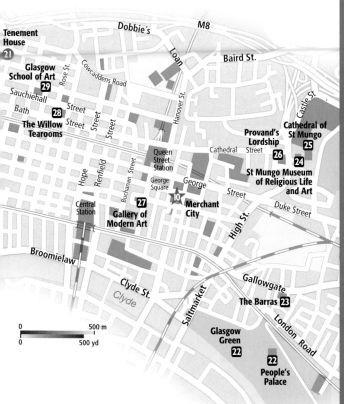

TOP 10

⭐ Kelvingrove Museum & Art Gallery ➤ 78

🔟 Merchant City ➤ 81

Don't Miss

🟤20 Burrell Collection ➤ 84

🟤21 Tenement House ➤ 87

At Your Leisure

22 People's Palace & Glasgow Green ➤ 90

23 The Barras ➤ 90

24 St Mungo Museum of Religious Life and Art ➤ 90

25 Cathedral of St Mungo ➤ 91

26 Provand's Lordship ➤ 91

27 Gallery of Modern Art ➤ 91

28 The Willow Tearooms ➤ 91

29 Glasgow School of Art ➤ 92

30 Botanic Gardens ➤ 92

31 Riverside Museum ➤ 92

32 The Tall Ship ➤ 92

33 Glasgow Science Centre ➤ 93

34 Scotland Street School Museum ➤ 93

35 House for an Art Lover ➤ 93

36 Hampden Park ➤ 94

37 Holmwood House ➤ 94

The Perfect Day

Art and culture instead of soot and smoke: Glasgow has undergone a massive image change. The following route will help you not to miss any of the highlights when you visit the former shipbuilding stronghold. For more information see the main entries (►78–94).

9:00am

Start on central George Square and take a look at the magnificent **City Chambers** and admire the impressive marble staircase (pictured right). Turn south and head for the shopping temple Italian Centre via John Street. Then stroll down Ingram Street, Trongate, High Street and Queen Street through the bustling and elegant ☆ **Merchant City** (►81) with its restaurants and shops behind the façades of the former trade centre.

11:00am

The Royal Exchange Square (pictured right) starts at the west end of Ingram Street, where you can visit the **27 Gallery of Modern Art** (►91). Its café offers an inviting place to take a nice break. Continue walking west and you soon arrive in the pedestrian-only Buchannan Street, where you can soak up the city centre atmosphere. Follow the shopping area north past the **Royal Concert Hall**, where Buchannan turns into Sauchiehall Street. Admire the Art Nouveau icon the **Willow Tearooms** (No 217) by the famous architect Charles Rennie Mackintosh as you wander along. When you reach the crossroads at Scott Street, you will also see one of his most famous works, the **29 Glasgow School of Art** (►92) in Renfrew Street.

1:00pm

When you are weary of wandering and browsing around the shops, **The Butterfly and the Pig**

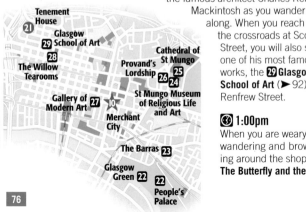

Botanic Gardens **30**

Kelvingrove Museum & Art Gallery **7**

Riverside Museum **31**

The Tall Ship **32**

Glasgow Science Centre **33**

House for an Art Lover **35**

Scotland Street School Museum **34**

Burrell Collection **20**

Hampden Park **36**

Holmwood House **37**

(151 Bath Street, about 300m back up the road) offers authentic Scottish hospitality, cosy wooden surrounds, and lots of jazz. After fortifying yourself, go up the steep street to the **29 Art School** and take a closer look at the Mackintosh building.

⏰ 3:00pm

Across Renfrew Street to the west, you reach the green Westend (after about a mile). On the right you pass by Kelvingrove Park before crossing the little Kelvin river and arriving at the palatial **Kelvingrove Museum & Art Gallery** (▶ 78). Take a moment to look into the magnificent hall; there is no entrance fee. In front of the gallery, about halfway along, you cross the street and cross over Regent Moray, Old Dumbarton and Ferry Street in 15 minutes to the Kelvin estuary in the River Clyde, where you will see Glasgow's most exciting example of modern architecture, the **31 Riverside Museum** (▶ 92), the work of the architect and designer Zaha Hadid. The silhouette of the **32 Tall Ship** (▶ 92) in front of it rounds off the post-industrial scene.

⏰ 5:00pm

Stroll along the Clyde towards the east. After a good 10 minutes you reach a trio of bridges. Cross the **Millennium Bridge** to the Glasgow Science Centre and to the **Waverley paddle steamer that is sometimes moored there**. With the Clyde now on your left, walk along until you reach the **Clyde Arc**, a bridge with an innovative curved design that is illuminated in the evening. Return along the north bank to Finnieston Street, where you can take a seat behind the panorama windows of the **India Quay** restaurants for a mild fish pakora.

⏰ 9:00pm

At the end of the evening, take a leisurely stroll after your meals further east along the Clyde until after about just over a mile (2km), you can take a nightcap at the traditional local **Scotia Bar** (Stockwell Street).

Glasgow

⭐ Kelvingrove Museum & Art Gallery

This diverse museum collection is the top free attraction in Scotland and brings together everything from natural history, through industrial exhibits to Egyptian mummies and African relics. The collection of armour is one of the finest in Europe and the art collection, featuring works by the Glasgow Boys, is one of the best in the UK.

The museum building, a magnificent turreted, red-sandstone fantasy, is an exuberant expression of late-Victorian confidence and aplomb. It's worth a visit just to admire the huge main hall, with its high vaulted ceiling and galleries, black-and-white tiled marble floor and the massive pipe organ set in an ornate arched recess.

Red stone Kelvingrove: one of Glasgow's most beautiful buildings

Museum Highlights
You could spend hours exploring, but if time is short here are some highlights. From the entrance hall turn left into the gallery holding the armour collection. You'll immediately

---

FREE ADMISSION – DONATION BOX NEAR THE EXIT
Kelvingrove is a collection of national importance but is funded entirely by the generosity of Glasgow taxpayers. Spare them a thought as you leave and put some small change, or better still notes, in the donations box.

A colourful mishmash: in Kelvingrove Museum a stuffed elephant is exhibited right next to a Second World War *Spitfire*

MACKINTOSH TEAROOM

Nine years of restoration has born fruit with the Mackintosh tearoom, a key exhibit in the ground-floor Mackintosh and Glasgow Style galleries. Between 1896 and 1911 Charles Rennie Mackintosh was commissioned to design several tearooms across the city by local tearoom mogul Miss Catherine Cranston. It was a competitive business and Mackintosh's beautiful interiors were intended to entice further custom. The Kelvingrove tearoom exhibit displays elements from several of his Glaswegian tearooms; you can see his style evolve through the furniture and fittings. To have tea in one of the originals, visit the Willow Tearooms (► 91 and 98).

see a huge **warhorse and rider** in 16th-century field armour made for the First Earl of Pembroke by the Greenwich Armoury. Gilded and decorated in the fashion of the day, it's thought to be the only surviving man and horse set, and was probably worn at the battle of St Quentin in France in 1557. In contrast to this ancient battledress is the white armoured spacesuit of an **Imperial Stormtrooper** from the *Star Wars* films.

Across the main hall, through the museum shop, is the 👥 **natural history collection**, including dinosaurs and fossils. Here in a glass case, under a magnifying glass and a bright light, is a **block of amber with a mosquito trapped within**. Michael Crichton, author of *Jurassic Park*, got the idea of using DNA from dinosaur blood sucked up by the insect before it was trapped, but the notes suggest that "such a technique is, in reality, well beyond present capabilities."

Glasgow

Another interesting exhibit is the **skeleton of the Baron of Buchlyvie,** a horse whose ownership was disputed in court. The judge ruled that the beast be sold at auction, where one of the disputing owners paid £9,500 for him, a record in the early 20th century. Two years later the Baron broke a leg and was put down. The break is still visible.

Art lovers also get their money's worth in the museum complex

Glasgow Art Collection

On the upper floors of the museum is Glasgow's **art collection,** covering Flemish, Italian, Dutch and British works, from the early Italian masters through Impressionists and Pre-Raphaelites to modern classics. Wander clockwise through each gallery or use the free map to guide you. Look particularly for works by **Charles Rennie Mackintosh** (► 14) and his contemporaries, including the **Glasgow Boys** – a group of artists who came together in the 1880s and spent their summers capturing the essence of the Scottish countryside. Members of the group included James Guthrie, John Lavery, George Henry, E A Hornel and James Patterson. You'll also find many examples of the **Glasgow Style** (► 14) in the form of paintings, sculpture and furniture.

Insider Tip

➕ 202 A4 ✉ Kelvingrove
☎ 0141 276 9599; www.glasgowmuseums.com
🕐 Mon–Thu and Sat 10–5, Fri and Sun 11–5
🍴 Café in museum (£)
Ⓠ Kelvinhall 🚌 Regular service from city centre 🚉 Partick
💷 Free, donations welcome

INSIDER INFO

In a small gallery you can see a **fascinating film** about the Native American Ghost Dance religion and the massacre of the Sioux people at Wounded Knee Creek in 1890. The **Ghost Dance Shirt,** an important religious talisman, was taken from one of the fallen at the massacre, exhibited in Buffalo Bill's Wild West Show, and finally donated to Kelvingrove. But it was returned to the Wounded Knee Survivors Association in 1998 and is now back in South Dakota. The shirt here is a replica presented to Kelvingrove by Marcella Le Beau, a Two Kettle Lakota Indian. It is not known if the gallery will remain in this form.

★ 10 Merchant City

Trendy Merchant City, once just containing warehouses and the homes of Glasgow's tobacco, sugar and cotton barons, is now filled with fashionable bars, restaurants and clubs. Wander idly through the streets absorbing the architecture and the ambience and then, if you enjoy browsing, continue indulgently along Argyle Street, Buchanan Street and Sauchiehall Street – the shopping area collectively known as Glasgow's "Golden Z".

Murals in Merchant City

The Merchant City spreads west from the old High Street in a grid pattern, but the best place to start a tour is George Square, right beside Queen Street Station.

After the Act of Union in 1707 (▶30) Scotland was allowed to trade with the colonies for the first time. Glasgow's merchants amassed huge fortunes, importing tobacco, sugar and cotton, which they ploughed back into the city, building warehouses, docks and mansions. By the 19th century Glasgow was the second city of the British Empire, and from then on its fortune fluctuated with that of the Empire.

Glasgow

The Heart of Glasgow

Glasgow City Chambers, a magnificent building with an opulent Carrara marble staircase, dominates **George Square**. Queen Victoria was certainly impressed when she opened it in 1888, and modern film-makers have cast its impressive Italian Renaissance façade, its high ceilings and massive marble staircases as law courts, embassies, palaces and even the Kremlin. It's still the administrative centre of Glasgow, and the council are so proud of it that they offer **free tours**, so take advantage of them if you can.

To the right of the City Chambers, between Cochrane and Ingram Streets, is the **Italian Centre**, an eclectic mix of pavement cafés, shops and wine bars. Versace- and Armani-clad citizens mingle with their equally stylish counterfeit counterparts, fresh from The Barras (➤ 90).

Hutcheson's Hall

At the corner of the next block stands elegant **Hutcheson's Hall**. Tall with a church-like spire, it was built in 1802 to replace a 17th-century hospice; statues from the original building were incorporated into the frontage. You can see a superb audio-visual presentation on the Merchant City at the visitor centre inside. There is also a designer gallery exhibition. The Hall, with its impressive staircase and portraits of Glasgow worthies, is often used for functions, but you can look round at other times.

The Corinthian

Built as a bank in 1842, **The Corinthian** has one of Glasgow's finest interiors. A 1929 conversion concealed most of the ornate features behind false walls and ceilings. It's now a

Corinthian Club: noble ambience in a setting steeped in history

fashionable watering hole and the trendiest of nightclubs, complete with classical figures and a Doric balustrade.

Trades Hall

With its green dome and classical façade, **Trades Hall** dominates Glassford Street. It was built between 1791 and 1794 by Robert Adam and his brothers James and William, although most of the interior is Victorian. Still occupied by its first owners, the Glasgow Trades Guild, its main attraction are the arms of the original guilds carved on the furniture and walls and visible in the stained-glass windows.

✚ 203 E2

Elegant Hutcheson's Hall on Ingram Street

⊠ Area west of High Street 🚇 Queen Street

Glasgow City Chambers
⊠ 80 George Square ☎ 0141 287 4018
🕐 Tours Mon–Fri 10:30 and 2:30 ✋ Free

Hutcheson's Hall
⊠ 158 Ingham Street ☎ 0141 552 8391 🕐 Mon–Sat 10–5 ✋ Free

The Corinthian
⊠ 191 Ingram Street ☎ 0141 552 1101 ✋ Free; charge for nightclub varies

Trades Hall
⊠ 85 Glassford Street ☎ 0141 552 2418 ✋ Free; but call for an appointment

INSIDER INFO

- In Buchanan Street look out for the Victorian-style **Princes Square shopping centre**. This is Glasgow's finest shopping experience: shops selling designer labels, expensive jewellery and fine crafts stand around an enclosed courtyard on tiered galleries. In the covered courtyard there are restaurants, cafés, bars and entertainment.
- **Babbity Bowster** (16–18 Blackfriars Street) is a late 20th-century conversion by Robert Adam of an 18th-century monastery (➤ 98). Babbity Bowster was an 18th-century Scottish dance and, appropriately, this is one of the best places for impromptu sessions of Celtic music, particularly if you come on a Saturday night. It's a great place to stay (there are a few bedrooms) or to eat, drink and relax in the bar, restaurant, café or garden.

 Insider Tip

20 Burrell Collection

This renowned collection of sculptures, paintings, ceramics, metal-work, tapestries, stained glass and much more spans all periods of history across three continents, and is probably the most diverse art collection ever assembled by a private individual.

The collection is housed in a building specially created by the architect Barry Gasson between 1971 and 1983. His brief – to design a modern gallery, incorporating Burrell's collection of porticos and doorways and recreating several rooms from Sir William's home – has resulted in a work of art in its own right. Pink Dumfriesshire sandstone, wood and glass have been used to produce a series of long external galleries combining light and space, while light-sensitive objects are displayed in the windowless core. Trees surrounding the gallery allow dappled light to fall on precious Ming vases and pottery from ancient civilisations. Medieval doors and windows are built into the fabric of the gallery so that you approach a richly carved, 14th-century stone doorway down a long corridor of light. The overall effect is an impressive symbiosis of modern architecture and art objects from times past.

Bronzes by Rodin line the inner courtyard

FINE ART CONNOISSEUR

Sir William Burrell (1861–1958) was a Glasgow shipping magnate, who amassed his fortune by ordering ships during times of depression and selling them when demand exceeded supply. As a youth with a passion for art and plenty of money, he started collecting objects at the age of 16, and would devote the rest of his long life to acquiring the very best. In 1944 Sir William and Lady Burrell gave the collection to the City of Glasgow, along with the money to build a home for it, and Burrell continued adding to the hoard until his death at the age of 96. After 80 years of collecting he had acquired around 8,000 objects, which equates to two a week, though it's difficult to comprehend that this incredible collection could be the lifetime achievement of just one man. Unfortunately, Sir William didn't live to see his collection displayed in such worthy surroundings.

The Highlights

Pass through the medieval stone entrance to find **bronzes by Rodin** lining the light inner courtyard, and in the centre, a massive **vase from the villa of the Emperor Hadrian** at Tivoli. Through the windows you can see the **dining room, hall and drawing room** from a 16th-century castle, part of the reconstruction of Burrell's home at Hutton Castle near Berwick-upon-Tweed. The rooms, arranged round the courtyard to allow light to shine through the windows, contain the main display of tapestries and were reproduced complete with the original furniture and 16th-century panelling,

Medieval portal from Hornby Castle

and are undoubtedly among the highlights of the collection. The windows are inset with precious stained glass, sculptures are arranged on the 16th-century oak buffet cupboards, and the great refectory table sits on a Persian flowered carpet.

From the courtyard you can walk clockwise round the building, passing through the **Ancient Civilisations collection**, with its pottery, carvings and statues from Mesopotamia, Egypt, ancient Greece and Rome, including a mosaic of a cockerel from the first century BC.

Continue into the **Oriental collection,** which includes Chinese bronzes as well as vases and ceramics from the Ming dynasty and an interesting pair of green-glazed, armoured

Glasgow

guardian figures from the same period. The **Medieval and Post-Medieval European Art collection** houses Burrell's prized tapestries and stained glass, examples surpassed only by the national collection at the Victoria and Albert Museum in London. Among the stained glass in the long galleries at the front and side of the building is an exquisite 15th-century small panel portrait of Edward IV's daughter Princess Cecily, and a German window of the Ten Commandments from the same period. The panel depicting the prophet Jeremiah, made for the abbey of St Denis outside Paris in around 1140, is one of the oldest surviving pieces of stained glass.

Stained glass from Burrell's magnificent medieval collection

Gallery No 8 contains one of the finest tapestry collections in Europe: 150 examples from the 15th and 16th centuries. They hang on great expanses of wall, carefully protected from the sunlight that streams through the stained-glass panels.

Behind the tapestries are the entrances to three period galleries: an **Elizabethan room**, a **17th- and 18th-century room** and a **Gothic domestic room**. The upper level houses a collection of striking **European paintings,** including works by Degas and Cézanne.

TAKING A BREAK

Visit the **tearoom**, downstairs near the stained glass collection. Or, if you're going to spend the day here, have lunch in the excellent restaurant.

➕ 202, off A1 ✉ Pollok Country Park
☎ 0141 287 2550
🕐 Mon–Thu and Sat 10–5, Fri and Sun 11–5
🍴 Café and restaurant (£–££)
🚌 Regular service from town centre, half-hourly park bus from park gates
🚆 Pollokshaws West or Shawlands 🎫 Free

INSIDER INFO

Insider Tip

- On a hot summer's day the **temperature** in the outer galleries can become uncomfortably high, so visit them early in the morning, then retreat to the cooler windowless interior at midday.
- Stairs lead up from the tapestries' gallery to a **collection of paintings** that includes masterpieces such as a Rembrandt self-portrait, the *Rehearsal* by Degas and Manet's *Women Drinking Beer*.

㉑ Tenement House

Tenement living was the norm for most Glaswegians from the mid-19th century right up to the 1950s, and here you can really get under the skin of Glasgow. Agnes Toward and her mother moved into 145 Buccleuch Street in 1911, where they stayed until the late 1960s. Amazingly, this tenement flat has never been altered since it was built in 1892. During her long life Agnes Toward never threw anything away, and her legacy is a fascinating social history of Glasgow.

When Agnes died her house was found to be crammed with the ephemera of a lifetime: letters, personal treasures and mementoes. She'd hoarded bills, receipts, bus and rail tickets and, tied in neat bundles piled high on the kitchen table, were old newspapers. When the National Trust for Scotland acquired the property they were able to reconstruct the history of her life in detail.

Despite the invention of modern kitchen devices, Miss Toward's kitchen retained its original character

The Heart of the Home
Visit the **kitchen** first, which is typical of Glasgow life at the end of the 19th century. Large families lived, slept, ate and socialised in such rooms, but Agnes had this room to herself after the death of her mother. The **bed** was concealed behind curtains by day and heated by an earthenware hot-water bottle at night. The large, black **coal range** was used for cooking and provided hot water and heating. In its day,

this range, with its regulated oven, hotplates and cast-iron pots and kettles, was at the leading edge of domestic technology. In the 1960s Agnes was still cooking on it and cleaning it daily with black liquid polish. The coal was stored in a large wooden bunker beside the food preparation area.

On the **shelves** are baking implements, a brass preserve pan and earthenware pots of jam. The old-fashioned **zinc washboard** is in the white sink and the **laundry** hangs on the pulley as if still waiting for the irons to heat up on the range.

In Edwardian Glasgow this was an affluent middle-class home. Miss Toward and her widowed mother lived on what her mother earned as a dressmaker, the income from taking in lodgers and Miss Toward's wages as a clerk. But the lovely 18th-century grandfather clock in the hall

The front room, or parlour, would be used only on special occasions

and the set of silver plate covers, incongruous in the kitchen of a Glasgow tenement, suggest that her family was once more comfortably off.

A 19th-century Snapshot

In the **parlour** the oval mahogany table, draped with red chenille, is set for afternoon tea with the best china. The fire is lit and teacakes, scones and shortbread are piled high on the plates. Windows draped in white lace curtains, the rosewood piano with brass candle-holders and mother Toward's sewing machine complete the picture of respectable gentlewomen keeping up appearances. In the **lodger's bedroom**, a traditional iron

No 19th-century middle-class parlour was complete without a piano

bedstead, high wardrobe and marble washstand with basin and jug are part of the original furnishings. Hot water for a morning wash and shave was brought from the bathroom.

The **bathroom**, with its deep bath and hot water on tap, was a rare luxury in late 19th-century Glasgow tenements, as most had only a draughty stairhead toilet shared by all the families in the block.

On your way out look for the brass plate advertising Mrs Toward's business at the entrance to the close.

✚ 202 C3 ✉ 145 Buccleuch Street
☎ 0844 493 2197; www.nts.org.uk
🕐 Mar–Oct daily 1–4:30
🚇 Cowcaddens 💷 £6.50

INSIDER INFO

■ Look out for the **chairs** – typical of the period, they are made of mahogany and stuffed with scratchy horsehair that pokes through the cover.
■ Check out the **box bed** behind the door in the corner of the parlour. This provided extra sleeping accommodation, but was rather unhealthy and was banned after 1900.

In More Depth There's an exhibition of some of **Miss Toward's treasures** in the National Trust for Scotland's rooms on the ground floor and a display telling the story of tenement housing in Glasgow. If you're in a hurry you can skip this or come back to it later.

At Your Leisure

22 People's Palace & Glasgow Green

Established as common land since 1178, Glasgow Green is the oldest public park in Britain, and has been the scene of many political meetings through the ages. Don't miss the People's Palace in the centre. This museum of social and working-class history is one of the city's gems, particularly the wonderful Winter Gardens, where you can listen to live music as you sip tea amid the tropical and subtropical plants. The richly patterned building at the end of the green, modelled on the Doge's Palace in Venice, was formerly Templeton's Carpet Factory.

🔲 203 F1 ⊠ Glasgow Green
☎ 0141 276 0788
⏰ Tue–Thu and Sat 10–5, Fri and Sun 11–5
🍴 Tearoom in Winter Gardens (£)
🚇 Argyle Street or High Street ♿ Free

23 🍴 The Barras

This combination of market and flea market is spread over several streets in a variety of buildings, sheds and halls. You'll find everything here from antique furniture, strange musical instruments and pirated computer software to fortune-tellers and fake designer clothing. Even snake-charmers have been known to make an appearance. Don't miss the oldest pub in town, the **Saracen's Head**, near the Barrowland Ballroom on the Gallowgate, which has been serving beer since 1755. Dr Samuel Johnson (1709–84) and his Scottish biographer James Boswell (1740–95) famously stopped here for refreshments.

🔲 203 F1 ⊠ Gallowgate and London Road between Ross Street and Bain Street
☎ 0141 552 4601; www.glasgow-barrowland.com ⏰ Sat–Sun 10–5
🍴 Various cafés, tea stalls and snack bars (£)
🚇 Glasgow Central, Queen Street ♿ Free

Insider Tip

Architectural detail from the People's Palace, which now houses Glasgow's social history museum

24 St Mungo Museum of Religious Life and Art

This modern building opposite Provand's Lordship houses an eclectic display of religious art and objects from around the world. The entrance is via the calm space of a Zen gravel garden. In the Gallery of Religious Art on the first floor exhibits include a woven Native American blanket, an Aboriginal Dreamtime painting and European ecclesiastical stained glass. A highlight is Salvador Dalí's oddly distorted painting of the crucifixion, *Christ of St John of the Cross.* Religious ceremony is explored on the second floor, and on the top floor the history of religion in Glasgow is revealed through an intriguing collection of objects.

203 F3 ✉ 2 Castle Street
☎ 0141 276 1625; www.glasgowmuseums.com
🕐 Tue–Thu and Sat 10–5, Fri and Sun 11–5
🍴 Café/restaurant (£) 🚇 High Street 🅿 Free

⑤ Cathedral of St Mungo

This medieval cathedral is reputedly built over the grave of Glasgow's founder, St Mungo (also known as St Kentigern), near the site of his seventh-century church. This is the only mainland pre-Reformation Scottish cathedral (begun in 1136) to have survived the Reformation, and its main features are the 15th-century stone screen, the vaulted crypt and the Blackadder aisle.

203 F3 ✉ Castle Street ☎ 0141 552 6891; www.glasgowcathedral.org.uk 🕐 Apr–Sep Mon–Sat 9:30–5:30, Sun 1–5:00; Oct–Mar Mon–Sat 9:30–4.30, Sun 1–4.30 🍴 Several in Merchant City (£) 🚇 High Street 🅿 Free

㉖ Provand's Lordship

Opposite Glasgow's Cathedral is the city's oldest house, built in 1471, the only one in Glasgow to survive from the medieval period. It was built as part of St Nicholas' Hospital but later became home to a canon of the Cathedral chapter. As he benefitted from monies from Balernock, he was known as the "Lord of Prebend of Balernock", which gradually became corrupted to "Lord of Provan", after which the house is named. The low-ceilinged, dark-wood medieval interior and the recreated medieval garden contrast vividly with the rest of Victorian Glasgow.

203 F3 ✉ 3 Castle Street
☎ 0141 552 8819; www.glasgowmuseums.com
🕐 Tue–Thu and Sat 10–5, Fri and Sun 11–5
🍴 Several nearby in Merchant City (£)
🚇 High Street 🅿 Free

㉗ Gallery of Modern Art

Four floors of modern art from around the world display the witty, dark, clever and surprising. This is one of the most consistently interesting modern art galleries in Britain. The mirror mosaic work on the pediment of this classical building is a perfect statement of Glasgow Style and a prelude to the varied collection inside. Look out for the papier-mâché statue of Her Majesty the Queen as a council-house tenant, complete with dressing gown, hairnet and curlers. Also worth seeing are the contemporary paintings, including works by Peter Howson, Scottish playwright John Byrne, and sculpture by Andy Goldsworthy.

203 C3
✉ Royal Exchange Square, Queen Street
☎ 0141 287 3050; www.glasgowmuseums.com
🕐 Mon–Wed, Sat 10–5, Thu 10–8, Fri, Sun 11–5
🍴 Café (£) 🚇 St Enoch, Buchanan Street
🚉 Queen Street, Central 🅿 Free

㉘ The Willow Tearooms

If you have time for just one cup of tea in Glasgow, have it here. Mackintosh designed these tearooms, along with several others, in 1904 for caterer Catherine Cranston. There's no better way to imagine yourself back in the city's Victorian heyday than to have afternoon tea in the mauve-and-silver high-backed chairs of the Room de Luxe (► 98).

Insider Tip

203 B4 ✉ 217 Sauchiehall Street, through a jeweller's shop and upstairs
☎ 0141 332 0521; www.willowtearooms.co.uk
🕐 Mon–Sat 9–5, Sun 11–5 🚇 Cowcaddens, Buchanan Street 🚉 Charing Cross 🅿 Free

Glasgow Cathedral was reputedly built over the grave of St Mungo

Glasgow

Mackintosh-designed Willow Tearooms

29 Glasgow School of Art

This is the earliest example of a complete Art Nouveau building in the UK. Mackintosh won the competition to design a new school in 1896 and everything, right down to the furnishings and fittings, is his work. It is considered by many Mackintosh buffs to be his greatest work. The façades of the north and west wings are the most impressive features of a building that really encapsulates the beauty of his style. In May 2014, a fire partially damaged the academy. Although it was possible to save the basic structure, the blaze destroyed the **Mackintosh Library**, in which it used to be possible to sit on the library's original chairs that were over 100 years old. Rebuilding work will last at least three to four years.

🚋 202 C3 ✉ 167 Renfrew Street
☎ 0141 353 4526; www.gsa.ac.uk
🍴 Willow Tearooms (£; ➤ 91; 98)
🚇 Cowcaddens 🚉 Queens Street
🎫 £10.50

A statue in Kibble Palace, the elegant glass conservatory at the centre of Glasgow Botanic Gardens

30 Botanic Gardens

These have been a peaceful oasis in Glasgow's West End since 1842. In bad weather head for the **Kibble Palace**, the massive but elegant glass conservatory at the centre, dating from 1873, now an A-listed building that underwent a full restoration in 2006. Tropical ferns, begonia and orchids flourish behind an unconventionally styled wrought iron framed glasshouse protected from the raw Scottish climate.

🚋 202, A5 ✉ 730 Great Western Road
☎ 0141 276 1614
🕐 7am–dusk; Kibble Palace: summer 10–6; winter 10–4:15 🍴 Café in Kibble Palace (£)
🚇 Hillhead 🎫 Free

31 Riverside Museum

Instantly recognisable thanks to its distinctive zinc roof and bold zigzag silhouette, the Riverside Museum on the north bank of the River Clyde was inaugurated in 2011. Zaha Hadid conceived the idea for what is probably Glasgow's most spectacular modern building. It replaces the old Museum of Transport and is full of everything that has wheels or a keel. One highlight is the reproduction of part of a 1930s street with an underground station, and another is the Tall Ship in front of the building.

🚋 202 off A3 ✉ 100 Pointhouse Road
☎ 0141 287 27 20; www.glasgowmuseums.com
🕐 Mon–Thu, Sat 10–5, Fri, Sun 11–5
🍴 Café (£) 🚇 Partick, Bus 3 🎫 Free

32 👥 The Tall Ship

The SV *Glenlee* (1886) moored in Glasgow Harbour is one of the last Clyde-built sailing ships afloat. Rescued from the scrap heap and

restored to exhibition standard, it shows life aboard a cargo vessel, and the holds have been recreated with the original sounds and smells. The maintenance of the museum ship is funded by the restaurant and café-bar. Entrance is free.

➕ 202, off A3
✉ Yorkhill Quay, 100 Stobcross Road
☎ 0141 222 2513; www.glenlee.co.uk
🕐 Mar–Oct 10–5; Nov–Feb 10–4
🍴 Café in Pumphouse Visitor Centre (£)
🚇 Kelvinhall 🚌 64 🚆 Finnieston 💷 Free

33 🎡 Glasgow Science Centre

The centre itself casts an unmistakable presence on the south bank of the River Clyde. On one side of the river the large blue Finnieston Crane pays tribute to Glasgow's heavy industrial glory days, while on the other the voluminous silhouette of the 330ft (100m) Glasgow Tower (the tallest free standing structure in Scotland) reaches for the heavens. The main part of the Science Centre is the shell-shaped Science Mall, which packs in more than 500 exhibits, including a virtual reality theatre that allows visitors to sink beneath the skin of the human body and explore its complexities. Visitors can also go up the Glasgow Tower, see the stars in the Planetarium or immerse themselves in the film action at the IMAX theatre. Unfortunately the Glasgow Tower next to it is often closed; when it is open the revolving tower offers a stupendous view. *Insider Tip*

➕ 202 off A3 ✉ 50 Pacific Quay ☎ 0141 420 5000; www.glasgowsciencecentre.org 🕐 10–5
🍴 Café £ 🚆 Exhibition Centre 🚇 Cessnock
🚌 23, 24, 88 and 89 🚌 23, 26, 90 💷 £10.50

34 Scotland Street School Museum

Mackintosh's Scotland Street is a great place for both kids and adults. Built in 1904, it was a school until 1979, and inside you'll find reconstructed classrooms from the Victorian and Edwardian periods, World War II and the 1960s, some during term time with pupils and teachers in period costume. For a real nostalgia trip, try out the historical playground toys.

➕ 202 A1 ✉ 225 Scotland Street
☎ 0141 287 0500; www.glasgowmuseums.com
🕐 Tue–Thu, Sat 10–5, Fri, Sun 11–5
🍴 Museum café (£) 🚇 Shields Road 🚌 89, 90
💷 Free

35 House for an Art Lover

In 1901 when Charles Rennie Mackintosh (► 14) and his wife Margaret entered a competition to design a "House for an Art Lover", they were unrestricted by finance or client specifications, and so let their imaginations run riot. The perfect proportions, the use of space, the careful balancing of dark and light, of lines and curves in the resulting House for an Art Lover represent the ultimate in Mackintosh design. The designs lay untouched for more than 90 years until Graham Roxburgh, a Glasgow engineer and Mackintosh enthusiast, came across them and initiated the idea of building the house, in collaboration with Glasgow City Council and Glasgow School of Art.

So at the end of the 20th century, modern artists and craftspeople from Scotland and beyond had the opportunity to work with the designs of one of Scotland's greatest architects to produce the original furniture, stencilling, gesso panels and decorative metalwork displayed in the house. Completed in 1996, it has an exhibition space and visitor centre, and also serves as a post-graduate study facility for Glasgow School of Art.

Glasgow

Alexander "Greek" Thomson's ornate cupola at Holmwood House

➕ 202, off A1
✉ Bellahouston Park, 10 Dumbreck Road
☎ 0141 353 4770; www.houseforanartlover.co.uk
🕐 Daily 10–5 🍴 Art Lovers' Café (£)
🚇 Ibrox Station 🚌 9, 36, 38, 54, 56
🚆 Dumbreck Station 💷 £4.50

36 Hampden Park

Football is at the very heart and soul of Glasgow, but unfortunately it is also the source of much rivalry between Celtic and Rangers, which can spill into violence that is intertwined with religion. But the national stadium at Hampden (one of the world's oldest and most famous), brings the country together. If you can get a ticket, experiencing the "Tartan Army" in full flow is a spine-tingling experience. When there are no games, there are regular tours of the stadium and the on-site museum that open up Hampden's fascinating history, and Scottish football traditions and cover the great European finals staged here, when the likes of Zinedine Zidane and Alfredo Di Stefano graced the turf.

➕ 202 off C1
✉ Hampden Park, Glasgow G42 9BA
☎ 0141 620 4000; www.hampdenpark.co.uk
🕐 Mon–Sat 10–5, Sun 10–5 (subject to events)

🚆 Mount Florida, King's Park 🚌 5, 7, 12, 31, 37, 44 and 75 💷 Combined ticket for museum & stadium tour £10, single ticket £7

37 Holmwood House

This is the finest example of domestic architecture by Alexander "Greek" Thomson, the architect whose designs helped to give Glasgow its distinctive look. Holmwood, located in the Cathcart area of Glasgow, was built in 1857–58 for the wealthy paper manufacturer James Couper, who gave Thomson a free hand in the design and got this gem in return. Thomson made the house asymmetrical, with the flat gable and large windows of the dining room on one side of the door. On the other side he created the appearance of a circular bay window by placing the free-standing columns of a Greek temple in front of the windows. The interior continues the classical theme, with original wallpaper in shades of russet depicting scenes from the Trojan War.

➕ 202, off C1
✉ 61–63 Netherlee Road, Cathcart
☎ 0141 637 2129; www.nts.org.uk
🕐 Apr–Oct Thu–Mon noon–5
🚌 44, 66, 374 🚆 Cathcart Station 💷 £6.50

Where to...
Stay

Prices
Expect to pay per standard double room per night, including breakfast:
£ under £70   **££** £70–£100   **£££** over £100

Abode Hotel £££
Abode's central Glasgow base, once a grand government building, has been spruced up with funky furnishings, well-designed bathrooms and all the latest gadgets. Dining is another strength. The hotel also offers several cost-effective family rooms.

✚ 203 D3 ✉ 129 Bath Street
☎ 0141 221 6789; www.abodeglasgow.co.uk

Citizen M ££
The mega cool chain also has a hotel in Glasgow. The form meets function interior style perfectly matches the online check-in. What is more, it is located in the same street as Mackintosh's Art Nouveau Art School, and thus very central. It's got great showers, too!

✚ 203 D3 ✉ 60 Renfrew Street
☎ 0141 404 94 85; www.citizenm.com

Crowne Plaza ££
Instantly recognisable from its mirrored glass exterior, the Crowne Plaza is one of the tallest buildings in Scotland. Built on the old Queens Docks, it's adjacent to the Scottish Exhibition Centre and has fine views of the Clyde. A huge mural of the Clyde's shipbuilding past is a feature of both of its restaurants. It also houses the Waterside health and leisure club. Most of the hotel's spacious bedrooms enjoy panoramic views over the river and city, and there are also useful family facilities. Ample parking is a bonus.

✚ 202, off A5 ✉ Congress Road
☎ 0871 942 9091; www.crowneplaza.com

Hotel Du Vin £££
Without doubt this hotel is one of the most impressive in Scotland. Four splendid Victorian town houses were combined to make a complete design statement, one where the golden rule has been to keep it simple, and where every detail has been carefully considered. Each of the 49 rooms has its own individual style with extras such as CD players, big beds, deep baths, fresh flowers, books, magazines and bathrobes.

✚ 202 by A5 ✉ 1 Devonshire Gardens
☎ 0844 7 36 42 56; www.hotelduvin.co.uk

Georgian House Hotel £–££
The accommodation and facilities in this small hotel are simple but offer good value for money. It's part of a quiet, tree-lined Victorian terrace near the Botanic Gardens (➤ 92). The 11 bedrooms are equipped in a modern style but retain many original features, and most are en suite. Breakfast is served in the first-floor lounge/dining room.

✚ 202 A5 ✉ 29 Buckingham Terrace, Great Western Road, Kelvinside ☎ 0141 339 0008; www.thegeorgianhousehotel.com

Glasgow Marriott ££–£££
Close to the city centre (by junction 19 of the M8), the Marriott offers a high standard of facilities, including a smart ground-floor bar/lounge, informal café and attractive restaurant. The hotel's leisure club has a gym and swimming pool, as well as beauty treatments and hairdressing.

Standard bedrooms are all good-sized, with generous beds, ample storage and air-conditioning. If your budget allows, book one of the hotel's luxurious suites.

➕ 202 C2 ✉ 500 Argyle Street, Anderston
☎ 0141 226 5517; www.marriott.com

Kelvingrove Hotel £–££

Just west of the city centre and close to the Kelvingrove Museum, this smart, family-run guest house is set into a terraced row of Victorian houses. Its 22 bedrooms include five family rooms. Service is friendly, dogs are accepted and reception is staffed around the clock. Breakfast is taken in a bright dining room.

➕ 202 A3 ✉ 944 Sauchiehall Street
☎ 0141 339 5011; www.kelvingrove-hotel.co.uk

Malmaison ££–£££

A sister hotel of its namesake in Edinburgh, this is part of an outstanding mini-chain of design-led hotels. All 72 bedrooms ooze stylish excellence, and come equipped with extras such as CD players and cable TV. The food is highly regarded, and the basement brasserie (➤97) has an energetic club-like appeal. You can also work out in the hotel's well-equipped gym.

➕ 202 C3 ✉ 278 West George Street
☎ 0141 572 1000; www.malmaison-glasgow.com

Merchant City Inn £

Economical accommodation is offered at Merchant City, in the former residence of Glasgow's tobacco merchants. All the rooms are en suite and have WLan. Family rooms made a stay affordable for small groups. Impressive stairway up which you still have to carry your luggage.

➕ 203 E2 ✉ 52 Virginia Street
◉ 0141 552 24 24; www.merchantcityinn.com

Millennium Hotel Glasgow ££

You can't get much more central in Glasgow than this handsome hotel on George Square. The grand Victorian exterior belies an interior that is firmly contemporary, including a glass veranda. There are 117 well-equipped bedrooms, plus a good brasserie and separate wine bar if you choose to dine in.

➕ 203 E2 ✉ George Square
☎ 0141 332 6711; www.millenniumhotels.com

Novotel Glasgow Centre ££

This city-centre hotel, close to the silvery SECC "Armadillo" building, is part of a well-respected chain, serving both business and leisure travellers. Bedrooms are brightly decorated and well equipped, and the facilities include a brasserie, and fitness club with sauna and gym. Limited parking available.

➕ 202 C3 ✉ 181 Pitt Street
☎ 0141 222 2775; www.novotel.com

Radisson SAS Glasgow £££

Convenience and comfort are paramount in the hotel situated in the city centre opposite the Central railway station. A huge glass-and-wood atrium forms the core of the building, leading to the lobby, two bars and two restaurants. There are 250 bedrooms, all with air-conditioning, high-speed internet access, safe, satellite TV and personal bar. The health club has a swimming pool, fitness studios, gym, sauna and treatment rooms.

➕ 203 D2 ✉ 301 Argyle Street
☎ 0141 204 3333; www.radissonblu.co.uk

Victorian House £

This guest house, part of a raised terrace row, is conveniently placed for easy access to Sauchiehall Street and the famous Glasgow School of Art. The 58 bedrooms, including some with polished wooden floors and bright modern styling, vary in size and décor, and most have adjoining bathrooms. Facilities include a lounge and a breakfast room, where guests can enjoy buffet-style meals.

➕ 202 C3
✉ 212 Renfrew Street ☎ 0141 332 0129;
www.victoriahotel-glasgow.co.uk

Where to…
Eat and Drink

Prices
Expect to pay per three-course meal per person, excluding drinks:
£ under £20   **££** £20–£30   **£££** over £30

RESTAURANTS

Fratelli Sarti £
One of a mini chain of family-run restaurants, Fratelli Sarti espouses authentic Tuscan cooking. It is informal, busy and pitched between a restaurant and a deli – have a quick snack or a three-course meal.

➕ 203 D3 ✉ 121 Bath Street ☎ 0141 204 0440; www.sarti.co.uk ⏱ Open all day

Gamba £–££
A stylish setting marks out this prize-winning basement restaurant, which serves the best of Scottish fish cooked in an unfussy manner. There is also an excellent wine list.

➕ 203 D3 ✉ 225a West George Street ☎ 0141 572 0899; www.gamba.co.uk ⏱ Lunch and dinner Mon–Sat, Sun dinner only

Hotel du Vin Bistro £££
Recline by the big bay windows and settle in for multi-award-winning Modern Scottish cooking and a comprehensive and well-thought-out wine list in the lavish surrounds of Glasgow's most luxurious hotel. The Buccleuch steaks are legendary. Booking is essential at weekends.

➕ 202, off A5 ✉ 1 Devonshire Gardens ☎ 0141 339 2001; www.hotelduvin.com ⏱ Breakfast, lunch and dinner daily

Malmaison ££–£££
This chic modern restaurant is in the crypt of a former church, now a hotel. Food is "homegrown and local" and dishes blend the modern flavours of France. Try the goat's cheese and celeriac soufflé and the yummy chocolate tart.

➕ 202 C3 ✉ 278 West George Street ☎ 0844 693 06 53; www.malmaison.com ⏱ Breakfast, lunch and dinner daily

Shish Mahal £–££
Fast, friendly service, excellent food and generous portions are typical of this North Indian restaurant. The fixed lunch menu is particularly good value. Reserve well ahead, especially at weekends.

➕ 196, off A5 ✉ 60–68 Park Road ☎ 0141 334 7899; www.shishmahal.co.uk ⏱ Lunch Mon–Sat, dinner daily

Stravaigin ££–£££
Hip and eccentric, this subterranean brasserie swings to a jazz beat and offers an eclectic menu that mixes flavours from Asia and Scotland. Try Vietnamese smoked chicken with mango and ginger summer rolls, grapefruit and mint salad and chilli peanut dressing. The wine list is global and down to earth.

➕ 202 A4 ✉ 28 Gibson Street ☎ 0141 334 2665; www.stravaigin.co.uk ⏱ Open all day

Two Fat Ladies at the Buttery ££–£££
Opened in 1869, this highly regarded restaurant is the oldest restaurant in Glasgow. Despite its age, it looks at traditional Scottish food through a surprisingly modern eye. The atmosphere is relaxed and the oak-panelled interior attractive. Make sure you leave room for desserts such as Scottish whisky tart with spiced rum sorbet.

➕ 202 B2 ✉ 652 Argyle Street ☎ 0141 221 8188; www.twofatladiesrestaurant.com ⏱ Lunch and dinner daily

Ubiquitous Chip £££

After 30 years, the Chip is a Glasgow landmark that still has a relaxed buzz with a plant-strewn, covered courtyard at its heart. An innovative dedication to the best Scottish produce goes from free-range Perthshire pork to organic salmon and venison haggis. Great brunch and breakfasts at weekends.

⊞ 202, off A5 ✉ 12 Ashton Lane
☎ 0141 334 5007; www.ubiquitouschip.co.uk
🕐 Open all day

CAFÉS

The 13th Note Café £

An unusual marriage of music venue and GM-free vegetarian café, aimed at appealing to families as well as Glasgow's gig-goers. Gigs take place downstairs (aged 18 and above only) while the café and art gallery welcome children until 6:30pm. Try the home-made croquettes and spring rolls, with vegetable curry or sweet-and-sour tofu to follow.

⊞ 203 E2 ✉ 50–60 King Street
☎ 0141 553 1638; www.13thnote.co.uk
🕐 Daily noon–midnight

Coffee, Chocolate and Tea £

Essential for the pleasures named above. The establishment's own coffee blend is roasted on location. Superb chocolate tart and muffins are served with Darjeeling tea of equal refinement.

⊞ 202 B3 ✉ 944 Argyle Street ☎ 0141 204 3161; www.coffeechocolateandtea.com
🕐 Mon–Fri, Sa 8–6, Sun 10–4

Café Gandolfi £

The long-established Café Gandolfi is a lively place with an unstuffy attitude. Stained-glass windows and wooden furniture contrast with the light, imaginative modern food. With a flexible all-day menu, it's also one of the city's best tea-rooms.

⊞ 203 E2 ✉ 64 Albion Street
☎ 0141 552 6813; www.cafegandolfi.com
🕐 Open all day

Tibo £

This "café" is all very Glasgow. It does great heart-warming breakfasts, brunches that are up there with the best and great-value lunches, while still managing to be the sort of place you'd like to return to for coffee, cake or even a decent dinner with a bottle of wine. Chic surrounds and affordable prices make this more than just a café.

⊞ 203, off F2 ✉ 443 Duke Street ☎ 0141 550 2050; www.cafe tibo.com 🕐 Open all day

The Willow Tearooms £

The Willow Tearooms is one of several quirky tearooms designed by Charles Rennie Mackintosh. The restored Room de Luxe sparkles with mirrors and grand windows and doors. Enjoy the 30 blends of loose-leaf tea, cakes, scones and sandwiches, as well as daily specials.

⊞ 203 D3 ✉ 217 Sauchiehall Street
☎ 0141 332 0521; www.willowtearooms.co.uk
🕐 Mon–Sat 9–5, Sun 11–5

PUBS & BARS

Babbity Bowster £

This famous pub, on Blackfriars Street, just to the west of Saltmarket, is in a stylish 18th-century town house designed by Robert Adam. There's live folk music on Saturday nights and several real ales.

⊞ 203 E2 ✉ 16–18 Blackfriars Street
☎ 0141 552 5055; www.babbitybowster.com
🕐 Open all day

Rab Ha's £–££

In the heart of the Merchant City, this refurbished Victorian hotel and bar takes its name from Robert Hall, a 19th-century local gourmand. Beers include Theakston's and Bellhaven Best, while bar meals include Scottish favourites such as haggis with neeps and tatties. The restaurant menu is more elaborate.

⊞ 203 E2 ✉ 81 Hutcheson Street
☎ 0141 548 6733; www.rabhas.com
🕐 Open all day

Where to...
Shop

Most shops open from 9/9:30am until 5:30/6pm, and many remain open until 7/8pm. Some open on Sunday, usually in the afternoon.

Shaped like a "Z", **Argyle Street**, **Buchanan Street** and **Sauchiehall Street** form Scotland's premier shopping area, with the best selection of stores in the UK outside London.

MAIN MALLS & CENTRES

The **Buchanan Galleries** (220 Buchanan Street; tel: 0141 333 9898) is a classy shopping centre, with a John Lewis department store. **St Enoch Centre** (55 St Enoch Square; tel: 0141 204 3900) has an array of high-street stores while **Merchant Square** (tel: 0141 552 3038) is a small mall in the Merchant City, with the exclusive Gift Merchant shop, plus restaurants and bars. More exclusive shops can be found at **Princes Square** (38–42 Buchanan Street; tel: 0141 221 0324; www.princes square.co.uk). The **Victorian Village** (93 West Regent Street; tel: 0141 332 9808; www.victorianvillage antiques.co.uk) is a collection of antiques shops.

CLOTHING

Designer clothes abound in the expensive boutiques of the **Italian Centre** on Ingram Street. **Cruise** (180–87 Ingram Street; tel: 0141 572 3232; www.cruisefashion.co. uk) has a huge range for men and women. Try **TK Maxx** (Sauchiehall Street; tel: 0141 331 0411) for affordable designer labels.

Meanwhile, there's **High and Mighty** (17 Trongate; tel: 0141 553 1081) for tall men, and **Soletrader** (164a Buchanan Street; tel: 0141 353 3022) sells every type of shoe. **Slater Menswear** (165 Howard Street; tel: 0141 552 7171) stocks more than 17,000 suits. **Slanj of Scotland** (67 St. Vincent Street; tel: 0141 248 7770) sells kilts – including black leather ones – and t-shirts with Scottish themes.

BOOKS

For new books **Waterstone's** (153– 157 Sauchiehall Street; tel: 0141 332 9105) has five floors, an internet café and reading areas. **Borders** (98 Buchanan Street; tel: 0141 222 7700) is also popular. **Voltaire & Rousseau** (12–14 Otago Lane; tel: 0141 339 1811) is good for second-hand gems, as is **Caledonia Books** (483 Great Western Road; tel: 0141 334 9663).

FOOD & DRINK

For whisky try the **Cask and Still** (154 Hope Street; tel: 0141 353 7420) or the **Whisky Shop** (Buchanan Galleries; tel: 0141 331 0022) in Princes Square. **Peckham's** is a great deli, with branches at 61–65 Glassford Street (tel: 0141 553 0666) and 100 Byres Road (tel: 0141 357 1454).

JEWELLERY

There is plenty of distinctively Scottish jewellery available – try the **Argyle Arcade** between Argyle Street and Buchanan Street. **Henderson The Jeweller,** has the best collection of silver jewellery in Mackintosh designs.

ART

National artists exhibit their work at the **Merchant Gate Gallery** (111 Saltmarket; tel: 0141 552 5847). You can also get paintings framed here.

Where to...
Go Out

CINEMA

The **Odeon Quay** (Springfield Quay, Paisley Road; tel: 0871 224 4007) has 12 screens and shows recent releases.

The **Glasgow Film Theatre** (12 Rose Street, tel: 0141 332 6535; www.gft.org.uk), housed in a lovely art deco building, shows independent, foreign and art house films.

THEATRE & MUSIC

Many of Glasgow's fine old theatre buildings have been closed, but a few remain. The **Citizens** (119 Gorbals Street; tel: 01441 429 0022; www.citz.co.uk) is Scotland's best, covering everything from Restoration comedies to the latest works by 21st-century playwrights. The **Tron** (63 Trongate; tel: 01441 552 4267) puts on productions of small touring companies as well as in-house shows, live music and occasional comedy.

For traditional performances, the **Theatre Royal** (282 Hope Street; tel: 0844 871 7647; www.ambassador tickets.com)is the venue for opera, ballet and all things highbrow, while the **King's Theatre** (297 Bath Street; tel: 0844 871 7648; www. ambassadortickets.com) presents musicals, both professional and amateur, and a great winter pantomime. The **Royal Concert Hall** (2 Sauchiehall Street; tel: 0141 353 8000; www.glasgowconcerthalls. com) is the headquarters of the Royal Scottish National Orchestra, also hosting rock and pop gigs as well as the Celtic Connections music festival (▶20).

The **St Andrew's in the Square** venue (1 St Andrew's Square; tel: 0141 548 6020), a Georgian gem, hosts concerts and ceilidhs throughout the year.

PUBS & CLUBS

Glasgow's pub scene is fantastic – from trendy Merchant City bars to West End student hang-outs and traditional working-class haunts. Don't miss the **Saracen's Head** (209 Gallowgate; tel; 0141 552 9306) for a slice of old Glasgow life. Best of the rest are the **Scotia Bar** (112 Stockwell Street; tel: 0141 552 8681), **Bargo** and **Babbity Bowster** (▶98) in the Merchant City and **The Curlers** (256–60 Byers Road; tel: 011 341 0737) in the West End.

The rock and pop scene is vibrant. **King Tut's Wah Wah Hut** (272a St Vincent Street; tel: 01441 221 5279) features the best circuit bands, with a few top names popping in occasionally, while the **Scotia** and the **Babbity Bowster** are best for folk and Celtic sounds.

Dancing has always been big in Glasgow. Nowadays it's not just hip hop and house – the city also has a thriving indie and rock music scene, and is a great place for a traditional ceilidh.

Try **The Garage** (490 Sauchiehall Street; tel: 0141 332 1120). Other good venues for the latest dance music include **Sub Club** (22 Jamaica Street; tel: 0141 248 4600), **Chinaski's** (239 North Street; tel: 0141 221 0061) **Blanket** (520 Sauchiehall Street; tel: 0141 332 0755) and the **Arches** (253 Argyle Street; tel: 0141 565 1000).

The best source for what's on is **The List**, available every two weeks from newsagents. The **Glasgow Evening Times** has daily listings and the weekend supplement of the **Saturday Herald** covers events nationwide for the next seven days.

Southern Scotland

 **Little Treats**

A Glowing Sunset

Even the Scots make the pilgrimage to **Culzean Castle** (▶ 115) to watch the West Coast's most spectacular sunset.

A Toast to Bonnie Prince Charlie

In age-old **Traquair House** (▶ 116) they still brew Jacobite ale dating back to 1745 – and at the beginning of August host a great beer festival.

Romantic Picnic

A picnic in the ruins of **Jedburgh Abbey** (▶ 116) promises an enchanting excursion in a medieval setting.

Getting Your Bearings

This is one of the prettiest but least visited parts of Scotland, with castles, towers and ruined abbeys nestling among rolling hills and pastoral lowlands. Rocky coves and sandy beaches are enhanced further by the glorious sunsets that gild the islands to the west. Inland, the wilderness of the Galloway Hills and the vast woodlands are a hillwalker's paradise, particularly beautiful in spring and autumn.

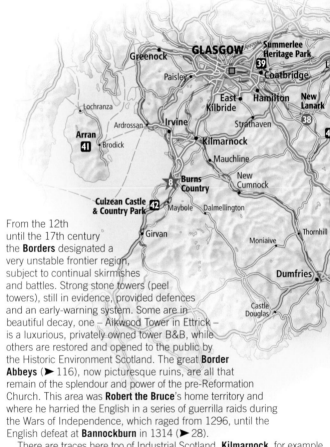

From the 12th until the 17th century the **Borders** designated a very unstable frontier region, subject to continual skirmishes and battles. Strong stone towers (peel towers), still in evidence, provided defences and an early-warning system. Some are in beautiful decay, one – Aikwood Tower in Ettrick – is a luxurious, privately owned tower B&B, while others are restored and opened to the public by the Historic Environment Scotland. The great **Border Abbeys** (► 116), now picturesque ruins, are all that remain of the splendour and power of the pre-Reformation Church. This area was **Robert the Bruce**'s home territory and where he harried the English in a series of guerrilla raids during the Wars of Independence, which raged from 1296, until the English defeat at **Bannockburn** in 1314 (► 28).

There are traces here too of Industrial Scotland. **Kilmarnock**, for example, was once filled with factories. It was here that Johnny Walker first blended whisky in the back shop of his grocery business in 1825. At **New Lanark** an entire industrial complex is preserved, while at **Wanlockhead** there is a superb museum of lead mining, complete with a mineshaft to explore along with other related buildings in this remote village.

Exquisite Rosslyn Chapel,
south of Edinburgh

North Berwick
Dunbar
St Abb's Head
47
BURGH
Dalkeith
Eyemouth
43 Abbotsford House
Duns
Lauder
Galashiels
44 Melrose
44 Kelso
44 Dryburgh
Selkirk
44 Jedburgh
Hawick
muir
Langholm

0   30 km
0   20 mi

Evening atmosphere in Melrose

Perfect Days in...

Three Perfect Days

Many visitors heading for Edinburgh, Glasgow and the Highlands miss out on this little-known region as they zoom past it on the motorway. If you're not quite sure where to begin your travels, this itinerary recommends a practical and enjoyable three days exploring Southern Scotland, taking in some of the best places to see. For more information see the main entries (► 106–117).

Day 1

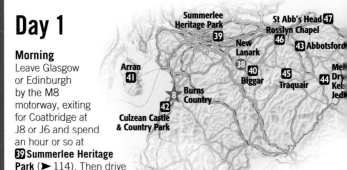

Morning
Leave Glasgow or Edinburgh by the M8 motorway, exiting for Coatbridge at J8 or J6 and spend an hour or so at **39 Summerlee Heritage Park** (► 114). Then drive south via the M74 to **38 New Lanark** (► 110) and spend a couple of hours exploring the old mills and houses of industrialist Robert Owen's Utopian dream. Take the riverside walk up to the Falls of Clyde if the weather's fine.

Afternoon
After a late lunch in the tearoom at New Lanark, take the A72 to **40 Biggar**, home to an amazing number of museums (► 114): there's even a museum of the local gasworks. A performance by **Purves Puppets** in the Victorian puppet theatre is a must. Should you have time, the **Moat Park Heritage**

Centre and the **Gladstone Court Museum** with its recreation of an historic pharmacy (pictured below left) are also worth visiting. Return on the A72 and head west on the A70 for the town of **Ayr** and your overnight stop.

Day 2

Morning
Just south of Ayr, you are in the heart of **Burns Country** (▶ 106) in Alloway. Visit the Robert Burns Birthplace Museum and the ruined Alloway Aulk Kirk (pictured right), thought to have provided the inspiration for the poem "Tam o' Shanter".

Head south on the A719, the scenic coastal road to Culzean. Stop to enjoy the views to the Isle of Arran and the Kintyre peninsula. Spend the rest of the morning at **42 Culzean Castle & Country Park** (▶ 115).

Afternoon
Head south on the A70 and A76 to **Dumfries** (▶ 108) via **Ellisland Farm**. Here you can visit the **Robert Burns Centre**, Burns' House and the **Mausoleum in St Michael's churchyard**. Have a coffee at **Gracefield Arts Centre** on Edinburgh Road, where you can also enjoy their current exhibits and browse in the excellent little craft shop, which sells work by local artists.

Day 3

Morning
From Dumfries takes the A701 to Moffat, turn off there on the A708. After the waterfall at **Grey Mare's Tail,** you come to St Mary's Loch, where you should not leave out **Tibbie Shiel's Inn**. Walter Scott and R L Stevenson left their names for posterity in the guestbook! The next stop along the way is the famous residence of Walter Scott, **Abbotsford House** on the River Tweed. By the A6091 is the picturesque town of **44 Melrose** (▶ 116) with its romantic abbey ruins and the nice pub restaurants not far away.

Afternoon
Dryburgh Abbey's ruins is just a bit further east along the Tweed. You can reach the magnificent Borders **Smailholm Tower** via the A6404. From here it is just an hour to the evening's east coast venue of **47 St Abbs Head**.

Burns Country

Robert Burns (1759–96), Scotland's national poet, was born in an "auld clay biggin" near the banks of the River Doon, with thick walls and tiny windows to protect against Scottish winters. You can see hundreds of similar long, low cottages across the southwest of Scotland. Restored to its original condition, Burns' cottage is now part of the Burns National Heritage Park at Alloway. In the cottage is the original manuscript of "Auld Lang Syne". Burns would recognise the cottages, but the boggy moorland from which he scratched a living has been transformed into fertile farmland.

Alloway

Start your tour at the **Robert Burns Birthplace Museum** in Alloway. After excellent films about Burns' life and an excellent audio-visual presentation of his greatest poem, "Tam o' Shanter", you can follow in Tam's footsteps to "**Alloway's Auld Haunted Kirk**" and the ancient **Brig o' Doon**. Burns' parents are buried in the auld kirk yard (old church-yard), and he often took the narrow road over the Brig o' Doon to Carrick shore.

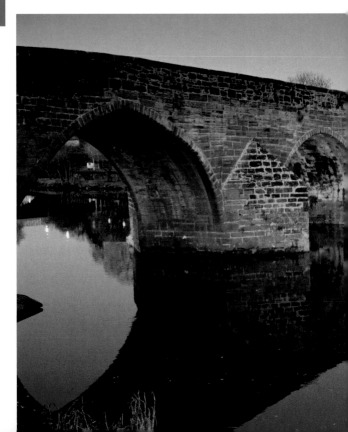

Burns was brought up on tales of legend and superstition told by his mother Agnes Broun. She was from **Kirkoswald** village, 14mi (23km) south of Ayr, where Robert went to school, and where he met the characters who were later immortalised in his poems. Their gravestones are in the yard of the ruined village church. Look out for Douglas Graham of Shanter Farm, the original Tam. Buried near by is "his ancient, trusty, drouthy, crony" Soutar Johnnie – cobbler John Davidson. His **cottage** and **workshop**, opposite the churchyard, have been restored, complete with tools.

Kilmarnock
Follow the trail north to **Kilmarnock**, where John Wilson's printing shop produced the first volume of Burns' poems in 1786. At the **Dean Castle** in the town is a rare original copy of the Kilmarnock Edition. A year later Burns moved a short distance to the farm at Mossgiel near **Mauchline**, where he wrote one of his best-loved poems, "To a Mouse", after ploughing up the nest of a fieldmouse.

Even during Burns' lifetime, you could cross the Devorgilla's Bridge to Dumbries

Mauchline
Burns met his future wife Jean Armour in Mauchline and regularly fell foul of the Kirk Session, made up of the church

Southern Scotland

elders, who judged the morals of their fellow parishioners and decided appropriate penalties. Burns retaliated against their hypocrisy with satirical verse. In the churchyard here is the grave of church elder Willie Fisher, ridiculed by Burns in "Holy Willie's Prayer" following his death in a ditch after a drinking session. Willie drank in Mauchline's **Poosie Nancy's Inn**, and it's still a great place to stop for a dram (a small whisky) before continuing to Dumfries.

 Insider Tip

Opposite:
A statue of
Burns stands
in front of
Greyfriars
Church in
Dumfries

Dumfries

Burns worked as an exciseman in Dumfries, and he would still recognise the broad sweep of the River Nith, **Devorgilla's Bridge**, the weir feeding the **watermill** and the **observatory.** The poet's statue stands in front of **Greyfriars Church**, looking down the High Street to the **Midsteeple**, the former town house where his body lay the night before his funeral. In his last home, now **Burns' House Museum**, you can see his desk and the bed in which he died on 21 July, 1796, aged 37, his health broken by years of unrelenting toil and poor diet.

TAKING A BREAK

In the Robert Burns' Centre in Dumfries (tel: 01387 264 808) is **Hullabaloo**, a lively café run by young people.

Robert Burns Birthplace Museum
✚ 205 E3 ✉ Murdoch's Lane, Alloway
☎ 01292 443 700; www.burnsmuseum.org.uk
🕐 Apr–Sep daily 10–5:30; Oct–Mar 10–5
🍴 Café and restaurant in the museum (££)
🚌 From Ayr bus station, Sandgate 🚆 Ayr 🎫 £9

Burns House
✚ 206 B2 ✉ Burns Street, Dumfries ☎ 01387 255 297
🕐 Apr–Sep Mon–Sat 10–5, Sun 2–5; Oct–Mar Tue–Sat 10–1, 2–5
🍴 Globe Inn near by (£) 🚆 Dumfries 🎫 Free

View of the
writing room
in the Burns
House in
Dumfries

INSIDER INFO

 Insider Tip

- Visit the eerie ruin of the **Auld Haunted Kirk o' Alloway**, if not, like Tam o' Shanter, at midnight, then in the long, atmospheric shadows of twilight.
- In Burns' favourite *howff* (an old Scots word for pub), **The Globe Inn in Dumfries**, his chair is still by the fireside and you can see his bedroom and the verses he scratched on the windowpanes with a diamond.

38 New Lanark

The merchant David Dale began to build his cotton mills at New Lanark in 1785 to take advantage of the narrow gorge in the River Clyde to power the mills. The elegant sandstone buildings were a welcome contrast to the usual working-people's slums. And for the large number of Highlanders, cleared from the north, this rural location must have seemed closer to home than the industrial heart of Glasgow.

As you descend the hill from the car park, the arresting panoramas of New Lanark's idyllic setting on the banks of the Clyde will stop you in your tracks. Almost unchanged since they were completed in the early 19th century, the beautiful buildings show a classical simplicity. Yet there's no mistaking their industrial purpose. The massive mill buildings ranged along the river, the channel carrying the water to drive the mills, and the rows of workers' tenements couldn't be further from a rural village scene. As you explore the village, the combination of industrial efficiency and clear sense of community is evident.

FROM APPRENTICE TO MERCHANT

David Dale (1739–1806) started as an apprentice weaver in Paisley before becoming a weaver's agent and eventually a merchant in Glasgow. He went into partnership with inventor Richard Arkwright (1732–92), and together they built the mills at New Lanark.

The tenements where New Lanark's workers lived

Owen's village store sold goods to the workers at reasonable prices

Dale's mill initially employed around 400 adults and 800 children, some of whom were only five or six years old, supplied by local orphanages. Child labour was the norm in that Dickensian world, but Dale actually provided well for the children in terms of hygiene, clothing, education and food.

A Social Experiment

New Lanark's **Visitor Centre** is housed in the **Institute for the Formation of Character**, which was built 30 years later by David Dale's son-in-law, the Welsh industrialist and social reformer Robert Owen (1771–1858) as part of "the most important experiment for the happiness of the human race that has yet been instituted at any time in any part of the world." This was the social hub of New Lanark, at the centre of a community of 2,500 people. It had a library and reading room and was used for adult education, concerts, carpet bowls, dances and weddings. It even served as a works canteen and a religious meeting place. It now houses the audio-visual **Millennium Experience**, guided by Harmony, a young girl from the future, who explains how Robert Owen's ideas and aspirations for a better future led him to develop his ideas at New Lanark.

Owen refused to employ children below the age of ten, but he enabled their mothers to work by providing a nursery where they could safely leave their babies and small children. Children continued in full-time education until 10 or 12. Dancing and singing were regarded as central to their education, and both punishments and rewards were banned. Thousands visited New Lanark in the years that followed to observe Owen's experiment. His competitors were scornful of Owen's initiatives, expecting his business to collapse, and were astonished when it flourished. Owen's belief that decent conditions would produce a more contented and efficient workforce, which would in turn improve business, was vindicated.

Southern Scotland

Insider
Tip

In the mill shop, Owen's workers could buy goods at reasonable prices, well below the inflated rates charged by the local grocers and butchers. The **village store** now sells everyday 1920s goods, such as enamel cookware or *soor plooms* (sour plums), and in the adjoining section see how different the choice would have been 100 years earlier. The nearby **millworkers' house** shows living conditions in the early 19th and 20th centuries, including the shared stairhead toilet and the communal wash-house.

The Mill

The mill itself has **working machinery** that once filled all these massive buildings. The great 19th-century spinning mule clatters noisily as one person controls countless spinning threads – a task that would once have been the work of hundreds of spinners.

When the mill closed in 1968, New Lanark quickly became derelict and the whole complex was very close to demolition when the **New Lanark Conservation Trust** was

A steam engine from the Victorian period

INSIDER INFO

■ It is well worth visiting the Scottish Wildlife Trust's 🅱 **Falls of Clyde Wildlife Reserve**, where the river flows through the gorge over a series of waterfalls, including the 86ft (26m) cascade of Corra Linn. There's a wide range of wildlife here, including badgers, foxes and roe deer. A treat in spring and summer is peregrine falcon-watching from a viewing area across the gorge from their nest. A new rooftop garden on top of Mile No 2 also offers wildlife sculptures and views of the Falls of Clyde.

In More Depth If you have time to spare, take a look **Robert Owen's house**, the only house in New Lanark "with more rooms than people".

The massive mill buildings are idyllically ranged along the banks of the Clyde

set up in 1973, and a long restoration programme began. The tenements have been transformed into comfortable modern flats, and the preserved shell of **Mill No 1** is now a luxury hotel, while the **Waterhouses** (formerly used to store the raw cotton) are rented as holiday apartments. The importance of the site was recognised by UNESCO, which placed New Lanark on its World Heritage list in 2001.

TAKING A BREAK

Stop for lunch or a coffee at **Owen's Warehouse,** which serves snacks and light meals at very reasonable prices. The **Mill Pantry** is also open from 10–5 for refreshments.

New Lanark World Heritage Site
✚ 206 B3 ✉ Lanark
☎ 01555 66 13 45; www.newlanark.org.uk
🕐 Apr–Oct 10–5, Nov–Mar 10–4
🍽 Café (£) ✋ £9.50

Falls of Clyde Wildlife Reserve
✚ 206 B3
✉ Scottish Wildlife Trust's Visitor Centre, The Old Dyeworks, New Lanark
☎ 01555 665 262; www.swt.org.uk
🕐 Reserve: Daily during daylight hours. Visitor centre: Daily
✋ £5

At Your Leisure

39 Summerlee Heritage Park

Based in the old Summerlee Ironworks, which was dug out from under 6m (20 ft) of industrial waste, this museum preserves and interprets the history of the steel and heavy-engineering industry that was once the lifeblood of the surrounding communities. It's certainly Scotland's noisiest museum, with engineers giving daily demonstrations of historic machines and making parts to restore others. In the exhibition hall you'll find a reconstructed tinsmith's shop, brass foundry and a spade forge, as well as an Edwardian photographer's studio and the interior of an old grocery shop. Even the tearoom was built in 1880 but moved here from Coatbridge in the 1980s. But pride of place goes to the large-scale re-production of the ironworks as they were in 1880, contained in a blast furnace structure with a viewing gallery. A £10 million redevelop-ment, completed in 2008, saw the addition of interactive displays and a new environmentally sustainable design for the main hall.

✚ 205 F4 ✉ Heritage Way, Coatbridge
☎ 01236 638 460
🕙 Apr–Oct daily 10–5; Nov–Mar 10–5
🍴 Tearoom at museum (£)
🚉 Coatbridge 🚌 Free

40 Biggar

The town of Biggar, on the A701 road just west of Peebles, was the birthplace of Albion Motors, once the largest truck manufacturer in Great Britain. Today it is famous for having more museums per head of population than anywhere in Scotland. **Moat Park** deals with the history of the area. The reconstructed Victorian street at **Gladstone Court** includes an ironmonger's store, a bank, photographer, chemist, dress-maker, watchmaker, milliner, print-er and bootmaker.

The **Greenhill Covenanters Museum** (Sat and Sun only 2:30–4) covers the religious strife of the 17th century, when the Scottish Presbyterian Covenanters fiercely resisted the imposition of an Episcopalian system on them.

Biggar Gasworks Museum tells of the works that supplied the town from 1839 until the arrival of natural gas from the North Sea in 1973.

The 🎭 **Biggar Puppet Theatre** nearby is home of **Purves Puppets**, established more than 35 years ago. The shows, aimed squarely at children, are guaranteed to delight.

✚ 206 B3
✉ Moat Park Heritage Centre, Kirkstyle
☎ 01899 221 050;
www.biggarmuseumtrust.co.uk
🕙 Easter weekend and May–Sep Mon–Sat 11–4:30, Sun 2–4:30; most museums open afternoons, check for details
🍴 Cafés and restaurants (£)
🚌 Bus from Peebles 🚌 From £1

Purves Puppets
✚ 206 B3 ✉ Broughton Road
☎ 01899 220 631; www.purvespuppets.com
🕙 Tue–Sat 10–4:30
🍴 Cafés in Biggar (£) 🚌 £8

41 Arran

The most southerly of the islands is sometimes called "Scotland in miniature" because of its moun-tainous, underpopulated north and lush, fertile south. The Arran glens are as varied as the mainland's, attracting climbers and walkers to easy pastoral rambles in Glen Rosa, or the more strenuous climbs of Glen Sannox and Goat Fell. Highlights include **Holy Isle** (reached by boat from Lamlash), with its Buddhist meditation centre, **Brodick** Castle and Gardens and the stone circles

Not far from Blackwaterfoot in the southwest of Arran is the picturesque bay of Drumadoon Point.

on **Machrie Moor**. In recent years Arran has also emerged as a foodie haunt. The bountiful island boasts two excellent cheese producers (the Arran Blue is world class), its own highly regarded whisky distillery, an award-winning brewery, an ice-cream maker, a boutique chocolatier and a company called Arran Provisions, which sells a wide range of Arran-themed consumables such as mustard and jam. Add in a sprinkling of excellent restaurants (with local seafood the highlight) and Arran is a great place to explore Scotland's rich culinary larder.

🕂 204 C3 🚢 Ferry from Ardrossan

Tourist Office
✉ By the Pier, Brodick
☎ 0845 225 5121; www.ayrshire-arran.com
🕐 Mon–Sat 9–5:30

42 Culzean Castle & Country Park

This spectacular clifftop castle, built by the renowned architect Robert Adam in the late 18th century, is the National Trust for Scotland's

most visited property. Wandering through the extensive grounds, which form Scotland's first country park, you'll find shore walks with caves to explore, woodland paths and mature parkland. In the house, the magnificent oval staircase and the circular saloon overlooking the Firth of Clyde are among Adam's most daring and brilliant designs. The Eisenhower exhibition recalls the former US president's role as Supreme Commander of the Allied Forces in Europe during World War II, after which he was given the use of an apartment in the building for life. The rooms here, including Eisenhower's suite, can be rented for the night.

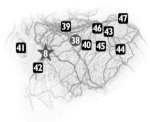

Southern Scotland

🕂 205 D3
✉ Maybole (on A719, approx 4mi/6.5km west)
☎ 01655 884 455; www.culzeanexperience.org
**🄲 Country park: 9:30–sunset; walled garden
and castle: 10:30–5; Visitor Centre: Apr–Nov
10–5:30; Dec–Mar Sat–Sun 11–4**
🍴 Restaurants and snack bars (£–££)
🚌 Ayr–Girvan via Maidens 🚉 Maybole
🎟 £15.50

🔢43 Abbotsford House
In this enchanting residence on
the Tweed, you can see Sir Walter
Scott's desk and everything that
inspired the creator of a mythical
Scotland with his 40 novels
(e.g. *The Bride of Lammermoor*
and *Ivanhoe*), such as Rob Roy's
sword or Bonnie Prince Charlie's
drinking cup.
🕂 207 D3 ✉ Melrose, Roxburghshire TD6 9BQ
☎ 01896 752 043; www.scottsabbotsford.com
🄲 Apr–Nov daily 10–4 🎟 £8.50

🔢44 Melrose, Kelso, Dryburgh & Jedburgh
These magnificent Border Abbeys
were founded by King David I

The ruins of Jedburgh Abbey

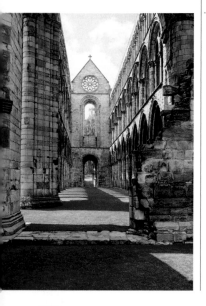

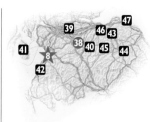

(*c.*1085–1153) and destroyed by
Henry VIII in 1545 in his attempt
to force a marriage between his
son Edward and Mary, Queen of
Scots. The friars were essentially
the king's men in the borders and
their abbeys became centres of
power and wealth. The heart of
Robert the Bruce (➤ 28) is buried
at **Melrose**, and Sir Walter Scott is
buried at Dryburgh. **Kelso** is the
most romantically ruinous, but
if you have time to visit only one,
make it **Jedburgh**, which remains
closest to its original medieval
splendour (➤ 183).
🕂 207 D3
🄲 Apr–Sep daily 9:30–5:30; Oct–Mar 9:30–4:30
**🚌 Edinburgh to Melrose; also Melrose to
Kelso and Jedburgh; postbus to Dryburgh
one-way only, Mon–Fri**

Kelso
🎟 Free

Jedburgh
☎ 01835 86 39 25 🎟 £5.50

Dryburgh
☎ 01835 82 23 81 🎟 £5.50

Melrose
☎ 01896 82 25 62 🎟 £5.50

🔢45 Traquair House
Dating from the early 12th century,
Traquair is the oldest continually
inhabited house in Scotland. Built
as a royal hunting lodge, it was
later fortified against border raiders.
Since 1700, it has been a family
home, and has changed very little.
Within the massive stone walls, the

Traquair has been a family home since the 18th century

house is a maze of corridors, tiny windows and secret passages.

When Bonnie Prince Charlie left on his way to Derby in 1745 to reconquer the Scottish and English throne, the Laird locked the famous Bear Gates and vowed never to open them again until the Stuarts were restored to the throne of Scotland, and thus the gates have remained closed ever since.

Also at Traquair, you can see the old brewhouse, which makes Traquair House ale in original 200-year-old oak casks.

➕ 206 C3 ✉ South of Innerleithen on the A709
☎ 01896 830 323; www.traquair.co.uk
🕐 Apr–Sep daily 11–5; Oct 11–5;
Nov Sat–Sun 11–3
🍴 Restaurant (£) 🚌 From Peebles 🖐 £8.60

46 Rosslyn Chapel

Founded in 1446 by the Third Earl of Orkney, this has all the splendour, in miniature, of the great French cathedrals and the richly carved interior features the world's finest collection of masonic carvings. Look for the "Prentice Pillar", reputed to conceal the Holy Grail, a legend that Dan Brown drew upon heavily in his novel *The Da Vinci Code*. If you ask, a guide will point out the death mask of King Robert the Bruce (► 28), carved into the stone, and tell you about the treasures of King Solomon's Temple and the Knights Templar, buried in the vault below. In addition to these associations, Scott's romantic poem, "The Lay of the Last Minstrel", is also connected with the chapel.

➕ 206 C4 ✉ Rosslyn, Midlothian
☎ 0131 440 2159; www.rosslynchapel.org.uk
🕐 Mon–Sat 9:30–6, Sun noon–4:45
🍴 Tearoom in visitor centre (£)
🚌 No. 15 from Edinburgh
🖐 £9; under 16s free

47 St Abb's Head

This magnificently wild and precipitous stretch of east coast with its many sea birds and butterflies is a nature reserve. To see it at its most beautiful, you should visit early in the morning or in the evening. To the north lie the spectacular ruins of Fast Castle (15 min.) and Tantallon Castle (45 min.). Accommodation can be found in Coldingham or Eyemouth.

➕ 207 E4
✉ www.nnr-scotland.org.uk/st-abbs-head

Where to...
Stay

Burt's £££

Burts was originally built in 1722 for a local dignitary, but over the years it has been transformed into this likeable, family-run former coaching inn. The setting, in the centre of a pretty market square in an historic town, has real picture-postcard charm, and the congenial bar (well stocked with single-malt whiskies) is a popular meeting place. The 20 en-suite rooms vary in size, but are comfortably modern, and the bar serves food that is a step up from standard pub grub.

➕ 207 D3 ✉ Market Square, Melrose
☎ 01896 822 285; www.burtshotel.co.uk

Castle Venlaw £££

This quietly luxurious hotel is located just above the Borders town of Peebles and is close enough to work well as an alternative base for visits to Edinburgh. The pick of the dozen idiosyncratic rooms is the Glenturret Honeymoon Suite, which comes complete (of course) with a four-poster bed and a bathroom that boasts underfloor heating, a bathtub for two and a Champagne cooler. The restaurant is first rate too, and small enough to make personal requests easy to accommodate.

➕ 206 C4 ✉ Edinburgh Road, Peebles
☎ 01721 720 384;www.venlaw.co.uk

Clint Lodge ££

Ideally located between Dryburgh Abbey and the Smailholm Tower on a quiet country road, this guesthouse belongs to the Duke of Sutherland. It is leased by Bill and Heather who make guests in the five rooms feel extremely welcome and serve great food.

➕ 207 D3 ✉ St Boswells
☎ 01835 82 20 27; www.clintlodge.co.uk

Craigadam £–££

Set on an organic sheep farm near Castle Douglas, Craigadam offers top-notch bed-and-breakfast in a gracious country house setting. There are ten large bedrooms, mostly overlooking a courtyard to the back of the main house. In the elegant panelled dining room the magnificent table can seat 15 people. Among the activities available to guests are fishing, snooker and croquet. Dinner is available by prior arrangement.

➕ 206 A1
✉ Craigadam, near Castle Douglas
☎ 01556 650 233; www.craigadam.com

Creggans Inn £££

This comfortable traditional inn offers spectacular views over Loch Fyne from the pretty bedrooms and the prize-winning candlelit restaurant. There are burgers in the bar, cream teas in the coffee shop and inviting lounges.

➕ 205 D5 ✉ Strachur
☎ 01369 860 279;
www.creggans-inn.co.uk

Dunure Inn ££

Nice gastro pub with six rooms in the west coast village between Ayr and Culzean Castle, which is nobly guarded by the ruined castle on a rocky promontory overlooking the harbour. Good food and a great location just one hour away from Glasgow.

🚩 205 D3 ✉ Dunure ☎ 1292 50 05 49

Fernhill ££–£££

This friendly, comfortable hotel enjoys a great location overlooking the harbour, and some of the 36 bedrooms have their own balcony to take full advantage of the views. Guests are served breakfast and dinner in the bright conservatory restaurant, with more sea views.

🚩 205 D1 ✉ Heugh Road, Portpatrick
☎ 01776 810 220; www.fernhillhotel.co.uk
🕔 Closed mid-Jan to mid-Feb

Hundalee House £

If you are entering Scotland in the south this stately residence set in a large park actually offers reasonably priced accommodation. The B&B is located so near to Jedburgh Abbey that it makes an evening visit well worthwhile. Capon Tree Townhouse by the Abbey offers a very fine menu.

🚩 206 A1 ✉ Jedburgh Roxburghshire
☎ 01835 86 30 11;
www.accommodation-scotland.org

Lochgreen House Hotel £££

This splendid country house has been developed into one of Scotland's finest hotels. Its position beside Royal Troon Golf Course provides good views over the fairways, expanses of woodland and immaculate gardens. The 40 rooms, in the main house and converted stables, show meticulous attention to detail. The Tapestry restaurant is highly regarded, with its combination of French techniques and Scottish ingredients.

🚩 205 D1
✉ Monktonhill Road, Southwood, Troon
☎ 01292 313 343; www.costley.biz

Macdonald Cardrona Hotel, Golf and Country Club ££–£££

Don't be put off by the slightly institutional appearance of this large hotel and country club, just south of Peebles. It has every facility, including an 18-hole golf course, indoor pool and a gym. You can also go walking, biking and fishing locally. Rooms are tidy, modern and fresh with rural views. The restaurant, Renwicks, serves a buffet breakfast and good evening meals. There are often out-of-season offers; check the website for details.

🚩 206 C4 ✉ Cardrona, Peebles
☎ 0844 879 9024; www.macdonaldhotels.co.uk

Popinjay Hotel & Spa £

Picturesque, inexpensive, friendly country guesthouse, only 20 minutes northwest of the World Heritage Site of New Lanark. It is located directly by the River Clyde and offers facilities that include a hairdresser, pool and massage.

🚩 205 F4 ✉ Rosebank
☎ 01555 860 18 60; www.popinjayhotel.com

Steamboat Inn ££

This rural country inn on the Solway coast is, as the name suggests, furnished in marine theme. It has two nice B&B rooms, delicious fish dishes and is located ten minutes away from the Sweetheart Abbey ruins.

🚩 206 B2 ✉ Carsethorn, south of Dumfries
☎ 01387 880 631; www.steamboatinn.co.uk

Tontine £–££

Set back from the main street in the market town of Peebles, the Tontine is a long-established hotel with 36 smart bedrooms, an inviting lounge, a bar with a clubby feel to it, and an elegant Adam dining room. The lasting impression is of the excellent hospitality and guest care. Look out for innovative activity packages, such as hiking and mountain-biking breaks.

Insider Tip

🚩 206 C4 ✉ High Street, Peebles
☎ 01721 720 892; www.tontinehotel.com

Where to...
Eat and Drink

Prices
Expect to pay per three-course meal per person, excluding drinks:
£ under £20   **££** £20–£30   **£££** over £30

RESTAURANTS

Aristas £££

Pretty Kirkcudbright is known as an artists' town – it is said that Robert Burns wrote the "Selkirk Grace" in this very hotel in 1794. The Aristas restaurant offers a concise menu of contemporary takes on traditional dishes, including some with a very Scottish theme, such as a starter of millefeuille of haggis with neep-and-tattie (turnip and potato) scones and a whisky reduction. Fish also features, and the wine list is good value. Children are welcome, and there's a beautiful garden.

➕ 205 F1 ✉ Selkirk Arms Hotel, Old High Street, Kirkcudbright
☎ 01557 330 402; www.selkirkarmshotel.co.uk
🕔 Lunch and dinner daily

Burt's Hotel Restaurant ££

With creative head chef Trevor Williams at the helm, this award-winning restaurant at the eponymous hotel is a real star in the picturesque Borders town of Melrose. Settle into the stylish surrounds and prepare for a culinary journey through the fertile Borders region. If you are lucky, fresh local lamb will be on the menu, alongside white fish and shellfish landed on the east coast just a few kilometres away. There's an excellent wine list too.

➕ 207 D3 ✉ Market Square, Melrose
☎ 01896 822 285; www.burtshotel.co.uk
🕔 Lunch and dinner daily

Kailzie Gardens Restaurant £

A handy pit stop after visiting Traquair House (➤ 116), this restaurant in converted stables offers some really good food in a relaxed setting. Lunchtime fare includes soups, sandwiches, pies and salads, but afternoon tea is a treat – it's hard to choose which tempting home-baked cake to have.

➕ 206 C4 ✉ Kailzie Gardens, Peebles
☎ 01721 722 807; www.kailziegardens.com/restaurant.html 🕔 Daily 10:30–5:30

Knockinaam Lodge £££

This old country hotel may have a dream albeit rather remote location in the southwest and a fixed menu with rather steep prices, but it is still well worth considering the extra mileage and cost. The high standard of the meals by long-standing local chef Tony Pierce means that the Michelin star has been a regular here for going on 20 years. The rooms are beautiful.

➕ 205 D1 ✉ Portpatrick
☎ 01776 81 04 71; www.knockinaamlodge.com
🕔 Lunch and dinner daily

The Roxburghe Hotel ££–£££

This top restaurant is set in the Jacobean mansion owned by the Duke of Roxburghe, surrounded by parkland close to the River Teviot. It's a popular base for shooting parties, and so it's not surprising that game features largely on the traditional menu, though it's cooked with a modern twist. You might find saddle of venison set on a bed of spinach and garnished with wild mushrooms, for example. Other menu items are likely to have been sourced from the extensive

Roxburghe estate, and the wine list includes clarets from the duke's private cellars at Floors Castle.

✚ 207 D3 ✉ Heiton, Kelso
☎ 01573 450 331; www.roxburghe.net
🕐 Lunch and dinner daily

The Sunflower ££

This intimate, friendly restaurant can be found down a side street in the centre of genteel Peebles. The Sunflower serves generous portions of unfussy world food cooked with finesse. The restaurant is open for dinner at the end of the week, when starters include smoked haddock chowder and mains, fillet of beef with a tasty herby mash. It's deservedly popular with locals, so reservations are necessary. It's a great place for a family lunch.

✚ 206 C4 ✉ 4 Bridgegate, Peebles
☎ 01721 722 420; www.thesunflower.net
🕐 Lunch Mon–Sat noon–3pm; dinner Thu–Sat 6–9; coffee and cakes Mon–Sat 10–12:30

Wheatsheaf at Swinton ££–£££

At heart, the Wheatsheaf is a village pub – it overlooks the green and the bar offers a warm welcome. But such is the restaurant's reputation that it's essential to book in advance. Scottish beef, duck, game and fish appear on a lengthy menu that is further extended with daily specials, and there's a certain experimental streak to the style that works well. Desserts are worth trying, the beer is good and there's a comprehensive wine list.

✚ 207 E4
✉ Main Street, Swinton ☎ 01890 860 257;
www.wheatsheaf-swinton.co.uk
🕐 Lunch Wed–Sun noon–2pm; dinner daily 5–9; bar: Mon–Tue 5pm–11pm, Wed–Thu 11am–3pm and 5pm–11pm, Fri–Sat 11am–midnight, Sun noon–10pm

PUBS & BARS

Creebridge House Hotel £–££

This pretty country house hotel makes a fine stop-off for light refreshment or a substantial meal.

In fine weather, tables on the front terrace look out over the lawn, otherwise the bar is welcoming. Real ales, more than 50 malt whiskies and a good wine list complement carefully prepared bar/bistro choices such as Dunsyre blue cheese soufflé or caramelised king scallops. Children are welcome.

✚ 205 E1
✉ Minnigaff, Creebridge, near Newton Stewart
☎ 01671 402 121; www.creebridge.co.uk
🕐 Lunch and dinner daily

The Crown Hotel ££–£££

The rambling bars, an open fire and dark, heavy furniture conjure up images of an old smugglers' haunt and contribute towards the popularity of this harbourside inn. The more modern-looking bistro is the place to eat: the menu is imaginative and slightly more expensive, but the quality of the cooking is high. Seafood features strongly.

✚ 205 D1 ✉ 9 North Crescent, Portpatrick
☎ 01776 810 261; www.crownportpatrick.com
🕐 Lunch and dinner daily

The Steam Packet Inn ££

The harbourside Steam Packet Inn, in a picturesque village on the Machars peninsula, serves good food, especially seafood, which is often landed by local fishermen. The bar area is pleasantly old fashioned, with several whiskies and real ales to choose from. If you wish to make a night of it, there are seven rooms at the Inn.

✚ 205 E1 ✉ Harbour Row, Isle of Whithorn, Newton Stewart ☎ 01988 500 334;
www.thesteampacketinn.biz
🕐 Lunch and dinner daily

Traquair Arms Hotel ££

The Bear ale served in the bar of this Victorian, town-centre hotel is brewed at the nearby Traquair House Brewery. The bar menu, which is available all day, makes good use of local ingredients. Soups, Aberdeen Angus beef, fish and game are backed up by a wide selection of vegetarian dishes. Omelettes, salads and baked potatoes are also available. There's a splendid range of desserts to finish, and the cheese-board is strictly Scottish.

✚ 206 C3
✉ Traquair Road, Innerleithen, Borders
☎ 01896 830229; www.traquairarmshotel.co.uk
🕐 Lunch and dinner daily

Where to…
Shop

DUMFRIES & THE SOUTHWEST

In Dumfries, visit **Greyfriars Crafts** (Buccleuch Street) and **Gracefield Arts Centre** (Edinburgh Road). A craft centre at **Drumlanrig Castle** near Thornhill (tel: 01848 330 248) sells jewellery, leather and ceramics. **Designs Gallery and Café** in Castle Douglas (179 King Street; tel: 01556 504 552) specialises in contemporary art and crafts.

Sulwath Brewery (tel: 01556 504 525; www.sulwathbrewers.co.uk) produces some of Scotland's most sought-after beer, including Criffel ale and Black Galloway porter. You can sample the beers and buy bottles at the brewery shop.

If you fancy sumptuous modern textiles, visit **Jo Gallant's** shop in Kirkcudbright (70 High Street; tel: 01557 331 130).

SCOTTISH BORDERS

This area is known for its excellent woollen goods. Try **Peter Scott** in Hawick (11 Buccleuch Street; tel: 01450 364 815) for knitwear.

The Scottish Borders are also renowned for traditional textiles and weaving. Smaller businesses, such as **Andrew Elliot Ltd** (tel: 01750 720 412; www.elliot-weave.co.uk) in Selkirk, offer bespoke services and high-quality products. You can design and commission your own tweeds and tartans, or buy from his selection of beautiful throws and blankets.

Where to…
Go Out

ACTIVITIES

The **Ice Bowl** in Dumfries (King Street; tel: 01387 251 300) offers curling, ice skating and indoor bowling, while the **Magnum Leisure Centre** in Irvine (tel: 01294 278 381) is one of the largest in Europe. **The Hub** (Glentress Forest; tel: 01721 721 736) in the Borders is one of Scotland's best equipped mountain biking centres, with routes to suit all levels. For angling, contact **Fish Tweed** for information (tel: 01573 470 612).

SPECTATOR SPORTS

FC Kilmarnock plays in the Scottish premiership, Scotland's top football league. Rugby union is so popular in the Scottish borders that even small towns have their own rugby ground.

MUSIC & THEATRE

Most towns have a nightclub, but don't expect sophistication. Concerts are held in the **Magnum Leisure Centre** at Irvine, the **Ryan Centre** (Farnhurst Road; tel: 01776 703 535) in Stranraer and in town halls. The **Theatre Royal** (66–68 Shakespeare Road; tel: 01387 254 209) in Dumfries is Scotland's oldest theatre. It stages amateur and visiting productions. The renovated **Gaiety Theatre** in Ayr is the largest theatre and arts centre in southwest Scotland.

Central Scotland

Little Treats

A Starter Mountain for Munro Collectors
The **Ben Lomond Munro** (➤ 128) on the east bank of the loch is perfect for a short, fairly easy, hike.

Fish & Chips for Everyone
Dangle your feet over the harbour wall in **Anstruther** (➤ 139) and allow your soul to soar as you munch on a treat from the "Wee Chippy".

A Drink with a View
Old fishermen's haunts are often dark and dismal, but the Ship Inn at Tay in **Dundee** (➤ 137) boasts a fine panorama window.

Getting Your Bearings

From Loch Lomond to the Angus Glens, the broad sweep of Central Scotland is a land of sharp contrasts. It offers rich farmland and industrial heartlands, a rugged coastline dotted with tiny fishing villages, bustling towns, ancient castles and sweeping battle-grounds, and a wild mixture of moor, mountain and loch.

Central Scotland has long been the playground of Glaswegians, drawn to the beauty of Loch Lomond or the hills around Arrochar. **Queen Elizabeth Forest Park** is a great spot for mountain biking, and is within an easy bus or train ride from Glasgow city centre.

Here, past and present, and fact and fiction, merge. From the Queen Elizabeth Forest Park, the **Trossachs** stretch east to **Stirling**, Scotland's ancient capital in the central plain. They extend north to the **Braes of Balquhidder**, haunt of Rob Roy MacGregor, Scotland's infamous outlaw immortalised by Sir Walter Scott's eponymous novel in the 19th century and more recently by Hollywood.

To the north is industrial **Dundee**, once famed for jam, jute and journalism but now rejuvenated as a conference and tourist centre. South across the long bridges of the River Tay in the Kingdom of **Fife** is **St Andrews**, which has been a university town and the home of golf since the 15th century. The region is ideal walking and cycling country, with probably more signposted cycling trails than anywhere else in Scotland.

To the north of Dundee, at **Kirriemuir**, you can visit the birthplace of author J M Barrie, and from Kirriemuir the Glens of Angus fan north into the arresting highland landscape of the **Grampian Mountains**.

Highland cattle in Trossachs National Park

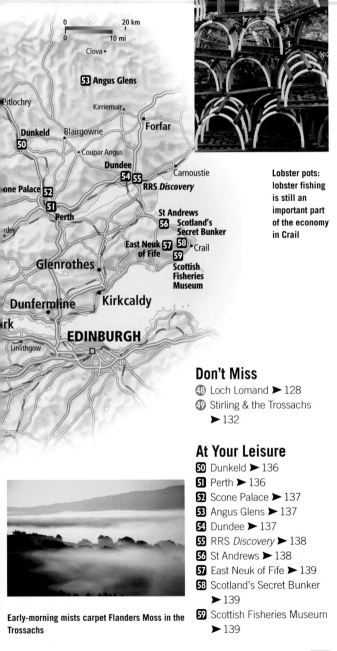

Lobster pots: lobster fishing is still an important part of the economy in Crail

Early-morning mists carpet Flanders Moss in the Trossachs

Central Scotland

Three Perfect Days

Stretching north of Glasgow and Edinburgh, the landscape is a picture of lowlands, hills and the fringes of the Highlands, with rivers and lakes, small industrial centres, fishing villages and spectacular coastline. The following route will ensure that you don't miss any of the highlights in Central Scotland. For more information see the main entries (➤ 128–139).

Day 1

Morning
Drive up the western side of **48 Loch Lomond** (➤ 128) along the A82 West Highland Way north to Crianlarich. Take the A85 to Lochearnhead then the A84 to Kingshouse. From here detour to the hamlet of **Balquhidder**, where Rob Roy MacGregor (➤ 133) lies buried in the tiny churchyard. Return to the A84 and head for Callander and a bar lunch at the Lade Inn at **Kilmahog**.

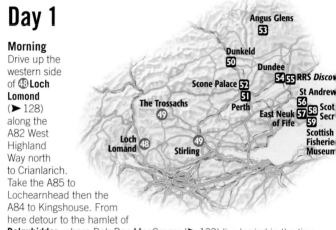

Angus Glens **53**

Dunkeld **50**

Dundee **54 55** RRS Disco

Scone Palace **52**
51
Perth

St Andre
56
East Neuk **57 58** Scot
of Fife **59** Secr

The Trossachs **49**

Scottish
Fisherie
Museum

Loch Lomand **48**   **49** Stirling

Afternoon
Rob Roy, Scotland's most famous cattle rustler, was born at Loch Katrine, and in nearby **Callander**, the tourist information centre has a small display about his life. Then drive through the **Queen Elizabeth Forest Park** on the meandering A821 to Brig o'Turk and via the Dyke's Pass to Aberoyle,

where you turn off on the B829 to the wonderful Loch Katrine (pictured opposite below) in the heart of the Trossachs. Take the A81 to 49 **Stirling** (➤ 132), where you can visit the castle, the atmospheric Old Town Jail and the Wallace Monument.

Day 2

Morning
Finish your tour of Stirling, before heading for Perth on the A9. **The Blair Drummond Safari Park** (➤ 138), just northeast of Stirling, is a good diversion for young families, with a funfair and a sea lion show. The highlight of the area is 52 **Scone Palace** (pictured right, ➤ 137), about 2mi (3km) north of town on the A93.

Afternoon
Head north on the A93 towards **Glenshee** and spend the rest of the afternoon driving round **the Glens**. Use a local map to pick any combination of roads you like. Or simply turn right on to the B951 through Glenisla to **Kirriemuir**, and from there follow the B955 and B956 around **Glen Clova**. That brings you back to Kirriemuir, from which you can get to 54 **Dundee** (➤ 137) via the A928 in 30 min.

Day 3

Morning
Visit the 55 RRS *Discovery* (pictured right, ➤ 138), next to which a spectacular new design museum (V&A Museum of Design) is currently being constructed (expected completion end of 2017; opening by June 2018). After a stroll through the streets and a visit to the cathedral and castle, have lunch at the **Seafood Restaurant** on the Bruce Embankment.

Afternoon
Leave St Andrews on the A917 and enjoy the scenic drive round the coastline of the 57 **East Neuk of Fife** (➤ 139). Don't miss the picturesque harbours at Crail and Pittenweem and the 59 **Scottish Fisheries Museum** at Anstruther (➤ 139). On your way back, take the B9131 to the 58 **Secret Bunker** (➤ 139) before heading back to St Andrews and its gorgeous West Sands beach.

48 Loch Lomond

One of the first acts of the Scottish Parliament was to protect the landscape by establishing national parks, and Loch Lomond and the Trossachs became Scotland's first in 2002. Not only is it an area of outstanding beauty, but it's accessible to all. A popular leisure choice for locals and tourists, it's still possible to find serene, isolated spots overlooking the waters.

Anyone desiring a good view of the area needs to aim high: Take the A811 from Balloch towards Stirling but turn off after 7mi (11km) on to the A837 to Drymen, Balmaha and then on to **Rowardennan**. The road stops at this point so it's much quieter than the busy A82 along the west side. From here you can climb **Ben Lomond** (973m/3,191ft), the highest mountain in the area and Scotland's southernmost **Munro** (see panel ➤ 130). From its peak, there is a superb view back over the loch.

Walking is the best way to appreciate the fauna and flora. You can continue walking from Rowardennan on the **West Highland Way**, a 95mi (152km) long-distance footpath that follows the banks of the loch as it winds its way via Inversnaid to the top of the loch and on to Crianlarich (www.west-highland-way.co.uk). Wildlife thrives in this unspoilt and tranquil area – waders, geese, capercaillie, golden eagles and sometimes white fallow deer all flourish in the vicinity of the loch. A quarter of all known British wild plant species are also found here.

A fire-coloured bed of reeds at Loch Arklet, a small lake to the east of Loch Lomond

The West Bank

If you prefer the busier areas with more facilities, try the villages of **Luss** and **Tarbet** on the west side of Lomond. Although they get busy, especially in summer, they don't usually feel crowded and offer plenty of hotels, tearooms and picnic spots, many with peaceful views of the loch and the surrounding mountains.

Just west of Tarbet is the village of **Arrochar**, whose nearby hills, have long been a popular haunt of climbers. Take to the hills and the open spaces are so vast that the countryside feels almost deserted despite the hundreds of climbers out Munro-bagging. Shade and shadow change with the seasons, making the lure of the lovely scenery around the loch hard to resist.

Loch Lomond's Islands

If you really want to get away from it all, explore some of Loch Lomond's 30-plus small islands. Some are inhabited, while others are nature reserves or Sites of Special Scientific Interest (SSSI). **Inchcailloch** belongs to Scottish Natural Heritage, and **Bucinch** and **Ceardach** to the National Trust for Scotland. The other islands are privately owned.

The largest is **Inchmurrin**, which was reputedly visited by Robert the Bruce, King James VI and Mary, Queen of Scots, as well as St Mirren, after whom it is named. You can explore the ruins of a seventh-century monastery as you undertake the various walks along the island's 2.5km (1.5mi) length. It offers rooms, a bar and restaurant (tel: 01389 850 245 to make a reservation).

Inchgalbraith island is an ancient "crannog", a loch dwelling built by Iron Age people as a safe haven. The name means "Island of the Galbraiths" and in medieval

INSIDER INFO

- To explore the islands, **take the Balmaha mail boat** from Sandy MacFarlane's boatyard, which his great-grandfather started 150 years ago. The boat serves the islands of **Inchtavannich, Inchmurrin, Inchcruin** and **Inchfad** on Monday and Wednesday to Saturday in July and August, leaving Balmaha at 11:30am and returning at 2pm. The one-hour stop on Inchmurrin is just long enough to explore a little and have lunch. A restricted service operates at all other times, so check with the boatyard (tel: 01360 870 214).
- You can also take a pleasant boat trip on the loch from Balloch, or if you're feeling adventurous, hire a speedboat, jet ski or canoe.
- If you don't have enough time for a boat trip, from the car park at Balmaha you can at least take one of the short **woodland walks** with wonderful views over the islands and Loch Lomond. Details and maps are available from the visitor centre.

Insider Tip

MUNRO-BAGGING
The terrain and changeable conditions of the Highlands are not to be underestimated, least of all when attempting to climb one of Scotland's Munros. A Scottish mountain over 914m (3,000ft) high is known as a Munro after Sir Hugh Munro (1856–1919), who catalogued the peaks, but while several thousand people have managed to summit all 284 Munros, Sir Hugh was not one of them. Many of the mountaintops, such as the notorious Inaccessible Pinnacle in the Cuillin range on the Isle of Skye, are for experts only, while some are distinctly unchallenging in favourable weather. Munro-baggers will try to climb them all, ticking each one off the list as it is conquered.

Loch Lomond

Daybreak at Balmaha, on Loch Lomond's eastern shore

times it was the base of their castle, now in ruins but visible through the trees as you approach by boat.

Inchfad was the site of an ancient illicit whisky still that did a brisk trade until a government cutter appeared on the loch in the mid-19th century. The still became legitimate and the island acquired a registered distillery, but only its ruins remain. If you take a trip on the mail boat, the boatman will tell you all about it, and is more or less a firsthand source, as it was run by his ancestor.

Insider Tip

A nature trail covers the whole island of **Inchcailloch**, which it takes about an hour and a half to stroll round and explore, together with the ruins of a 14th-century chapel and burial ground. There are great views over the loch from the highest point on the island, and at Port Bawn on the south side there are picnic tables, barbecue facilities and a superb beach. The **ferry service** runs on demand from the boatyard at nearby **Balmaha**, which also rents out various boats and fishing tackle, and sells fishing permits as well as daily cruises round the nature reserve islands.

TAKING A BREAK

For a real treat with fabulous views, try the informal **Colquhoun's** restaurant (tel: 01436 860 201) that belongs to the Lodge on Loch Lomond Hotel, in the pretty village of Luss.

Opposite: Ben Lomond, the highest peak in the area towers over the lake of the same name

✚ 205 E5

National Park Gateway Centre
✉ Loch Lomond Shores, Ben Lomond Way, Balloch
☎ 01389 751 035; www.lochlomondshores.com
🕐 Daily 10–5

④⑨ Stirling & the Trossachs

Stirling Castle at the eastern edge of the Trossachs has been perched on its plug of volcanic rock for centuries, a lone sentinel overseeing Scotland's central lowland plain as far as the eye can see and guarding the gateway to the Highlands. Its strategic significance made it the scene of many battles from the 12th century onwards, as successive waves of English forces swept north and were repelled.

The current **castle**, with its **chapel** and **palace**, dates mainly from the 16th century and is dominated by the **Great Hall**. The main feature, however, is the **spectacular view** from the esplanade, and if you take the Back Walk around the castle you can enjoy a full panorama of the surrounding countryside. For an explanation of the principal hills and battlesites, there's a viewfinder on **Ladies' Rock** in the cemetery below the castle. This vast historic burial ground beside the **Church of the Holy Rude** is an attraction in its own right, containing the remains of Stirling's most prominent citizens, and an assortment of ancient gravestones. A little down the hill is the **Old Town Jail**, where actors recreate the once horrifying conditions of this 19th-century prison.

Stirling Castle has guarded the "Gateway to the Highlands" for centuries

Stirling & the Trossachs

Old Stirling Bridge dates from the 15th century and replaces an older wooden one, where William Wallace defeated the English in 1297. This success is commemorated at the **National Wallace Monument**, a striking tower just outside the town, set, like the castle, on a rocky outcrop.

Another important battle on the outskirts of Stirling was the decisive Scottish victory at **Bannockburn** in 1314 where the boggy ground decimated the English cavalry, while the Bannock Burn (stream) prevented easy withdrawal. You can wander round the field, and there are exhibitions and an audio-visual of the battle. At the centre is an equestrian statue of Robert the Bruce (➤ 29).

The Trossachs Trail

From Stirling, the Trossachs stretch out to Loch Lomond and Crianlarich in the west, to Loch Tay in the north and through Callander, Aberfoyle and Loch Katrine. Pick up a **Trossachs Trail leaflet** and map from the

Detail from the facade of Stirling Castle

tourist office on Stirling's Castle Esplanade and head for **Callander**, an essential first stop because of what you can learn there about "Rob Roy". This Robin Hood figure was born by Loch Katrine. There is a small exhibition in the town's tourist information centre. Robert MacGregor, ("Roy" is from the Gaelic *rua*, meaning "red", because of his red hair), was a cattle drover. He ran a protection racket, extorting money from other drovers to ensure their safety while travelling through MacGregor land. Despite

A statue of Robert the Bruce commemorates the Scottish victory at Bannockburn

his turbulent life, he died in old age in his cottage. You can visit his grave in the old churchyard at **Balquhidder**. Go north along the A84 and then turn right at Kingshouse.

Ben An overlooks Loch Katrine

Area Highlights

Visit Scotland's only natural lake, the **Lake of Menteith**, and take a boat trip out to the island to explore **Inchmahome**, a ruined Augustine priory founded in 1238. Mary, Queen of Scots, was hidden here in 1547 before she was exiled to France. In the church chancel, admire the double effigy of Walter, Steward of Menteith and his wife, shown in a last embrace.

Nearby **Aberfoyle** is the home of the **Scottish Wool Centre**, with presentations explaining how different breeds of sheep played a part in building the Scottish wool industry, sheepdog displays and demonstrations of spinning.

From Aberfoyle, wander the hills to the **Duke's Pass** for spectacular views over the area and the visitors' centre for the **Queen Elizabeth Forest Park**. Covering an immense 303km² (117mi²), this apparent wilderness stretches from the eastern shores of Loch Lomond to rugged Strathyre. It's home to red and roe deer and wild goats. There are forest trails, woodland walks, mountains to climb and strenuous bike trails, as well as a carriage ride for those who enjoy more sedate exploration.

TAKING A BREAK

There's an excellent restaurant at the visitor centre in the Queen Elizabeth Forest Park.

The tranquil waters of the Lake of Menteith, Scotland's only natural lake

Stirling Tourist Information Centre
✚ 206 A5 ✉ 41 Dumbarton Road, Stirling ☎ 08707 200 620
🕐 Apr, May Mon–Sat 9–5; Jun, Sep Mon–Sat 9–5, Sun 10–4; Jul, Aug Mon–Sat 9–7, Sun 10–4; Oct–Mar Mon–Sat 10–5
🚌 From Glasgow and Edinburgh 🚉 Stirling

Visit Scotland Information Centre
✚ 206 A5 ✉ Ancaster Square, Callander ☎ 018777 330 342
🕐 Daily Apr–Jun, Sep–Oct 10–5; Jul–Aug 10–6; Nov–Mar 10–4
🚌 From Stirling

Stirling Castle
✚ 206 A5 ✉ Stirling ☎ 01786 450 000; www.historic-scotland.gov.uk
🕐 Apr–Sep 9:30–6; Oct–Mar 9:30–5 🍴 Café in grounds 💷 £14.50

Wallace Monument
✚ 206 A5 ✉ Abbey Craig Hillfoots Road, Causewayhead
☎ 01786 472 140; www.nationalwallacemonument.com
🕐 Jan–Mar, Nov–Dec 10:30–4; Apr–Jun, Sep, Oct 10–5; Jul–Aug 10–6
🚌 From Stirling 💷 £9.50

Scottish Wool Centre
✚ 205 E5 ✉ Off Main Street, Aberfoyle
☎ 01877 382 850; www.scottishwoolcentre.co.uk 🕐 Daily 9:30–5:30

INSIDER INFO

Insider Tip

- Take a trip around Loch Katrine on the **Victorian steamer** *Sir Walter Scott* (Mar–Oct). Scott's novel *Rob Roy* and his romantic poem "The Lady of the Lake", which was set on the loch, have long drawn visitors to this area. As Loch Katrine supplies Glasgow with much of its water, the West of Scotland Water Authority, which owns and runs the boat, allows no other powered craft.
- Behind Balquhidder church there's a stile leading to a forest road. Turn right at the first junction to climb a small hill above the church with views to the **Braes of Balquhidder** and secluded **Balquhidder Glen.** Along the road is **Iverlochlarig**, where Rob Roy died, and it was along the 24km (15-mile) glen that his funeral procession marched on New Year's Day, 1735.

At Your Leisure

The dramatic waterfall at the Hermitage Woodland Walk, near Dunkeld

50 Dunkeld

At the heart of this delightful village is a square of 17th-century white-washed cottages, rebuilt after the Battle of Dunkeld in 1689. From here it's a short stroll along the river to the partially ruined cathedral (services are still held). There are many wonderful riverside and wood-land walks around Dunkeld, for example along the Tay and across Thomas Telford's bridge to the neighbouring village of **Birnam**. The last ancient oak from Birnam Wood – as featured in the prophecy of Macbeth's death in Shakespeare's play – stands beside the river. The **Hermitage Woodland Walk** takes in many exotic trees, and Britain's tall-est – a Douglas fir over 210ft (64m) tall – stands close to the curious **Ossian's Hall**, an elegant 18th-cen-tury folly on a rocky outcrop over a dramatic waterfall. In contrast, nearby **Ossian's Cave** is a primitive roofed cell built from natural rock formations. You can pick up trail leaflets and more information at the National Trust for Scotland (NTS) shop in the Ell House, named after the brass measure on the wall, which medieval merchants used to measure cloth.

✚ 210 C2
🍽 Cafés and tearooms in the village (£)

NTS The Ell Shop
☎ 0844 493 192
🕐 Apr–Oct Mon–Sat 10–5:30, Sun 12:30–5:30; Nov–23 Dec Mon–Sat 10–4:30, Sun 12:30–4:30

51 Perth

Perth is one of Scotland's most his-toric cities, being both the former capital and also where the country once crowned its kings. In 2010 the royal burgh celebrated its 800th anniversary and these days it always appears in surveys as one of the places that Scots themselves would most like to live. Scotland's former capital is now a prosperous market town and makes a good base for exploring. While here, visit the restored Victorian oatmeal mill at **Lower City Mills** and the **Black Watch Regimental Museum**.

Bell's Cherrybank Gardens has one of Britain's best collections of heathers. Popular **Branklyn Garden** (NTS) on the Dundee Road covers just less than 1ha (2.5 acres) with a superb collection of alpine plants and rhododendrons, Perth is also a green city, with a riverside walk, and its centre is neatly flanked by two leafy parks, the North Inch and South Inch. Kinnoull Hill overlooks the city and is also alive with walking trails, which boast some sweeping views.

Insider Tip

➕ 210 C1

Tourist Information
✉ West Mill Street
☎ 01738 450 600; www.perthshire.co.uk
🕐 Apr–Jun and Sep–Oct 9:30–4.30;
Jul–Aug daily 9:30–6; Nov–Mar Mon–Sat 10–4

Lower City Mills
✉ West Mill Street ☎ 01738 62 7958

Black Watch Regimental Museum
✉ Balhousie Castle, Hay Street
☎ 0131 310 8530; www.theblackwatch.co.uk/index/museum 💷 £7.50

Bell's Cherrybank Gardens
☎ 01738 472 800; www.rampantscotland.com/visit/blvisitbells.htm

Branklyn Garden
✉ 116 Dundee Road
☎ 01738 625 535; www.branklyngarden.org.uk

52 Scone Palace
Scotland's monarchs were crowned here on the **Stone of Destiny** (also known as the Stone of Scone) until it was stolen by Edward I of England in 1296 and only returned 700 years later in 1996 (➤ 56). The present building dates from the 16th century but was restored and extended in the 19th century. The grand rooms, with magnificent ornate ceilings and French period furniture, contain an amazing collection of porcelain, clocks and 16th-century needlework, yet still manage to retain the feel of a family house. The grounds

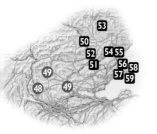

are a delight, with parklands, peacocks and a children's playground.
➕ 210 C1
✉ A93, 2mi (3km) northeast of Perth
☎ 01738 552 300; www.scone-palace.co.uk
🕐 Apr–Oct daily 9:30–5;
Nov–Apr Fri 10–4 grounds only
🍴 Restaurant and tearoom (£–££)
🚌 Limited service from Perth 🚉 Perth
💷 £10.50

53 Angus Glens
The glens of Angus are atmospheric even in torrential rain, but when the sun shines, a blue vista stretches out before you. Hillsides thick with heather are dotted with sheep and deer, while burns tumble to the winding rivers below. This is walking country at its best: there are ten Munros (➤ 130) and a wealth of wildlife and plants. The glens fan out over 30mi (48km) from Kirriemuir and Blairgowrie to Braemar and Balmoral. Drive up Glenshee from Blairgowrie on the A93 to view the majestic scenery as the road rises to over 600m (1,968ft) past the Devil's Elbow, a double hairpin bend now bypassed by the road. Quiet B-roads meander up through the glens from the pleasant low-lying towns of **Alyth, Kirriemuir** and **Edzell**. You can leave your car at one of the car parks and explore the glens on foot if the weather is up to it.
➕ 210 C2
✉ North of Blairgowrie and Kirriemuir

54 Dundee
The ancient city of Dundee is a fun, down-to-earth place with many fine buildings and a thriving theatre scene. It is a far more attractive and modern city than its reputation as the centre of "jute, jam and journalism" would suggest. Highlights include the **McManus Galleries**, where you can see the oldest-known astrolabe (an instrument used to make astrological measurements), dating from 1555; 👫 **Sensation: Dundee**, a hands-on science centre for all ages dedicated to understanding

the five senses, and the innovative **Dundee Contemporary Arts centre**, which hosts a lively, exciting programme of events, experimental films and exhibitions.

The old jute industry is recalled in the restored mill at the **Verdant Works**, with its noisy textile machines. At 1pm the wailing of the "bummer", the factory whistle that once regulated the lives of Dundee's families, is achingly evocative for some. The industry once employed 50,000 people in the city. Today, however, Dundee is better known as a centre for high technology, in the fields of science and electronics.

➕ 211 D1

McManus Galleries
✉ Albert Square, Meadowside
☎ 01382 307 200; www.mcmanus.co.uk

Contemporary Arts Centre
✉ 152 Nethergate
☎ 01382 909 900; www.dca.org.uk

Verdant Works
✉ 27 West Henderson's Wynd
☎ 01382 309 060; www.verdantworks.com

👫 ON LAND AND SEA

■ The **Blair Drummond Safari Park** (tel: 01786 841 456; www.blair drummond.com; end Mar–end Oct 10–5.30; £14) combines wildlife enclosures – containing creatures from chimpanzees to camels – with waterslides, bouncy castles and other activities where kids can let off steam. During the summer holiday season there are festivals and special events every week.

■ If you're in St Andrews with children, then the **Aquarium** (tel: 01334 474 786; daily 10–6; www.standrews aquarium.co.uk; £10) is a must. With its underground walkways, pools, shark displays and all manner of other marine creatures, it's a great place for all the family.

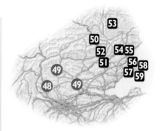

55 RRS *Discovery*

Built in Dundee's Panmure shipyard in 1901, the Royal Research Ship *Discovery* carried Captain Scott's (1868–1912) first expedition team, including a young Ernest Shackleton, to the Antarctic in 1900–1904, where they survived two years trapped in the ice but managed to carry out pioneering work, including the discovery of 500 new kinds of marine animal. Fully restored after years rotting on the Thames in London, it is Dundee's main attraction and a fascinating glimpse into the life of the intrepid explorer.

➕ 211 D1
✉ Discovery Point, near the Tay Road Bridge
☎ 01382 309 060; www. rrsdiscovery.com
🕐 Apr–Oct Mon–Sat 10–6, Sun 11–6;
Nov–Mar Mon–Sat 10–5, Sun 11–5
🍴 Café in visitor centre (£)
🚉 Dundee 💷 £9

56 St Andrews

St Andrews, with its medieval cobbled streets and narrow alleys is home to Scotland's oldest university, founded in 1411. Guided tours in summer include the eerie ruins of the 12th-century cathedral where Robert the Bruce worshipped (for details tel: 01334 476 161).

Insider Tip

The Royal and Ancient Golf Club is another venerable institution. The world's oldest golf club, it is also the headquarters of the game and attracts international golfers. The British Open has often been played here. If you have a handicap certificate you can play a round on the famous Old Course (➤ 144 for reservation details) either by booking far in advance or by entering the daily lottery for a place. Near by is the British Golf Museum, with all manner of memorabilia from ancient to modern.

🕂 211 D1

Tourist Information
✉ 70 Market Street
☎ 01334 472 021; www.visitfife.com
🕔 Apr–Jun Mon–Sat 9:30–5:30, Sun 11–4; Jul–Aug Mon–Sat 9:30–7, Sun 10–5; Sep–Oct Mon–Sat 9:30–5, Sun 11–4; Nov–Mar Mon–Sat 9:30–5 🍴 Numerous cafés, restaurants and tearooms (£) 🚌 Regular service from Leuchars, Dundee or Edinburgh 🚉 Leuchars

57 East Neuk of Fife
The coastline of this small corner of Scotland is best seen at a walking or cycling pace, or you could take an afternoon drive down the coast from St Andrews. Highlights are the fishing villages of Crail, Anstruther, Pittenweem and St Monans, where cottages with red-tiled roofs and crow-stepped gables crowd around picturesque harbours littered with nets and lobster pots. There are coastal walks to view the massed seabirds nesting on the rocks, or you can go diving in the clear waters below, which are swarming with different species of sea life.

🕂 207 D5 ✉ Fife coast, south of St Andrews

58 🍴 Scotland's Secret Bunker
This underground command post, designed as the administrative centre of Scotland in the event of a nuclear attack, was one of Scotland's best-kept secrets until it was officially revealed in 1995. Now, signposts everywhere point to it. The entrance, through a small, nondescript building resembling a traditional Scottish farmhouse, doesn't prepare you for the labyrinth below. Once through the massive steel bomb doors, built to withstand the full force of a nuclear explosion, you can wander, via 150m of tunnels, round a maze of

The waterside homes of Pittenweem, the East Neuk of Fife

dormitories, communications equipment and control rooms, and even have a cup of tea in the NAAFI (canteen). This was to be the base of important people from all over Scotland, such as government ministers, scientists and technicians. Up to 300 people could live in here, working and sleeping in shifts in order to maximise on space.

🕂 211 E1
✉ 3mi (5km) north of Anstruther
☎ 01333 310 301; www. secretbunker.co.uk
🕔 Mid-Mar–Oct daily 10–5
🍴 Café in bunker (£) 🎫 £11

59 Scottish Fisheries Museum
Contained in a number of harbour-front buildings dating from the 16th to the 19th centuries, this museum recounts Scotland's long fishing tradition in exhibits that include a reconstruction of the interior of a fisherman's cottage and a display about the local "Zulu" fishing boats, including a 78ft (24m) example, which made its last trip in 1968. Opposite, in the harbour, you'll find a traditional Fifie fishing boat.

🕂 211 D1 ✉ Harbourhead, Anstruther
☎ 01333 310 628; www.scotfishmuseum.org
🕔 Apr–Sep Mon–Sat 10–5:30, Sun 11–5; Oct–Mar Mon–Sat 10–4:30, Sun noon–4:30
🍴 Tearoom (£)
🚌 From St Andrews to Leven 🎫 £8

Where to...
Stay

Prices
Expect to pay per standard double room per night, including breakfast:
£ under £70   ££ £70–£100   £££ over £100

Apex City Quay Hotel & Spa ££–£££

As part of Dundee's regenerated city centre, this stylish modern hotel offers warm hospitality and good service to match its excellent facilities. These include fine contemporary dining, an indoor pool, gym and excellent spa. Rooms are well appointed, with wide-screen TVs, DVD players and walk-in power showers.

✚ 211 D1
✉ 1 West Victoria Dock Road, Dundee
☎ 01382 202 404; www.apexhotels.co.uk

Arden House ££

Arden House was used as the doctors' house in the popular 1960s British TV series *Dr Finlay's Casebook*. Now a well-run, comfortable bed-and-breakfast, the Dr Finlay associations are worked into a theme, but are not overdone. The substantial, stone-built house stands in a quiet location, just a short walk uphill from the main street of Callander. There are just six en-suite bedrooms.

✚ 206 A5 ✉ Bracklinn Road, Callander
☎ 01877 330 235; www.ardenhouse.org.uk.
Ⓒ Closed Nov–Easter.

Breadalbane House £

At the south end of the enchanting Loch Tay, this Dutch-run B&B concealed behind a typical Highland façade reveals itself to be a modern guesthouse. As a base to explore the Trossachs for a day, this location and room prices (5 rooms) are ideal. The Falls of Dorchart (rapids) are close by.

✚ 210 A1 ✉ Killin
☎ 01567 82 01 34; www.adamohotels.com

Cromlix House £££

A long, winding drive through the 12km² (4.6mi²) estate is a magnificent prelude to the charms of this outstanding Victorian mansion. In winter, log fires ensure that the impressive public rooms are kept warm, while in the summer months, you can enjoy a game of croquet or tennis, or perhaps a spot of trout and salmon fishing. This exclusive establishment belongs to tennis pro Andy Murray.

✚ 206 A5 ✉ Kinbuck by Dunblane
☎ 01786 822125; www.cromlix.com

Drovers Inn & Lodge £–££

Since 1705, cattle drovers have been stopping here, north of Loch Lomond by Ardlui, for a wee dram and a good night's sleep. Today, it is also popular with hikers on the West Highland Way between Glasgow and Fort William. Accommodation has remained affordable and very down-to-earth: a must! In the pub building, the rooms are a cosy testimony of times gone by, the rooms in the lodge next door are more modern. *Insider Tip*

✚ 209 F1 ✉ Inverarnan ☎ 01301 70 42 34;
www.thedroversinn.co.uk

Easter Dunfallandy House £–££

There are just three bedrooms at this comfortable bed-and-breakfast, which offers a high standard of hospitality, and superb views over Ben-y-Vrackie mountain and the Tummel valley. The Scottish breakfasts are a gourmet's delight.

Insider Tip

🔲 210 B2 ✉ Logierait Road, Pitlochry
☎ 01796 474 031; www.dunfallandy.co.uk

Forest Hills Hotel & Resort £££

You can enjoy all the great indoor and outdoor facilities of a resort complex at this popular hotel, situated in the heart of the Trossachs with wonderful views of Loch Ard. When you're exhausted from swimming, sailing, quad biking, abseiling and archery, relax in the Jacuzzi or the solarium, or in the restaurant overlooking the landscaped gardens.

🔲 205 E5 ✉ Kinlochard
☎ 0844 879 9057;
www.macdonaldhotels.co.uk

The Gleneagles Hotel £££

This top-class hotel is set in beautiful countryside surrounded by its famous golf courses, leisure facilities, including a country club and health spa, and well-tended grounds with opportunities for everything from archery to falconry. Sumptuous afternoon teas are served in the drawing room, and for dinner there's a choice of two top-notch restaurants. Luxurious suites have every comfort, and standard rooms are well designed and equipped.

🔲 205 E5 ✉ Auchterarder
☎ 01764 662 231; www.gleneagles.com

Hazelbank £–££

For a less expensive but still very comfortable stay in the home of golf, try the small Hazelbank hotel. With just ten en-suite rooms available in the honey-coloured stone townhouse, you may need to book well in advance around large events. Golf and accommodation packages are available; the hotel is just a two-minute walk from the first tee on the Old Course.

🔲 211 D1
✉ 28 The Scores, St Andrews
☎ 01334 472 466; www.hazelbank.com

Isle of Eriska Hotel £££

On a private island with vehicle access from the mainland via an iron bridge, Eriska is a nature-lover's dream, with beaches, woodlands and moors. The baronial house is furnished with style. Service and hospitality are impeccable. There's a six-hole golf course, a swimming pool, gym, putting, clay-pigeon shooting and tennis. All 17 bedrooms are spacious and thoughtfully equipped. Seafood features strongly in the renowned restaurant.

🔲 209 E1
✉ Ledaig by Oban, Isle of Eriska
☎ 01631 720 371;
www.eriska-hotel.co.uk

The Lodge on Loch Lomond £££–£££

The setting is idyllic and the panoramic views taken for granted in this low-slung, modern building hugging the shore of Loch Lomond. The hotel is entirely pine clad, including its 46 bedrooms, which range from suites to family and standard rooms, many overlooking the loch. Uniquely, each room has its own sauna, although those in standard rooms are single size only. Fishing and boating are gentle pursuits that the hotel can arrange.

Insider Tip

🔲 205 E5 ✉ Luss
☎ 01436 860 201;
www.loch-lomond.co.uk

The Parklands Hotel ££

This award-winning, four-star hotel overlooking Perth's leafy South Inch Park offers a stylish setting and two recommendable restaurants: the Number 1, The Bank, a popular and informal bistro. The 15 rooms are modern and comfortably furnished. The location speaks for itself.

🔲 210 C1
✉ 2 Leonard's Bank, Perth
☎ 01738 622 451;
www.theparklandshotel.com

Where to...
Eat and Drink

Prices

Expect to pay per three-course meal per person, excluding drinks:

£ under £20   **££** £20–£30   **£££** over £30

RESTAURANTS

Cellar Restaurant ££–£££

This cosy restaurant with candles, rough stone walls, a tiled floor, heavy oak furniture and an open fire is considered to produce some of the best seafood to be found in Scotland. Chef Peter Jukes keeps it simple, using prime ingredients; new season's crab is especially good. Booking required.

➕ 211 D1 ✉ 24 East Green, Anstruther
☎ 01333 310 378; www.cellaranstruther.co.uk
🕐 Lunch Fri–Sat; dinner Tue–Sat,
also Mon Jun–Aug

Craig Millar@16 West End ££

This little seafood bar in St Monans is a great place to break for refreshment if you're exploring the picturesque old fishing villages of the East Neuk. It's located in a 400-year-old former fisherman's house, close to the edge of the harbour, with fabulous views from the terrace to the Isle of May and across the Firth of Forth. Taste delights such as seared scallops with mango and sweet chilli salsa or perhaps curried shellfish risotto.

➕ 211 D1 ✉ 16 West End, St Monans
☎ 01333 730 327; www.16westend.com
🕐 Wed–Sun lunch 12:30–2; dinner 6:30–9

Creagan House ££–£££

This welcoming 17th-century farmhouse restaurant, which also has rooms, is located in the heart of Queen Elizabeth Forest Park. The tiny dining room serves fresh produce that is grown locally and cooked in a bold, innovative, French-influenced style. Five en-suite bedrooms are thoughtfully equipped with extra touches. Smart-casual dress code for dinner.

➕ 210 A1 ✉ Strathyre
☎ 01877 384 638; www.creaganhouse.co.uk
🕐 Dinner only, Fri–Wed; closed Feb and 2 weeks in Nov

Herrmann's Restaurant £–££

With a menu offering *Wiener Schnitzel* or *Jager Schnitzel* followed by apple strudel, it is pretty obvious that the chef made his way to Stirling from the Alps. Tirolean Herrmann Aschaber also has a Scottish side, however, his local specialities include: Cullen Skink and freshly caught fish. The wine list is discerning and good.

➕ 205 F5 ✉ Stirling, 58 Broad Street
☎ 01786 45 06 32; hermanns-restaurant.co.uk
🕐 Daily noon–2, 6–10

Kind Kyttock's Kitchen £

Kind Kyttock is the heroine of an early Scots poem, who served good food and drink to weary travellers. This long-established tearoom follows faithfully in her footsteps, drawing folk from afar to enjoy substantial snacks of omelettes, baked potatoes, salads and some impressive baking. Afternoon tea is excellent, the scones perfect. That Scottish treat, cloutie dumpling, also gets the thumbs up.

➕ 206 C5 ✉ Cross Wynd, Falkland, Fife
☎ 01337 857 477 🕐 Tue–Sun 10:30–5:30

Monachyle Mhor £££

Tom Lewis' converted farmhouse is full of rustic charm and character, set amid some 800ha (1,976 acres) of tranquil farmland at the loch-head of a beautiful glen. The view from the conservatory restaurant alone is beyond compare, looking out over Loch Voile and Loch Donie. The kitchen offers some exemplary cooking, with simple dishes that rely on natural flavours enhanced by a careful choice of herbs, fruits and vegetables. Snacks are served in the bar at lunchtime. No children under 12. Enjoy – this is a real gastronomic temple.

🔲 210 A1 ✉ Lochearnhead, Balquhidder
☎ 01877 384 622; www.mhor.net 🕒 Lunch and dinner daily; closed Jan to mid-Feb

The Peat Inn ££–£££

Created from the original coaching inn, the beautifully located Peat Inn is one of the most charming restaurants-with-rooms in Scotland. It has a reputation for fine cooking, the focus resting on local and seasonal ingredients such as Anstruther lobster and Shetland salmon. The smooth staff are genuinely hospitable and the eight luxurious bedrooms come highly recommended.

🔲 211 D1 ✉ Peat Inn, Cupar
☎ 01334 840 206; www.thepeatinn.co.uk
🕒 Tue–Sat lunch 12:30–1:30; dinner 7–9

63 Tay Street ££

This award-winning fine-dining eatery, which has excellent Perthshire chef Graeme Pallister at the helm, is located down by the River Tay in Perth and is regarded by most locals as one of the best eateries in town. It embraces the "Slow Food" movement, for which local produce is key. The lamb comes from famous Scottish chef Andrew Fairlie's brother, the venison is perfectly cooked and the wines are a well-thought-out accompaniment. This is a light and airy restaurant where you will want to linger for a while.

🔲 210 C1 ✉ 63 Tay Street, Perth
☎ 01738 441 451; www.63taystreet.com
🕒 Tue–Sat lunch noon–2; dinner 6:30–9

PUBS & BARS

An Lochan Tormaukin Country Inn ££–£££

Stone walls, natural timbers and exposed beams make the bar of this 18th-century drovers' inn a cosy place to be – especially on chilly days when there are blazing log fires. It's in a beautiful setting, in the midst of the Ochil hills, with good opportunities for walking, fishing and golf near by. An inventive range of dishes are served every day, and there's a blackboard menu of daily specials. Children welcome.

🔲 206 B5 ✉ Glendevon
☎ 01259 781 252; www.tormaukinhotel.co.uk
🕒 Mon–Sat 11–11, Sun noon–11pm

Lomond Country Inn £–££

A small, privately owned hotel on the slopes of the Lomond Hills offers a friendly welcome and panoramic views across Loch Leven to the island where Mary, Queen of Scots, was imprisoned. Established for more than 100 years, it's located in a small village near Scotlandwell. Enjoy real ales and a wide choice of whiskies by the log fire in the bar, or eat in style in the restaurant, to make the most of the views. There's a deck for summer dining, too.

🔲 206 B5 ✉ Kinnesswood
☎ 01592 840 253 🕒 Lunch and dinner daily

Insider Tip

The Ship Inn £–££

Beach-cricket is just one of the activities that make this traditional-looking pub such a fun place in the summer. It's right on the waterfront at Elie, a small town famed for its golden sands, and there's a watersports centre close by. Barbecues take place in the beer garden, and children and dogs are welcome. The food is great, with a variety of excellent bar meals served all week from noon–2 and 6–9. Fresh fish is a major speciality.

🔲 205 C5 ✉ The Toft, Elie
☎ 01333 330 246; www.ship-elie.com
🕒 Mon–Sat 11am–11pm, Sun 12.30pm–11pm

Insider Tip

Where to…
Shop

ARTS & CRAFTS

In Fife, don't miss the excellent **Crail Pottery** (75 Nethergate; tel: 01333 451 212) and **Griselda Hill Pottery** (tel: 01334 828 273) in the village of Ceres, which makes and sells Wemyss ware, including the traditional startled-looking cats.

Crieff Visitors Centre (Muthill Road; tel: 01764 654014) has a good selection of mugs, plates and coffee pots. It is also the last of Caithness Glass' own outlets, and a small workshop allows you to see glass being blown. The visitor centre also sells Dartington Crystal.

If you get as far as Dunoon, pop into **Dunoon Ceramics** (164–65 Argyll Street; tel: 01369 702 662), which produces the tartan and Mackintosh design mugs you'll come across in all the gift shops. They're less expensive here and factory seconds are also available.

GOLF GEAR & CLOTHING

Auchterlonies (2 Golf Place, St Andrews; tel: 01334 473 253), stocks classic golfing clothes.

The **St Andrew's Golf Company** (8 Golf Place; tel: 01334 474 710) lets you try putters on the indoor green or have your swing analysed by computer. Clubs, carts and clothing are all sold at this large outlet.

The **David Brown Gallery** (9 Albany Place; tel: 01334 477 840) sells golfing antiques and is crammed with silver-ware, prints and vintage golfing books.

Where to…
Go Out

GOLF

There's hardly a town in Scotland without a golf course. Most are municipally owned and not very expensive. Ask at the local tourist office for details.

Rosemount at Blairgowrie (tel: 01250 872 622) is a fine course, as is the **King James VI** course at Moncrief Island (tel: 01738 445 132) in the middle of the River Tay, or the more expensive and famous **Gleneagles** (tel: 01764 662231, ▶ 141).

The legendary **Old Course** at St Andrews (▶ 141; tel: 01334 474 371) is every golfer's dream. However, if you wish to feel like Tiger Woods at the British Open, you'll have to take part in a draw the day before to get a place and you'll need a handicap certificate.

Or you could opt for the tree-lined course at **Ladybank** (tel: 01337 830 814), designed by "Old Tom" Morris (▶ 19).

THEATRE

Perth Theatre (tel: 01738 621 031) is excellent and the place to see up-and-coming young stars.

Pitlochry Festival Theatre (tel: 01796 484 626) is open summer and autumn for touring productions.

Local newspapers usually carry a "what's on" section. Notice boards in village halls are also useful, as are local tourist offices. Look out for fly-posters, often the only source of information on a ceilidh or event.

Highlands & Islands

 **Little Treats**

Slumber under a Thatched Roof
On the **Hebrides** (▶ 151), three old farm-houses with peat fires provide simple but stylish accommodation (www.gatliff.org.uk).

Film-like Settings
The romantic eye-catcher on the route to **Skye** (▶ 150) is the Eilean Donan Castle – a stone bridge crosses over to it.

Perfect Island Fortune
You will like it here: Sligachan Hotel (www.sligachan.co.uk) on **Skye** has over 100 sorts of whisky and a campsite for those also wanting a taste of "the great outdoors."

Getting Your Bearings

The Highlands and Islands are the Scotland of legend and post-cards, of heather-clad hillsides, snow-capped mountains and sparkling lochs. On a sunny day the still waters of the lochs reflect the massive peaks and serried ranks of crags, and hills flank the glens into the distance. When the mist settles, great shoulders of rock suddenly loom before you and the black waters ripple with a chill north wind.

Here you can drive for great distances on single-track roads without meeting another soul, and at your journey's end you might find a perfect beach of silver sand in a sheltered bay or a tiny hamlet of low stone cottages smelling of peat smoke. Explore the colourful harbours of the little fishing ports and then take a ferry to the islands.

The moors and cliffs of the Highlands shelter thousands of **birds**, including puffins, oystercatchers and curlews. Herds of **deer** roam freely, their russet colours blending into the bracken and peat of the moors. You'll see mature stags with impressive antlers, shaggy highland cattle with serious-looking horns and **sheep** virtually everywhere.

The pace is different and sometimes unpredictable, but that gives you the chance to appreciate the region all the more.

The Old Man of Hoy on the island of Hoy, Orkney

Getting Your Bearings

The lush green of Calgary Bay on the Isle of Mull.

Shetland Islands **69**

68 Orkney Islands

Stromness

Thurso

John o'Groats

Tongue

Wick

Lairg

Ullapool

Fraserburgh

Elgin

Dingwall

Peterhead

Portree

Inverness **65 66** Culloden Moor

Drumnadrochit

Grantown-on-Spey

60

Loch Ness

Aberdeen **67**

Mallaig

Road to the Isles

Kingussie

Cairngorms

Braemar

4

Fort William

Pitlochry

Ballachulish

Forfar

ermory

Mull **64**

6

Glen Coe

Perth

DUNDEE

3

Oban

Crianlarich

Jura **62**

Dunoon

61 Islay

0   50 km
0   30 mi

Five Perfect Days

For many, they represent the essence of Scotland: the Highlands the Scottish islands enchant visitors with their rugged landscapes, dry whiskies and hospitable local inhabitants. This itinerary helps ensure that you will not miss any of the highlights in North Scotland. For more information see the main entries (➤ 150–171).

Day 1

Morning
From Crianlarich on the A82, drive right across the bleak Rannoch Moor and through ⭐ **Glen Coe** (➤ 162) to Glencoe itself. Join the walkers in the bar at the **Clachaig Inn** (➤ 163) for a hearty lunch of Scottish dishes.

Afternoon
Spend the afternoon exploring Glen Coe in more detail. Starting from the visitors' centre, you should have time for the forest walk to **Signal Rock** or the short climb up the **Devil's Staircase** from Altnafeadh. Then continue on the A82 northeast to Fort William.

Day 2

Morning
Take a leisurely drive along the A830 ⭐ **Road to the Isles** (➤ 155), to Mallaig, stopping at Glenfinnan for the **Monument** (➤ 155) and also to admire the white sands of **Morar**. Take the 30-minute ferry crossing from Mallaig (summer only) to Armadale on the ⭐ **Isle of Skye** (150).

Afternoon
Stop for lunch at the **Hotel Eilean Iarmain** (➤ 173) at Isle Ornsay, about 6mi (10km) to the north along the main A851 road. Continue to **Portree** along the A87, enjoying the unrivalled scenery. If you have time, take a detour west along the A863 at Sligachan for views of the Cuillin Hills and the coast. Short detours off this route will take you to the **Talisker Whisky Distillery** in Carbost (➤ 151) and **Dunvegan Castle** (pictured right ➤ 151). Alternatively, carry straight on to Portree and spend the time wandering around its picturesque harbour before spending the night in one of its hotels or guesthouses.

Shetland **69**
Islands

68 Orkney
Islands

Outer
Hebrides

Inverness **65 66** Culloden
Moor

Skye
Loch
Ness **60**

Aberde·
67

Road to
the Isles

Cairngorms

Iona **63** Mull

Glen Coe

62 Jura

61 Islay

Day 3

Morning

On a Monday, Wednesday or Friday you can take the scenic route around the Trotternish Peninsula in the north, taking in the **Old Man of Storr** (right, ➤ 150) and the **Skye Museum of Island Life** (➤ 150), as well as stunning coastal views to Wester Ross and the ⭐**Outer Hebrides** (➤ 151) and then catch the 2pm ferry. But on a Tuesday, Thursday or Saturday you have to go direct to Uig because the ferry leaves at 9:40am. Alternatively, you could spend the time on Skye before catching the 6pm ferry from Uig for the two-hour trip to Tarbert. Have lunch either at the Uig Hotel or the Harris Hotel in Tarbert.

Afternoon

Do a trip anti-clockwise through the lunar landscape of East Harris on the Golden Road (A859) to the west coast. Stop at **St. Clement's Church** in Rodel. Enjoy the drive along the famous **West Coast Beach to** Luskentyre. Look out for a B&B on the way to Callanish Standing Stones on Lewis.

Day 4

Morning

Go and see the **Standing Stones** (➤ 152) at sunrise and then set off for the **Blackhouse Villages** of **Gearrannan** and later **Arnol** (➤ 152). Catch the next ferry from Stornoway to ferry to **Ullapool** (➤ 190). Have lunch on the boat during the three-hour journey.

Afternoon

From **Ullapool** drive to Inverness southeast along the A835, stopping at the Falls of Measach about 20km (12.5mi) away. Spend the night in ㊸**Inverness** (➤ 167), where there is plenty to see.

Day 5

Morning

Take the A82 south alongside ㊿**Loch Ness** (➤ 164) to Drumnadrochit. Take time to visit the **Loch Ness Exhibition Centre** and **Urquhart Castle** (panel ➤ 165). Then the route takes you back to Inverness. Go via the A9 and A95 to Dufftown where you will find yourself surrounded by about half a dozen distilleries.

Afternoon

Meander through **Scotland's ski resorts** to Ballater, then follow the River Dee to Aberdeen with an optional stop at **Crathe's Castle**.

★ Skye & Outer Hebrides

The Hebrides, the islands off the west coast of Scotland, are at the heart of Gaelic culture. Renowned for their music, culture and legendary hospitality, this is where you can really get away from it all and relax, so take time to enjoy the islands. The high lonely peaks, the broad moorlands teeming with wildlife, the smell of peat, ancient brochs (circular stone towers) and long, narrow, winding roads are distanced from mainland pressures by the surrounding sea. Car ferries and some bridges make the visit easier.

Skye

Skye is the most accessible of the islands: there are regular car ferries or you can cross at any time by the toll bridge at Kyle of Lochalsh.

In the northern part of Skye is the **Trotternish peninsula**, and it's worth meandering around this fascinating coastline. On the eastern side the **Old Man of Storr**, a distinctive 161ft (49m) sheer column of rock, appears precariously balanced below the Storr mountain. Further north, the spectacular **Kilt Rock waterfall** drops 298ft (91m) to the sea, while among the pinnacles and strange rock formations of the Quiraing you enter a weird and wonderful landscape of legends and giants. More prosaically, the **Skye Museum of Island Life**, housed in a number of thatched buildings, shows island

The Table at the Quiraing on Skye's Trotternish peninsula

Dunvegan Castle: ancestral seat of the MacLeods

life as it was about 100 years ago. For a taste of the life of the Scottish Laird, visit **Dunvegan Castle**, a stronghold that has been in the same family for nearly 800 years.

The most dramatic sight, visible throughout the Islands and from the mainland, is the jagged outline of the **Cuillins**, a massive mountain range that dominates the landscape. The range includes 12 Munros (➤ 130).

The combination of Munros and weird rock formations of the Trotternish peninsula make Skye the ideal place for **hillwalkers and climbers**, but there are also plenty of less challenging walks – check with the local tourist board for information. **Birdwatchers** may be lucky to hear the cry of the corncrake, a once common bird that is now extremely localised.

Skye's greatest attraction is its **scenery**, but if it disappears into low grey clouds and fine drizzle, you can always visit the award-winning 🐍 **Skye Serpentarium** near Broadford. This unique collection of reptiles will captivate the whole family, and if you wish you can even hold a snake. Alternatively, take a tour of the **Talisker Whisky Distillery** at Carbost and sample the distinctive peaty dram.

Insider Tip

THINGS TO DO

On the island of **Raasay**, the house where Dr Johnson and James Boswell lodged in 1773 on their tour of the Hebrides is now an outdoor centre offering kayaking, sailing, rock climbing and cycling. You can spot wild otters from the hide at Kylerhea Otter Haven, south of Kyle of Lochalsh on Skye. The **Brightwater Visitor Centre** at Kyleakin (tel: 01599 530 040) provides an introduction to the wildlife of Skye and access to the island of **Eilean Ban** (under the bridge), once home to writer Gavin Maxwell.

The Outer Hebrides

The rugged Western Isles – **Lewis** and **Harris**, **North** and **South Uist**, **Benbecula** and **Barra** – stand between the harsh Atlantic Ocean and Skye and the other inner islands. The flat windswept peat bog and moorland of Lewis contrasts with the mountainous, rugged contours of adjoining Harris. To appreciate the strange beauty of Harris, take the Golden Road to Leverburgh from the ferry port at Tarbert. Twisting and turning along the coast, through a moonscape of ancient rock, this single-track road

is possibly the most scenic drive in the Hebrides. If you have time, visit the **Seallam Visitor Centre** at Northton, which has an interesting permanent exhibition about the islands.

Lewis

On Lewis you'll find the **Standing Stones of Calanais** (or Callanish) once buried in a peat bog, which have stood above this bay for more than 4,000 years. Although the original purpose of this complex pattern of massive stones is a mystery, the central cairn (mound) is known to have been a burial place for many years.

Further north is **Dun Carloway Broch**, built around 2,000 years ago. This high, round, fortified house was built with a double drystone wall to withstand the Atlantic gales.

Blackhouses were long and low for the same reason. **The Arnol Blackhouse**, occupied until the 1960s, shows a crofter's way of life, with the animals living in the byre at the other end of the house. You can stay in a black-house, with modern facilities, at **Gearrannan Blackhouse village** (www.gearrannan.com). If you wish to see how Harris Tweed is made, visit the **Lewis Loom Centre** close by in Stornaway.

The old bridge on the A863 in Sligachan complements Skye's famous mountain panorama Skyes to create a romantic ensemble

➕ 208 C4

Tourist Information Centres

Skye: ✉ Bayfield Road, Portree, Skye ☎ 0845 225 5121; www.visithebrides.com
🚢 Car ferries to Skye from Mallaig or Glenelg; passenger ferry from Gairloch
Lewis: ✉ 26 Cromwell Street, Stornoway ☎ 01851 703 088

Skye Museum of Island Life
✚ 208 C5 ✉ A855 north of Uig ☎ 01470 552 206; www.skyemuseum.co.uk
🕐 Apr–Oct Mon–Sat 10–5 🚌 Bus from Portree to Kilmuir 💷 £2.50

Dunvegan Castle
✚ 208 C4 ✉ A850 ✉ A850 north of Dunvegan, Skye
☎ 01470 521 206; www.dunvegancastle.com 🕐 April–mid-Oct 10–5:30
🍴 (£–£££) 💷 £11

Skye Serpentarium
✚ 212 C1 ✉ The Old Mill, Harrapool, Broadford
☎ 01471 822 209; www.skyeserpentarium.org.uk
🕐 Easter–Oct Mon–Sat 10–5 Jul–Aug daily
🚌 Bus from Kyle, Kyleakin and Armadale 💷 £4.50

Talisker Distillery Visitor Centre Information
✉ Carbost, Isle of Skye
☎ 01478 614 308; www.discovering-distilleries.com/talisker
🕐 Apr–Oct Mon–Sat 9:30–5; Jul–Aug also 11–5, regular tours (last tour 4pm);
Nov–Mar 10–4:30; tours 10:30, noon, 2, 3:30 💷 £8

Larger than Stonehenge and yet not so well-known: the Standing Stones of Calanais

Seallam Visitor Centre
🔁 An Taobh Tuath (Northton), Harris ☎ 01859 520 258; www.seallam.com

Calanais (Callanish) Standing Stones and Visitor Centre
🔁 212 B4 ✉ A859 at Calanais, Lewis
☎ 01851 621 422; www.historic-scotland.gov.uk
🕐 Open access to stones. Visitor centre: Apr–Sep daily 10–6;
Oct–Mar Wed–Sat 10–4 🍴 (£) 🚌 Bus from Stornoway

Dun Carloway Broch and Visitor Centre
🔁 212 B4 ✉ A858 south of Carloway, Lewis
☎ 01851 710 395; www.historicscotland.gov.uk
🕐 Open access to broch. Visitor centre: Apr–Sep Mon–Sat 10–5
🚌 Bus from Stornoway

The Black House, Arnol
🔁 212 B4 ✉ 42 Arnol, Barvas, Lewis
☎ 01851 710 395; www.historic-scotland.gov.uk
🕐 Apr–Sep Mon–Sat 9:30–5:30; Oct–Mar Mon–Sat 10–4
🚌 Bus from Stornoway 💷 £4.50

Lewis Loom Centre
🔁 212 C4 ✉ 3 Bayhead, Stornoway, Lewis
☎ 01851 704 500 🕐 Daily 9–6 💷 £2.50

Grasslands, moors and lakes dominate the landscape scenery of the Hebrides, which also includes Harris

INSIDER INFO

- There is strict **Sunday observance** throughout the Isles, especially on Lewis and Harris, so don't be surprised if attractions are closed on Sundays, even during peak seasons.
- The best way to see Skye and the Outer Hebrides is with an **8- or 15-day Island Rover Ticket** from Caledonian MacBrayne Ferries. Follow the **Road to the Isles** (➤ 155), explore the small Isles, then take the **Skye ferry** to Armadale. From Uig, cross to Tarbert on Harris or Lochmaddy on North Uist. Then take the ferry from Stornaway to Ullapool.
- **Dunvegan Castle** contains a few curiosities, such as the **Fairy Flag.** This faded fragment of silk, which ensures victory in battle, was reputedly given to a chief of MacLeod by his wife, a fairy.

⭐ The Road to the Isles

Whether you're heading for the Isle of Skye or simply want to enjoy the spectacular Highland landscape, the Road to the Isles is one of the most romantic and historic journeys in Scotland. Drive or take the train from the foot of mighty Ben Nevis through dramatic loch and mountain scenery to the busy fishing port of Mallaig along the A830.

Steam trains have been puffing across Glenfinnan Viaduct since 1901

Around Fort William
Start just outside **Fort William**, opposite the Ben Nevis Distillery, and head west on the A830. Just north of Fort William is the village of **Banavie**, site of the unmissable **Neptune's Staircase** on the Caledonian Canal – Thomas Telford's spectacular engineering feat of eight locks raises boats 64ft (20m) over just 1.1mi (5km).

Insider Tip

Glenfinnan Monument
About 19mi (30km) from Ben Nevis, the Glenfinnan Monument at the head of Loch Sheil marks the spot where Bonnie Prince Charlie raised his standard in 1745. More than 1,000 Highlanders gathered in this lonely place to greet him as his rowing boat crept from the mists. The picturesque railway station at Glenfinnan houses the **Glenfinnan Station Museum**, with a display of memorabilia.

Glenfinnan to Loch Morar
As you travel west, the landscape becomes increasingly more rugged, while the sea lochs create constantly

changing perspectives of land and water. It was not until the early 19th century that a road allowing coach travel penetrated this far. The 12th-century monks at Arisaig called this high rocky countryside the Rough Bounds. At **Loch Nan Uamh**, look out for the **railway viaduct** and the **Prince's Cairn** marking the spot where Bonnie Prince Charlie left for France following the failure of the Jacobite rising.

At **Arisaig** you can take a ferry to the small isles or walk along the pure white beaches. Stop at **Morar** (B8008) to walk along the silver sands, looking for the legendary monster of Loch Morar, or just to watch a magical sunset over the islands.

Ben Nevis looms mightily over Loch Linnhe

Mallaig

Mallaig is the end of the road and it's worth spending some time here. Wander through the **harbour** by the boats and nets and listen to the clank of chains and the screech of the seabirds. Fishing is the lifeblood of Mallaig and you can watch boats unloading their catch. For an account of how the herring-fishing industry changed the town, visit the **Mallaig Heritage Centre**. You may also be able to join a **tour** on one of the fishing boats licensed to take passengers, or take a trip into Loch Nevis on Bruce Watt's mail boat.

🏰 OFF TO HOGWARTS

The **Jacobite Steam Train** rattles between Fort William and Mallaig twice a day during the summer, passing through spectacular landscape. It crosses the impressive 380m-long Glenfinnan viaduct with its 21 semicircular spans made of mass concrete (picture ▶ 155). Does the scene look familiar? Yes, the Hogwarts Express in the Harry Potter film crosses over this bridge (departure times ▶ right).

TAKING A BREAK

At Mallaig eat fresh fish at one of the tearooms or restaurants on Main Street: the **Cornerstone Café** is particularly good and at the Tea Garden Café, you can sit outside.

➕ 209 E3

Fort William Tourist Information Centre
✉ 15 High Street ☎ 0845 225 5121
🕐 Apr–May Mon–Sat 9–5, Sun 10–5; Jun Mon–Sat 9–6, Sun 9:30–5; Jul–mid-Sep Mon–Sat 9–6:30, Sun 9:30–6:30; Mid-Sep–Nov Mon–Sat 9–5, Sun 10–4

National Trust for Scotland Information Centre
✉ Glennfinnan, A830, 18mi (29km) west of Fort William
☎ 0844 4 93 22 21 🕐 Apr–Jun, Sep–Oct daily 10–5; Jul–Aug 9:30–5:30
✋ Monument: £3.50

Jacobite Steam Train
☎ 0845 1284681; www.westcoastrailways.co.uk
🕐 Departs from Fort William mid-May to end Oct Mon–Fri 10:15 and 2:40; end of Jun to beginning of Aug also Sat, Sun ✋ single £34, return £58

Glenfinnan Station Museum
☎ 01397 722 295; www.glenfinnanstationmuseum.co.uk
🕐 Jun–mid-Oct daily 9–5

The evening light casts a glow over the sands of Morar

Mallaig Heritage Centre
✉ Station Road, Mallaig ☎ 01687 462 085; www.mallaigheritage.org.uk
🕐 Opening times vary weekly; check website for details

INSIDER INFO

■ The viewpoint on the hill behind the visitors' centre at **Glenfinnan** is the best place to watch steam trains cross the impressive viaduct or for taking a photograph of the monument and Loch Sheil, particularly in the early morning when the sun shines through the mist.

■ In Arisaig take the local road left, off the A830, to **Rhue peninsula** for superb views towards the islands of Eigg, Muck, Rum and Canna.

⭐5 The Cairngorms

The Cairngorm Mountains take their name from Cairn Gorm, a peak of 1,245m (4,084ft). An incredibly varied landscape, the area was designated Scotland's second national park in 2003. Here you'll find alpine tundra, heather and moorland and remnants of ancient Caledonian pine forests.

A Centre of Activity

Whether you're based in one of the sleepy villages or in the brash resort of Aviemore, you'll find plenty to do, from fly fishing on a remote inland loch, training for the rigours of mountaineering at Glenmore Lodge or enjoying a drive through the historic Spey Valley.

The **Cairngorm plateau** has five of the highest peaks in Scotland, ranging from 1245 to 1309m (4,085–4295ft), and is one of the best areas in Britain for rock and ice climbing. In summer the area attracts watersports enthusiasts with sailing, windsurfing and canoeing at the **Loch Morlich Watersports centre** about 7mi (12km) from Aviemore. There's more of the same at the watersports centre on **Loch Insh**, which also has a dry-ski slope and mountain bikes to hire.

Right: The red squirrels are among the rare species that can be seen in the Cairngorms

Scots pine against the backdrop of the snow-covered Ben Macdhui

Aviemore, Scotland's premier ski resort, is home to a number of rare wildlife species, including the Scottish wild cat, red squirrels, pine martens and the threatened capercaillie.

Aviemore was purpose-built in the 1960s to cater for the growing number of skiers attracted to the slopes of Cairn Gorm, and is currently undergoing a revamp, with much of its concrete development having been demolished and replaced with new more attractive housing.

At 🏠 **Leault Farm** south of Aviemore at Kincraig, dog trainers demonstrate the skills of their Scottish border collies during 45-minute shows (every day at 2:15). Each dog has its own set of whistles that provide signals for specific tasks trained by the farmer. Sheep and ducks are herded through the course – an authentic Highland experience for the entire family.

At the centre of the Cairngorms is one of the finest outdoor recreation centres in the Highlands, **Rothiemurchus Estate**, which has belonged to the Grant family since the early 16th century. Here you can try off-road driving or clay-pigeon shooting, or go walking, birdwatching, mountain biking or fishing. You could easily spend days here, but make sure you see the largest section of almost completely **natural Caledonian pine forest** in Scotland, stretching for more than 20mi (32km). These forests once covered most of the country.

At **Loch an Eilein** are the remains of a 15th-century castle, and at the visitor centre you can learn all about 200 years of the great estate of Rothiemurchus. Elizabeth Grant of Rothiemurchus has left a fascinating account of life here 200 years ago in her book *Memoirs of a Highland Lady*, which is on sale here.

Insider Tip

Quieter Pastimes

Farther south, in the beautiful Spey Valley, is the little town of **Kingussie,** which, together with nearby **Newtonmore**, is home to the **Highland Folk Museum**. The museum covers all aspects of Highland life, such as farming, in reconstructed buildings that include a smokehouse, mill and a blackhouse from the Hebridean islands. Nearby, the impressive ruin of **Ruthven Barracks**, built to quell Highland unrest after the

Jacobite rebellion of 1715, stands proud and roofless against the sky. It was captured by Bonnie Prince Charlie's army in 1746, who blew it up when news reached them of defeat at Culloden. From Ruthven you can walk a stretch of **General George Wade's military road** (➤ 189), which crosses the perfectly preserved Wade Bridge near Dalwhinnie.

Above: The Cairngorms provide ideal walking country for people of all abilities

TAKING A BREAK

Superb restaurants and tea-rooms abound. Try **Grantown-on-Spey** where there are good hotel-restaurants around the town square north of the centre.

✚ 210 C3

Aviemore Tourist Information Centre
✉ Grampian Road ☎ 0845 225 5121
🕐 Jun–mid-Jul Mon–Sat 9–6, Sun 10–5;
Mid-Jul–mid-Sep Mon–Sat 9–6, Sun 9:30–5;
Mid-Sep–May Mon–Sat 9–5, Sun 10–4
🍴 Cafés and restaurants (£–££)
🚌 From Inverness, Glasgow and Edinburgh stop on Grampian Road, Aviemore

Cairngorm National Park Authority
✚ 210 C4
✉ 14 The Square, Grantown-on-Spey
☎ 01479 873 535; www.cairngorms.co.uk;
free app for Cairngorms:
http://visitcairngorms.com/app

Right: The Rothiemurchus Estate is one of the best outdoor recreation centres in the Cairngorms

INSIDER INFO

- In summer take the **chairlift** to the Cairngorm plateau and then walk the short distance to the summit. On a clear day you can see past Loch Morlich to Aviemore and beyond.
- To get away from the bustle of Aviemore. base your trip at one of the quieter villages in the area: nearby **Coylumbridge** is in the heart of Rothiemurchus Estate and the fine Georgian town and ski resort of **Grantown-on-Spey** is particularly popular with anglers looking for trout and salmon.
- The **osprey**, a fish-eating hawk, was not seen in Britain for 50 years, but in 1954 a pair built a nest near Loch Garten and returned each year. Other nesting pairs have now become established in the Highlands. The **Loch Garten** site is part of the **Abernethy Forest reserve** belonging to the Royal Society for the Protection of Birds (RSPB) and during the nesting period (April to August), visitors can view the birds from a hide equipped with a closed-circuit television link to their nest.
- The Cairngorms region is **ideal walking country** for people of all abilities. There are plenty of low-level walks and nature trails, especially on the **Rothiemurchus Estate** and around **Loch Morlich**. For the more adventurous, **Lairig Ghru** is the finest mountain pass in Britain, carved by glaciers. Running 20mi (32km) from near Coylumbridge to the Linn of Dee near Braemar, it links Speyside with Deeside. But this route is challenging and suitable only for experienced, properly equipped walkers, as even in summer a change in the weather can bring the risk of exposure. For a shorter option there's a six-hour hike up to the pass from Coylumbridge and back.

⭐6 Glen Coe

The novelist Charles Dickens (1812–70) imagined Glen Coe as the "burial ground of a race of giants", and it is one of the few places where non-hillwalkers or climbers can experience the sheer mass of the mountains close up. It is usually teeming with visitors, but its vast spaces never feel crowded. For less ambitious hikers there are short, low-level trails that take you off-road, and the walk to the Signal Rock from the Clachaig Inn or the walk around Loch Achtriochtan are not strenuous.

The mood of the glen changes with the weather and the seasons, often dramatically in a day. On a clear spring day, the snow-capped peaks, high white clouds and blue sky reflected in **Loch Achtriochtan** light up the whole glen. At dawn and dusk the low light and long shadows highlight the deep cracks and craggy mountaintops, while either side is patched with light in shades of emerald and dark olive. And when it's dark and overcast, the mountains are veiled in mist and cloud.

The great bulk of **Buachaille Etive Mór** guards the entrance to the glen from the bleak expanse of **Rannoch Moor.** From there the road curves around below the massive peaks

THE MASSACRE OF GLENCOE

On 13 February 1692, government troops, led by Captain Robert Campbell of Glenlyon, who had been billeted with the MacDonald clan, rose at dawn and slaughtered their hosts. Aside from the savagery of the attack, it was the breach of the code of Highland hospitality towards all, even an enemy, that made the Campbell name a byword for treachery for centuries. Some 38 people were killed and hundreds more, including women and children, escaped to the hills, although many perished in the winter snows. Most of the MacDonalds escaped, including the sons of the old chief.

Buachaille Etive Mór, at the entrance to the glen

Winter scene in the Highlands by Loch Leven

flanking the broad floor, to tiny **Loch Achtriochtan**, whose community was at the centre of the Massacre of Glencoe. (William III of England had the rebellious MacDonald clan slaughtered here in 1692, ➤ 162). As the road curves away again around the woodlands at the visitor centre, look for the **Signal Rock**, a 60–90-minute walk through the forest, where the fire was lit to signal the start of the massacre. Another relatively easy walk for this area is the Devil's Staircase from the Altanafeadh lay-by. The glen opens up at Glencoe with a view up the broad waters of **Loch Leven**. On the shores near here the old chief was shot in his bed and his wife was brutally attacked.

TAKING A BREAK

The **Clachaig Inn** (tel: 01855 811 252) is the best place for a bar lunch or evening meal. It's a little basic, but popular with walkers and has a great atmosphere. Scenes from the third Harry Potter film were shot near here.

➕ 209 E2–F2

Glen Coe Visitor Centre
➕ 209 E2 ✉ Just over a mile (2km) east of Glencoe
☎ 00844 493 222; www.Glencoe-nts.org.uk
🕐 Mid-Mar to Aug 9:30–5:30; Sep–Oct 10–5; Nov to mid-Mar Thu–Sun 10–4
🚌 Glasgow to Fort William; the train goes through the glen ✋ £6.50

INSIDER INFO

Get away from the summer crowds by taking the B-road by Buachaille Etive Mór to Glen Etive to picnic by **Loch Etive.**

⑥⓪ Loch Ness

The beauty of the steep tree-lined banks of Loch Ness makes a striking backdrop to the moody waters below. The best way to see the loch is aboard the Nessie Hunter cruise boat.

In its ice-cold depths, 699ft (213m) below the surface, scientists discovered a living population of Arctic charr, fish undisturbed since the last Ice Age. Of course, the main tourist attraction is another supposed inhabitant of the loch. Only the most hardened cynic could look out over these mysterious waters without looking for a glimpse of Nessie, the legendary monster.

LOCH NESS VITAL STATISTICS
is the largest water reservoir in Great Britain
Length: around 23mi (37km)
Width: 2mi (3km)
Depth: 230–250m (754–820ft)

A Monster Hit

Nessie first appeared when the Irish missionary and abbot St Columba (*c*.521–97) allegedly drove away a sea monster in AD565. But it was not until the construction of the A82 road in the 1930s that sightings increased, as did the appearance of indistinct and somewhat dubious photographs. More recently, highly sophisticated scientific equipment has failed to find any conclusive proof. The evidence amassed about the teeming life below the surface of these still, dark waters is presented in a fascinating multi-media display at the **Loch Ness Exhibition Centre** on the A82 in Drumnadrochit.

The ice-cold water of Loch Ness reaches depths of 250m (800 ft)

The now-ruined Urquhart Castle was once one of the largest castles in Scotland

TAKING A BREAK

At **Brackla**, just beyond Abriachan off the A82 between Inverness and Drumnadrochit, is the family-owned **Clansman Hotel** (tel: 01456 450 326), which has a superb panorama bar overlooking Loch Ness and the small marina.

➕ 210 A4
✉ Between Inverness and Fort Augustus

Loch Ness Exhibition Centre
✉ Drumnadrochit ☎ 01456 450 573; www.lochness.com
🕐 Feb–May daily 9:30–5; Jun and Sep 9–6; Jul–Aug 9:30–6; Oct 9:30–5; Nov–Jan 10–3:30
✋ £7.45, family ticket £22.50

Nessie Hunter Cruise Boat
✉ Lock Ness Exhibition Centre
☎ 01456 450 395; http://loch-ness-cruises.co.uk
🕐 Good Friday–Oct; daily, every hour (depending on demand) 9–6
✋ £15

INSIDER INFO

- The best view of the loch is from **Urquhart Castle** (open summer daily 9:30–6, winter 9:30–4:30; £7.90) near Drumnadrochit.
- About 2mi (3km) south of Urquhart Castle, on the loch side of the road, stands the **Cobb Memorial**, a cairn commemorating John Cobb, who died on 29 September 1952 while breaking the world water-speed record in his speedboat *Crusader*.
- Follow the well-marked forest paths from pretty **Invermoriston** to where the **River Moriston** tumbles over waterfalls towards Loch Ness. The partly ruined **Telford bridge**, spanning the falls, can still be crossed on foot.

At Your Leisure

Restored in the early 20th century, Iona Abbey is still a spiritual retreat

61 Islay

This wildly beautiful island is serious malt whisky country, with no fewer than eight distilleries. The water, peat and generations of skill and knowledge produce the distinctive smoky flavours of Bowmore, Lagavulin and Laphroaig whiskies. As well as a distillery visit on the most southern island of the Inner Hebrides, look out for the 18th-century round church. *Insider Tip* Birdwatching is another attraction, and the RSPB site has guided walks. There is also a great deal to see that is of historical interest on the island.

➕ 204 A4 ✈ From Glasgow Mon–Fri two flights daily, Sat one flight
⛴ Car ferry from Kennacraig to Port Ellen

Bowmore Tourist Information
✉ The Square ☎ 08707 200 617
🕐 Apr–Jun Mon–Sat 10–5, Sun 2–5;
Jul–Aug Mon–Sat 9:30–5:30, Sun 2–5;
Sep and Oct Mon–Sat 10–5;
Oct–Mar Mon–Fri 10–3

RSPB
✉ Gruinart 01496 850 505

62 Jura

If you want to know where George Orwell wrote his classic *1984*, go and stay on the Isle of Jura. With 6,000 deer, only 200 inhabitants, the Paps mountains, one distillery, one walled exotic garden, otters and one road, it is the place to get away from it all and experience an ideal piece of the Highlands. From Kinuachdrachd in the northeast, a 2mi (3km)-hike takes you to the northern tip, where you might catch sight of the infamous Corryvreckan Whirlpool, classified as violent and dangerous; the maelstrom is very audible after low tide.

➕ 204 B5 ⛴ Car ferry from Islay

Tours
☎ 01496 820 231; www.juraislandtours.co.uk
✉ Jura House
🌐 www.isleofjura.scot/jura-house-garden

63 Iona

Just a five-minute trip by passenger ferry from Fionnphort on Mull, Iona has been a place of pilgrimage since the days of St Columba. It's still a religious retreat, and a sense of peace surrounds the 12th-century abbey. Iona was supposedly the burial place of the kings of Scotland, including Duncan and Macbeth, but there's no evidence to support this. A more recent and poignant memorial is the simple headstone of John Smith (1938–94), former leader of the Labour Party, carved on a mighty boulder at St Oran's Chapel. If you get the chance, take the boat trip to **Staffa**, with its massive basalt columns and the incredible Fingal's Cave, which inspired Mendelssohn-Bartholdi's overture *The Hebrides.*

🚩 208 C1 🚢 From Fionnphort, Mull

🍴 The Coffee House, west of the Abbey (£)

64 Mull

If Mull is your first introduction to the Hebrides, take a slow winding drive around the island's narrow winding roads to appreciate the wonderful scenery as you glimpse the sea and the islands or small lochs glistening in the glens between the hills. You'll need to allow yourself a couple of days to be able to wander past the brightly coloured houses that line **Tobermory** harbour, visit Toronsay Castle, with its extensive gardens and Venetian statues and admire the rugged cliffs at Loch na Keal.

Mull is also something of a nature lover's paradise, with miles of unspoilt countryside just waiting to be explored by the adventurous. Mull is home to the only Munro in the isles outside Skye, Ben More. A walk up the mighty slopes may well be accompanied by sightings of deer and, if you are lucky, a Golden Eagle. The island has also become Scotland's premier whale-watching destination. Sightings of whales are by no means guaranteed, but there are also dolphins and porpoises in the waters and the chance to espy myriad wild sea birds, including, if you are very lucky, a sea eagle.

Insider Tip

🚩 208 C2 🚌 Infrequent buses to Fionnphort and Tobermory

🚢 Oban and then ferry to Craignure

Craignure Tourist Office

✉ The Pier ☎ 0845 225 5121

🕐 Apr–Jun, Sep, Oct Mon–Sat 8:30–5, Sun 10–5; Jul, Aug Mon–Sat 8:30–7, Sun 10–7; Nov–Apr Mon–Sat 8:30–5, Sun 10–noon, 3:30–5

65 Inverness

Situated on the River Ness at the head of the Great Glen, Inverness is the shopping centre of the Highlands. It is the largest town in the Highlands and predominantly dates back to the 19th century; most of the older buildings were regularly destroyed during times of turbulence. Even the castle dates only from 1836, although its attractive setting was the site of an 11th-century defensive fort of some

Brightly painted houses line Tobermory harbour on the Isle of Mull

Highlands & Islands

kind. In the ⛴ **Titanic Maritime Museum,** children can board scale models of famous ships and try their hand at Morse code and as machine operators. In the Kiltmaker Centre, you can also try on some Scottish plaid.

🔶 210 A4 🔲 Inverness

Inverness Tourist Information Centre
✉ Castle Wynd ☎ 0845 225 5121
🕐 Sep–Jun Mon–Sat 9–5, Sun 10–4;
Jul–Aug Mon–Sat 9–6, Sun 10–5

Titanic Maritime Museum
✉ 16 Clachnaharry Road
☎ 01463 716839; www.shipspace.com
🕐 Daily 10–3 🎫 Free

66 Culloden Moor

This is the site of the last battle that was fought on British soil. It took place in 1746 and is where the Jacobite cause finally foundered. The battlefield has been restored to its condition at that fateful time. Flags mark the lines of Government and Jacobite forces and each clan and regiment is faithfully located. It's easy to see why the battle charge of the Highlanders, in this boggy ground against heavy artillery, was doomed to failure from the outset. Near the cairn lie the mass graves of the Highlanders, and a melancholy air of desolation still clings to this bleak and barren moor. There is an excellent Visitors' Centre here.

Inscription on the memorial cairn at Culloden

🔶 210 B4 ☎ 0844 493 2159; www.nts.org.uk
🕐 Apr–May, Sep–Oct daily 9–5:30;
Jun–Aug daily 9–6; Nov–Dec 10–4; Jan closed
🍴 Restaurant in visitors' centre (££)
🔲 Inverness 🎫 £11

67 Aberdeen

The townscape of Europe's offshore oil capital is dominated by the harbour, airport and very often the dramatic interplay of light on the many granite façades. That is why Aberdeen is often called the *Silver City by the Sea*. Sited between the mouths of the rivers Don and Dee, it is home to 230,000 inhabitants Footdee (known locally as "Fittie") is a homogenous housing project on the Dee estuary, originally built by the architects of Balmoral Castle to rehouse the fishing community. Fish has been the mainstay of Aberdeen for centuries and if you head for the harbour between 6 and 8, you'll discover that it still plays a role today. If it rains during your stay, visit the **Maritime Museum** or the **Aberdeen Science Centre**. The cathedral-like Marishal College, now the headquarters of the local city council, is the world's second largest granite building.

🔶 211 F3

Aberdeen Science Centre
🔶 201 F1 ✉ 179 Constitution Street
☎ 01224 640340; www.satrosphere.net
🕐 Daily 10–5 🍴 Café on site (£)
🔲 Aberdeen 🎫 £6

Aberdeen Maritime Museum
🔶 201 F1 ✉ Shiprow ☎ 01224 337 700;
www.aagm.co.uk 🕐 Tue–Sat 10–5, Sun
noon–3 🍴 Café (£) 🔲 Aberdeen 🎫 Free

68 Orkney Islands

The Orkney Islands comprise of 67 on the whole fairly small islands and about 75% of their 20,000 inhabitants live on Mainland. Designated a World Heritage Site in 1999, the island attractions include a 12th-century cathedral and some fine Neolithic remains.

Skara Brae: Neolithic house

🏠 Skara Brae
In a country littered with neolithic remains, standing stones, chambered tombs and prehistoric relics, Skara Brae on Mainland is still an overwhelming archaeological site. This small village takes you to the heart of a community living at the dawn of history, showing how the people lived, ate and slept.

The excellent interpretation centre explains how Skara Brae was revealed to the world in 1850 when a great storm uncovered it, how the landscape and climate have changed over the millennia and how the evidence has helped to recreate an ancient way of life. In the reconstructed house outside you can creep through the low narrow passages, walk round the central hearth and imagine the smoke drifting up into the restored rafters tied together with twine. The box beds are complete with heather mattresses and warm fleece, the stone dresser is adorned with ornaments and shells, while nearby a lobster lies as if ready to eat.

The walk to the village itself is a timeline to the past. Start from a depiction of Neil Armstrong on the moon, past the invention of the telephone and the American Declaration of Independence. Go back past the fall of Rome and the birth of Christ, then further back past the Parthenon in Athens and the construction of the Pyramids in Egypt to Skara Brae at the end of the line, 5,000 years ago. Yet in this little cluster of roofless dwellings, built in mounds of midden (refuse) for stability and warmth, the past somehow seems very near.

Maeshowe
When the neolithic chambered tomb at Maeshowe was built 5,000 years ago, 6mi (10km) from Kirkwall on Mainland, it was aligned with such precision that the midwinter sunset, streaming along the narrow entrance tunnel, lit the back wall of the chamber. The mound was excavated in 1861, revealing a central chamber with three small chambers in the walls but no prehistoric remains.

The tomb had suffered the depredations of the Vikings centuries before. It is unclear whether or not they took anything, but they left masses of ribald Runic graffiti on the walls. Talented jeweller Sheila Fleet has used then for her enchanting jewellery designs (www.sheilafleet.com).

The Stones of Stenness & Ness of Brodgar
Also on Mainland, these dramatic standing stones, standing at a maximum height of 19ft (6m) are visible from miles and date from at least 3100 BC, making them one of the earliest stone circles in Britain. Archaeologists are currently excavating a large site next to them, the Ness of Brodgar.

The Ring of Brodgar
This site is only a short drive northwest of the Stones of Stennes. Although the stones here have never been fully excavated, it is generally believed that they date from 2500–2000 BC and are, therefore, the last of the Neolithic ceremonial rings built in the area. Built in a true circle, measuring nearly 341ft (104m) across, there may have been as many as 60 stones, although there are only 27 now. The tallest one measures 4.15ft (6m).

The people of Lamb Holm tracked down the original builders to restore the Italian Chapel when it began to deteriorate

St Magnus Cathedral

This stately sandstone cathedral in Kirkwall was founded by Jarl Rognvlad in 1137 in honour of his uncle, St Magnus, who had been canonised in 1135. It took more than 300 years to complete, and has architectural details ranging from Norman to early Gothic. It contains the remains of both Magnus and Rognvlad.

The Italian Chapel

This delightful chapel in Lamb Holm is an inspiring example of faith and dedication. Italian prisoners of war, with nowhere to worship and using little more than concrete, wire and paint, constructed it from two Nissen huts during World War II. The interior, by artist Domenico Chiocchetti, is a masterpiece of *trompe l'œil* stonework and windows, with a magnificent fresco altarpiece behind a wrought-iron screen.

Scapa Flow

The natural harbour of Scapa Flow, surrounded by Hoy, South Ronaldsay and Mainland, has been used since Viking times. But it was the scuttling of the remains of the German fleet here on 21 May, 1919 by Admiral von Reuter that made it the world's premier wreck-diving location. Most of the fleet was salvaged but seven wrecks remain, some highly accessible and others only 30ft (9m) deep.

✚ 214 C4 ✉ www.scapaflow.co.uk
🚗 Car ferry from Scrabster to Stromness
✈ Flights from Orkney, Aberdeen, Inverness and Glasgow

Orkney Tourist Board

✉ West Castle Street, Kirkwall
☎ 01856 877 856; www.visitorkney.com
🕐 May and Sep daily 9–6; Jun–Aug daily 8:30–8; Oct–Apr Mon–Sat 9–5
🍴 Plenty of cafés, restaurants and tearooms in Kirkwall (£–££)

Skara Brae

✚ 214 C4 ✉ Sandwick
☎ 01856 841 815; www.historic-scotland.gov.uk
🕐 Apr–Sep daily 9:30–5:30; Oct–Mar 9:30–4
🍴 Café (£) 💷 £7.10

Maeshowe

✚ 215 D4 ✉ by Tormiston Mill (limited parking)
☎ 01856 761 606; www.historic-scotland.gov.uk
🕐 Apr–Sep daily 9:30–5; Oct–Mar 10–4. Hourly tours must be booked in advance.
🍴 Café nearby at Tormiston Mill (£) 💷 £5.50

St Magnus Cathedral

✚ 215 D4 ✉ Broad Street, Kirkwall
☎ 01856 874 894; www.stmagnus.org/
🕐 Daily; Sunday service 11.15; hosts music event throughout the year – check for details

The Italian Chapel

✚ 215 D4 ✉ Lamb Holm just off the A961
🕐 Apr–Sep daily 9am–10pm; Oct–Mar 9–4:30
💷 Free; donations welcome

Scapa Flow

✚ 215 D4 ✉ Scapa Scuba dive shop, Lifeboat House, Stromness
☎ 01856 851 218; www.scapascuba.co.uk

69 Shetland Islands

In fine weather, Shetland, Scotland's most northerly outpost, is inde-

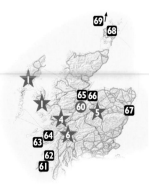

burned and everyone parties all night in halls throughout Lerwick. You can get an idea of the custom at the Up-Helly-Aa exhibition near St Sunniva Street. Get a glimpse of Shetland's Scandinavian past at the fascinating and multi-layered Viking settlement of Jarlshof to the south of Lerwick close to the airport.

The distinctive Shetland **fiddle music** has evolved through the playing of Aly Bain and others. Remnants of an older style can still be heard and you may come across some old men playing in the strangely discordant style of Papa Stour. **The Lounge Bar** in Lerwick is a good place to hear local traditional musicians.

 Insider Tip

scribably beautiful, but when the weather changes it disappears in grey. Travel the length of the islands to the north to appreciate the bright greens, the sandy beaches and the sparkling blue sea. Look out for seals, porpoises and nesting sea-birds, including puffins and black guillemots.

Lerwick

The narrow flagstoned main street of Lerwick, Shetland's largest town, has lots of narrow wynds (alleys) and passages branching to the busy and colourful harbour or up through the houses huddled on the hillside.

Shetland's annual fire festival, **Up Helly Aa**, is held in January regardless of the weather. More than 1,000 men carrying blazing torches drag a Viking longship through the darkened town. Finally, the craft is

A view over Sandsayre pier with Mousa in the distance

Mousa Broch

On the tiny island of Mousa, reached by boat from Leebitton in Sandwick, is the best-preserved broch in Britain, built approximately 2,000 years ago. You can still climb the dark winding stairs in the thick stone walls to the top, where only the roof is missing.

🗺 216 B2 ☎ www.mousa.co.uk

✈ To Sumburgh from Edinburgh and Glasgow

🚢 From Aberdeen to Lerwick (some via Kirkwall)

Shetland Islands Tourism

🗺 216 B3 ✉ Market Cross, Lerwick

☎ 01595 693 434; www.visitshetland.com

🕐 Apr–Sep Mon–Fri 8–6, Sat–Sun 8–4;
Oct–Mar Mon–Fri 9–5

Where to…
Stay

Prices
Expect to pay per standard double room per night, including breakfast:
£ under £70   **££** £70–£100   **£££** over £100

Busta House ££–£££

Set in pleasant grounds overlooking Busta Voe, this historic laird's home dates from the 18th century. High standards are evident throughout, but especially in the 20 country-house-style bedrooms. Day rooms include several lounges, a traditional bar well stocked with malts (and popular for taking light meals), as well as the attractive Pitcairn Restaurant

✚ 216 B4
✉ Brae, Shetland
☎ 01806 522 506; www.bustahouse.com

Eilean Donan Guesthouse and Restaurant £

One of Ullapool's many bed-and-breakfasts hides a secret: John Macrae in the kitchen. The rooms in this quiet guesthouse are comfortable if not lavish, but it is his cooking that keeps guests coming back for more. The dinner menu depends on what is available daily – fish is a speciality in this port town – while breakfasts are perfect insulation against the west-coast sea breezes.

✚✚ 213 E3
✉ 14 Market Street, Ullapool
☎ 01854 612 524; www.ullapoolholidays.com

Gearrannan Blackhouse Village £ and ££

It does not get more authentic than this. In this former farming village on Lewis' west coast, four thatched stone cottages have been turned into self-catering accommodation (£££). There is also hostel accommodation available for £15 per person, which includes a family room. The houses bear the names of the last crofters.

✚ 212 B4   ✉ Carloway, Lewis
☎ 01851 64 34 16; www.gearrannan.com

Glenmoriston Town House Hotel ££–£££

Guests at this riverside hotel in Inverness enjoy exceptional standards of service and customer care. Behind the traditional stone façade, bold contemporary designs give it a smart, stylish air, and the 30 modern bedrooms have every facility. You can unwind in the cocktail bar, and dine in the sophisticated restaurant.

✚ 210 A4
✉ 20 Ness Bank Road, Inverness
☎ 01463 223 777;
www.glenmoristontownhouse.com

The Globe Inn £

Ideal for travellers in Aberdeen looking for something reasonable in a central location; this popular pub with live music has seven nice rooms; the breakfast is so so.

✚ 211 F3   ✉ 13 North Silver Street
☎ 01224 622 893;
www.theglobeinn-aberdeen.co.uk

Highland Cottage ££

Visitors receive a warm personal welcome at this small hotel in the island's capital, Tobermory. The six en-suite bedrooms reflect an island theme, and are furnished with antique beds and thoughtful extras. Guests have the use of a lounge on the first floor, with an honesty bar, or can relax in the conservatory. Excellent meals are served in the dining room. No children under 10.

✚ 208 C2
✉ Breadalbane Street, Tobermory, Isle of Mull
☎ 01688 302 030; www.highlandcottage.co.uk

Hotel Eilean Iarmain ££–£££

Set right beside an old stone pier, this is a small hotel of charm and character on the shores of a sea loch, with spectacular views. There are 12 cosy bedrooms with antique furniture and individual styling, plus four delightful suites in the converted stable block. Candlelit dinners take place in the dining room, where fresh seafood and game from the estate feature large. Shooting, fishing and whisky tastings are some of the activities to indulge in.

✚ 209 D4
✉ Isle Ornsay, Sleat, Isle of Skye
☎ 01471 833 332; www.eileaniarmain.co.uk

Inverlochy Castle £££

Inverlochy is one of the most impressive destination hotels in the world – the Great Hall sets the tone of Victorian grandeur and it remains a castle built for comfort rather than defence. Antiques are everywhere, in the public rooms and in the luxurious bedrooms, each complete with sofas, armchairs, fresh flowers and enormous bathrooms. Views over the gardens and loch are stunning. Three elegant dining rooms, each decorated with furniture presented as gifts from the King of Norway, are the setting for inventive, ambitious cooking.

✚ 209 E3 ✉ Torlundy, Fort William
☎ 01397 702 177;
www.inverlochy castlehotel.com

Kinloch House ££–£££

Idyllically located just west of the Perthshire town of Blairgowrie, this small hotel has 18 rooms and offers top rates of service and comfort, including an excellent

restaurant. The furnishings are elegant, the lounges inviting, the bathrooms opulent, the bar is stocked with an impressive range of whiskies, and there's even a beauty and fitness centre and a swimming pool. What more could you want?

✚ 210 C2 ✉ Blairgowrie
☎ 01250 884 237; www.kinlochhouse.com

Old Minister's House £

A cosy manse dating from 1906, this bed-and-breakfast is beautifully furnished and stands in well-tended grounds. There are four, attractive en-suite bedrooms. Hearty breakfasts are served in the dining room. Children under 12 are not allowed.

✚ 210 B3 ✉ Rothimurchus, Aviemore
☎ 01479 812 181;
www.theoldministershouse.co.uk

Pool House Hotel £££

This splendid hotel is set on the shores of Loch Ewe, looking across to the famous gardens at Inverewe, and makes a fabulous base for exploring the area. During World War II it was actually used as the Command Headquarters of the Russian Arctic and North Atlantic Convoys. There are just five spacious suites, each one individually designed and furnished. The nautical theme continues in the dining room, and you can even try your hand at sea-fishing from the jetty at the front of the hotel.

✚ 213 D2
✉ Poolewe, Highland
☎ 01445 781 272; www.pool-house.co.uk
🕙 Closed Jan–Feb

Stromness Hotel £–££

A grand hotel with a musical vein, offering modern, jazz and folk, in a lively Orkney town. Ask for rooms with a view of the harbour.

✚ 215 C4
✉ The Pierhead, Stromness
☎ 01856 85 02 98;
www.stromnesshotel.com

Where to...
Eat and Drink

Prices
Expect to pay per three-course meal per person, excluding drinks:
£ under £20   ££ £20–£30   £££ over £30

Applecross Inn £–££

Good food is the hallmark of this venerable pub, set in an area of natural beauty on the seashore in Applecross village. Behind the simple whitewashed walls is a cosy temple to hospitality, with convivial company and top-quality seafood, fresh from the local catch. Sandwiches and home-made soup are available for a snack meal, but it's well worth taking your time and sampling the main menu, with treats such as king scallops with crispy bacon and garlic butter, or marinated squat lobsters in tempura batter with salad and red pesto.

🔒 209 D4
✉ Shore Street, Applecross, Wester Ross
☎ 01520 744 262; www.applecross.uk.com/inn
🕒 Daily. Bar meals noon–9; restaurant 6–9

Crannog Seafood ££

Fort William's finest restaurant is one of the best places in the country to try fresh local seafood with consistently high standards. The restaurant, with views across Loch Linnhe, is filled with the heavenly scent of cooking; the emphasis is on simple, freshly prepared dishes, such as mussels in white wine and herb-crusted cod. In addition to the restaurant, the Crannog has a busy smokehouse and shop selling smoked Scottish seafood.

🔒 209 E3 ✉ The Pier, Fort William
☎ 01397 705 589; www.crannog.net
🕒 Daily lunch noon–2:30; dinner 6–9

The Creel ££

The appeal of Joyce and Alan Craigie's remote island restaurant lies in the sheer quality of local ingredients. Orkney beef, North Ronaldsay lamb and seafood are all used to good effect in a repertoire that calls on the Mediterranean and beyond for inspiration. Scotland, however, cannot be beaten for cloutie dumplings, beremeal bannocks and soda bread – all are irresistible. Reserve a window table for views over the bay.

🔒 215 D4
✉ Front Road, St Margaret's Hope, Orkney
☎ 01856 831 311; www.thecreel.co.uk
🕒 Apr–Sep Tue–Sun 7–9; closed Oct–Mar

Lochleven Seafood Café ££

Scotland's seafood is world class. Here it is served as it should be – simply cooked with minimum fuss. Stop by for a lunch of grilled king scallops and oysters with a chilled white wine and a view of the loch, or come back in the evening when the service gets slicker and feast on a massive seafood platter that is as close to seafood heaven as lovers of fish and crustaceans will ever get. They have their own boat and also sell fresh seafood that visitors can take away to enjoy elsewhere.

🔒 209 F2 ✉ B863, near Kinlochleven
☎ 01855 821 048;
www.lochlevenseafoodcafe.co.uk
🕒 Subject to change, telephone in advance

Moorings Hotel £–££

This striking modern hotel stands right beside the famous flight of eight locks on the Caledonian Canal known as Neptune's Staircase – so it's a great place to relax with a drink and watch the boating folk working hard. The restaurant uses the best local produce, including fresh west-coast seafood and high-land game. Bar meals are hearty, offering the likes of paella-style seafood and saffron risotto, and rich game pie. Children are welcome, and the Mariners cellar bar stays open late through the milder summer evenings.

🚹 209 E3 ✉ Banavie, by Fort William
☎ 01397 772 797; www.moorings-fortwilliam.
co.uk ⏰ Lunch and dinner daily

Old Inn £–££

Looking out across Gairloch harbour to the islands of Rona, Raasay, Skye and even the Outer Hebrides, this country inn has been serving customers since 1760. The building has been carefully restored to reveal and retain original features such as fireplaces and thick stone walls. Enjoy the best fresh scallops, lobsters, mussels and other seafood in the bar or restaurant. You can stay here, too: rooms include four-postered and family rooms. Children and dogs are welcome. There's live music in the bar every Friday night during the summer and frequently in the winter, too.

🚹 213 D2 ✉ Gairloch
☎ 1445 712 006; www.theoldinn.net
⏰ Lunch and dinner daily

The Oyster Shed £

In the 1980s, not far from the Talisker distillery, a fisherman set up an oyster farm, and it has become so popular over the year that he and his family have had to continually add to his shop and simple kiosk-restaurant. While you eat, you can learn all about oysters (£1) and lobsters from the experts.

🚹 208 C5 ✉ Carbost, Skye
☎ 01478 64 03 83; www.skyeoysterman.co.uk
⏰ Daily 10–5

The Plockton Hotel £–££

One of a row of whitewashed cottages on the waterfront at Plockton, this hotel has a good reputation for its food. There's lots of fresh seafood on the menus, including herring pan-fried in oatmeal and locally caught wild salmon in season, but plenty of other options too, including venison, beef and locally smoked ham. There are 15 bedrooms and children are welcome.

🚹 209 D4 ✉ 41 Harbour Street, Plockton
☎ 01599 544 274; www.plocktonhotel.co.uk
⏰ Daily lunch and dinner

Skoon Art Café £

More of a wonderful cottage-café in the middle of nowhere than a restaurant. Go there for lunch and fight the air of melancholy on Harris' Golden Road with soup, salmon, a selection of Scottish cheeses and cake. It serves the best coffee far and wide. *Insider Tip*

🚹 212 B4 ✉ Geocrab, Harris
☎ 01859 53 02 68; www.skoon.com
⏰ Tue–Sat 10–5

Summer Isles Hotel ££–£££

This is an oasis, with something for everyone. For an informal meal, eat in the popular bar, where diners can tuck into the freshest of fresh crab and squat lobster. For something grander, visit the Michelin-starred restaurant. Wherever you eat, there are the same great views out over the water to the eponymous Summer Isles. *Insider Tip*

🚹 213 E3 ✉ Achiltibuie Achiltibuie
✉ 01854 622 282; www.summerisleshotel.co.uk
⏰ Daily lunch noon–2:15; dinner 8pm

Three Chimneys Restaurant £££

This wonderful stone crofter's cottage stands in rugged countryside, enjoying views of the sea and distant mountains. A growing following enjoys the fresh seafood and honest cooking that is on offer here. A keynote of the tried-and-tested menu is the quality of the local and regional ingredients.

🚹 212 B1 ✉ Colbost, Isle of Skye
☎ 01470 511 258; www.threechimneys.co.uk
⏰ Lunch mid-Mar–Oct Mon–Sat;
dinner Feb–Dec daily; closed Jan

Where to…
Shop

TARTANS & TWEEDS

Tweeds and knitwear are specialities of the Inner Hebrides. And there is no better place to buy Harris tweed than on the Isle of **Harris**, which is actually the only place it is produced. Signs all along the Golden Road advertise locally made tweed.

You can also buy it by the metre (as well as watch demonstrations of how it is made) at the **Lewis Loom Centre** (► 152). On Orkney, **Judith Glue's** (25 Broad Street, Kirkwall; tel: 01856 874 225) sells Orcadian knitwear, jewellery, pottery and stoneware.

CRAFTS

Besides **Sheila Fleet's** runes jewellery, there is also a **crafts trail**: www.orkneydesignercrafts. com/craft-trail.

FOOD

Brodie Country Fare (tel: 01309 641 555), on the road from Nairn to Forres, sells cheeses, chutneys and other deli delights. **Moniak Castle Wineries** (tel: 01463 831 283), at Inverness, creates a variety of country-style wines, liquors and preserves from plants such as birch and elderflower and from strawberries.

There are many whisky shops and distilleries. Try the **Whisky Shop** in Dufftown (1 Fife Street; tel: 01340 821 097 or the **Highland Park Distillery** (tel: 01856 874 619) in Kirkwall.

Visitors with a sweeter tooth can buy Walkers shortbread from the factory shop in Aberlour-on-Spey.

Where to…
Go Out

CONCERTS & CEILIDHS

During the summer the Highlands are jumping. The best events are the local ceilidhs (traditional Gaelic social gathering) held in village halls, but you'll need to search for them. Ask at tourist offices or look out for posters.

The **Ceilidh Place** (14 West Argyle Street; tel: 01854 612 103) in Ullapool is the best place in the Highlands for live traditional music and dancing, which takes place every evening during the summer.

In Aberdeen try the **Lemon Tree** arts centre, café and restaurant (5 West North Street; tel: 01224 641 122). In Inverness the excellent **Johnny Foxes** (26 Bank Street; tel: 01463 236557), by the riverside, holds regular live music nights.

THEATRE

Mull Theatre (tel: 01688 302828) is still one of the smallest theatres in Scotland, despite new, larger premises at Druimfin, just outside Tobermory. Advance reservations are recommended.

The **Eden Court** (Bishops Road, Inverness; tel: 01463 234 234) is among the top provincial theatres in Britain, staging classical drama, dance, pop music and opera. It also hosts ceilidhs and piping events in the summer.

Aberdeen has the **His Majesty's Theatre** (Rosemount Viaduct; tel: 01224 641 1222), while the **Garrison Theatre** (Market Street, Lerwick; tel: 01595 692 114) is Shetland's main performing arts venue.

Walks & Tours

1 THE WHISKY & CASTLE TRAIL

Drive

DISTANCE 83mi (134km) **TIME** 4–6 hours depending on stops
START/END POINT Huntly, on the A96 about 37mi (60km) northwest of Aberdeen 211 D4

Scotland is famous for its ancient castles and for its whisky, and this tour of Speyside covers both. Scotland's Malt Whisky Trail and Scotland's Castle Trail have been specially devised and sign-posted by the Aberdeen and Grampian Tourist Board. Free maps for both trails, and also for the Victorian Heritage, Stone Circles and Coastal Trails, are available from local tourist information offices. The two trails are too extensive to cover in full here, so this tour combines some of the highlights of both.

1–2
Huntly stands at the confluence of the rivers Bogie and Deveron and offers some fine fishing. Set in parkland beside the River Deveron is the roofless **Huntly Castle,** with a magnificent south front, massively inscribed across the beautiful oriel windows. Its ornate heraldic doorway has carved coats of arms stretching up the tower, but the religious figures are sadly defaced. You can still see the motte and bailey of the original 12th-century wooden keep and the shape and position of the medieval tower

The stone carvings on Huntly Castle

house that replaced it. The ruins of the 17th-century palace vividly fuel the imagination. What was life like behind these walls? Narrow stairs lead from the steward's room to the lord's chamber above. In the basement there is a 16th-century graffiti, and looking down into the dungeon pit will cause a shiver.

Take the A920 about 12mi (20km) east to **Dufftown** and follow the signs to the visitors' car park at the **Glenfiddich Distillery** just north

of town. This is the only Highland distillery to use a single source of spring water and also to bottle its own product on site. The **free tour** (Mon–Sat) covers the entire process, from malting the barley, the preparation and fermentation of the mash to distillation in the huge copper stills. In the bottling plant you can see the green triangular bottles being filled, corked and capped. There is a free whisky tasting at the end.

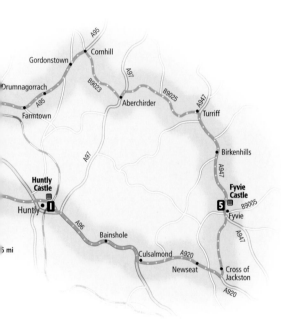

Note that Scotland has severe **drink-driving laws**, so don't drink if you're the driver. (The permitted blood alcohol level is 0.8 mg.) Instead of accepting the complimentary drink at the end of the distillery tour, ask for a miniature to enjoy later.

Full steam ahead: Whisky production in Glenfiddich

Walks & Tours

Stone figurine in the grounds of Fyvie Castle

2-3

From Dufftown head north on the A941 towards **Craigellachie**. Look out for the **Speyside Cooperage** on your left, where you can watch highly skilled coopers at work Monday to Friday. Each year, they repair some 100,000 oak casks, which will be used to mature

Insider Tip

Scottish whiskies. Standards of workmanship are high: the coopers are paid by the barrel so there are few complaints. After watching them work, visit an exhibition of the history and traditions of this ancient craft. This is also a handy place to stop for a picnic, with tables near the car park. The Cooperage is on the edge of Craigellachie. Thomas Telford's **19th-century cast-iron bridge** spans the River Spey here.

3-4

From Craigellachie take the A95 northeast towards **Keith** and follow signs to the **Strathisla Distillery**, 200m from the railway station. Enjoy a **guided tour** round the oldest working distillery in the Highlands (it has been in business since 1786), which produces the legendry Chivas Regal. Learn about whisky blending then enjoy a dram.

4-5

Continue northeast on the A95 for about 13mi (20km). At the hamlet of Cornhill, turn right on to the B9023. In another 5mi (8km) turn left on to the A97, then right on to the B9025 for 6mi (10km) to Turriff. At Turriff turn right on to the A947 towards Fyvie 8mi (13km) away. On your left just before the town is **Fyvie Castle**, originally dating from the 13th century and a fine example of Scottish Baronial architecture. It has been extended and improved over the centuries, and it's said that five of its owners added a tower bearing their name. The great 16th-century spiral staircase is the best example in Scotland. Rising up the Gordon Tower to the dining-room, its steps are 10ft (3m) wide, supposedly enabling horses to be ridden up them. Inside the castle are portraits, fine armour and 16th-century tapestries, while outside there is an ice house, a racquets court and a walled garden outside.

TAKING A BREAK
While in Craigellachie, try the riverside **Highlander Inn** (10 Victoria Street; tel: 01340 881 446) for home-cooked dishes).

5–6

Stop briefly in Fyvie to see the striking Tiffany window at St Peter's Kirk. Then drive another kilometre (0.5mi) on the A947 and turn right on to the local road. Drive for 4mi (7km) via the hamlet of Cross of Jackston to the junction with the A920 and turn right. After another 7mi (11km) turn right on to the A96 and continue for 9mi (14km) to return to **Huntly**.

Aberdeen Tourist Information Centre
✉ 23 Union Street, Aberdeen
☎ 01224 288 828;
www.maltwhiskytrail.com

Fyvie Castle
✉ Near Turriff
☎ 01651 891 266; www.nts.org.uk
🕑 Apr–Jun, Sep–Oct Thu–Tue noon–5;
Jul–Aug daily 11–5
Garden: daily 9–sunset ✋ £12.50

Glenfiddich Distillery, Dufftown
✉ A941, 1mi (1.5km) north of Dufftown
☎ 01340 820373;
www.glenfiddich.com
🕑 Mon–Fri 9:30–4
✋ Tour from £10

Huntly Castle
☎ 01466 793 191;
www.historic-scotland.gov.uk
🕑 Apr–Sep 9:30–5:30;
Oct –Mar except Thu 10–4 ✋ £5.50

Speyside Cooperage Visitor Centre
✉ Dufftown Road, Craigellachie, Aberlour
☎ 01340 871 108;
www.speysidecooperage.co.uk
🕑 Mon–Fri 9–4 ✋ £3.50

Strathisla Distillery
✉ Seafield Avenue, Keith
☎ 01542 783 044; www.chivas.com
🕑 Mar–Nov Mon–Fri 9:30–5, Sun noon–5,
Jan–Mar Mon–Fri 10–noon, 1–2
✋ Tour £7.50 🛑 no kids under 8

Snow-covered barrels at the Glenfiddich Distillery, Dufftown

2 SIR WALTER SCOTT'S BORDERS
Drive

DISTANCE 80mi (130km)	**TIME** Half a day
START/END POINT Abbotsford ✚ 206 C3	

An Edinburgh lawyer, Sir Walter Scott was the pioneer of the historical novel in Britain, and his work portrayed a Scotland of romance and myth (► 22).This tour explores some of the places associated with him, and also takes in the evocative and historic Border Abbeys (► 116).

❶–❷
Start at Scott's home, originally a farmhouse, beside the River Tweed in **Abbotsford**, in which his descendants still live here today. Most of his furniture, historical relics, weapons and armour are on display and the highlight is the great library of 9,000 books. After visiting the house, walk through the gardens and alongside his beloved river.

Take the B6360 out of Abbotsford and after 2mi (3km) turn left on to the A7 to **Selkirk**. In the Market Square you can visit Scott's **courtroom** (tel: 01750 20096) where Scott sat in judgement as the county sheriff. An exhibition tells of his life and writings.

❷–❸
Return to the A7, turn left and continue via Galashiels to the village of Stow. Turn right on to the B6362 and drive via Lauder to the junction with the A697 and turn right. After 3mi (5km) turn right again on to the A6089, signposted to Gordon. At the crossroads in Gordon, turn right on to the A6105 and after about 4mi (7km) turn left on to the B6397 and follow it for 4mi (7km) to Smailholm. From here follow the signs south on the local road to 16th-century **Smailholm Tower** (tel: 01573 460 365), on a crag beyond Sandyknowe farm, home of Scott's grandfather, where young Walter convalesced after contracting polio. It was here that he first heard the old tales, ballads and legends that gave him a love of Scottish history and a taste for adventure. One of his earliest works, inspired by his visit to Smailholm Tower, was a collection of songs and ballads, published as the *Minstrelsy of the Scottish Border*. A display within the tower illustrates that work.

❸–❹
Return to the B6397 and continue to the junction with the A6089 and turn right for Kelso. Stroll round the wide market square surrounded by fine Georgian buildings then briefly look at the ruins of **Kelso Abbey**. Leave Kelso on the A698 and after 9mi (14km) turn left on to the A68,

Dryburg Abbey was Scott's "romantic" ruins

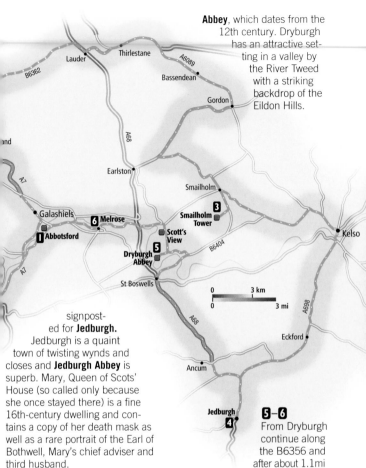

Abbey, which dates from the 12th century. Dryburgh has an attractive setting in a valley by the River Tweed with a striking backdrop of the Eildon Hills.

signposted for **Jedburgh**. Jedburgh is a quaint town of twisting wynds and closes and **Jedburgh Abbey** is superb. Mary, Queen of Scots' House (so called only because she once stayed there) is a fine 16th-century dwelling and contains a copy of her death mask as well as a rare portrait of the Earl of Bothwell, Mary's chief adviser and third husband.

4-5
Return on the A68 north from Jedburgh and at St Boswells turn right on the B6404. After about 2.5km (1.5mi) turn left on to the B6356 and shortly afterwards turn left and follow the signs for **Dryburgh**

TAKING A BREAK
Picnic on the well-kept lawns of Dryburgh Abbey or try **Burt's Hotel** (Market Square, Melrose; tel: 01896 822 285), a former coaching inn with a good selection of malt whiskies.

5-6
From Dryburgh continue along the B6356 and after about 1.1mi (5km) you'll come to **Scott's View**, his favourite vista. Take the next local road on the left, keep left at the next junction and fork left. Take the B6360, then immediately join the A68. At the roundabout take the A6091 towards **Melrose** to visit the richest of the abbeys. The heart of Robert the Bruce is said to be buried under the altar.

6-1
Leave Melrose on the B6374, turn left on to the B6360 and then right on to the A6091. Turn left on to the A7 and left again on to a local road. Follow the signs back to **Abbotsford**.

3 THE STREETS OF GLASGOW

Walk

DISTANCE 6mi (10km)   **TIME** 4 hours
START/END POINT George Square, opposite Queen
Street Station (►82) ✚ 203 E2

Glasgow's reputation is riding high.
It is a former "European City of
Culture", it was awarded a global
award for excellence in applying
technology to regeneration of the
city in 2004, and it hosted the
Commonwealth Games in 2014.

The 17th-century Tolbooth Steeple guards
the old High Street

1–2

The tour starts at **Queen Street
Station**, behind which there is also
a multi-storey car park. From the

south side of the station cross
into vibrant George Square. The
square is dominated by the
Victorian **City Chambers,** built in
Italian Renaissance style (►82).
Turn left, then left again up
Hanover Street and turn right on
to Cathedral Street, which gets very
busy. At the end of the road cross
over into a little square encircling
12th-century **Glasgow Cathedral**
(►91). Overlooking it are the
elaborate Doric columns and neoclassical temples of the cemetery
known as the Necropolis, modelled
on the Père Lachaise cemetery in
Paris. Opposite the cathedral, in
the High Street, is the 15th-century
Provand's Lordship, Glasgow's oldest house (►91) and below it is
the **St Mungo Museum** (►90).

2–3

Turn left from the cathedral (or
right from Provand's Lordship) and
carry on down the High Street for
about 800m until you reach the
distinctive 125ft (38m) **Tolbooth**

Window detail from Provand's Lordship, Glasgow's oldest house

The Streets Of Glasgow

❸–❹

A large, red complex built in 1889, this was originally **Templeton's Carpet Factory**. With its ornate arched windows, turrets, delicate mosaics and tiles it looks more like a palace than a factory; the architect William Leiper modelled it on the Doge's Palace in Venice. It is bold and uncompromising – just like Glasgow itself. Walk all the way round the building, turning right and up the path on the other side. Just past the sandstone edifice that houses the **People's Palace** museum, take the track on the left to stroll across **Glasgow Green,** reputedly the oldest public park in Britain.

Pass the spire, go right on to Greendyke Street then left to Saltmarket. Turn right, then left at the Tolbooth Steeple to head back along Trongate. You soon reach the main shopping area of Argyle Street. Turn right into Buchanan Street and past the stylish Princes Square arcade until you reach Gordon Street.

Steeple, on the right just past the Glasgow Cross. Built in 1626, it marked the centre of Glasgow until Victorian times and is the only remnant of a church that was burnt down by drunken members of the local Hell Fire Club. Cross into London Road and continue for about 1km (0.5mi), then turn right to reach the Templeton Business Centre.

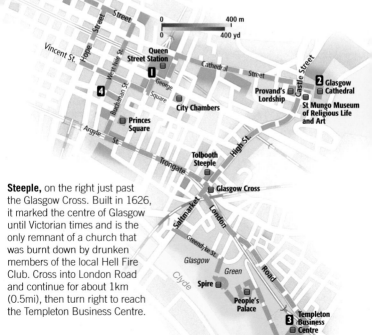

Walks & Tours

TAKING A BREAK
Pop into Mackintosh's famous **Willow Tearooms** (▶ 91) for a grand selection of tea and cakes.

4–5

A little way along, turn right into **West Nile Street** and keep walking until you reach **Sauchiehall Street.** Turn left, then go as far as the main road. Cross over and continue along Sauchiehall Street. Walking down this long street takes you past the **Grecian Chambers** designed by the renowned Scottish architect Alexander "Greek" Thomson, past Charles Rennie Mackintosh's **Willow Tearooms** (▶ 91) and out into the West End. The city's wealthier residents began to move here in the 19th century, when industrialisation brought rapid growth to Glasgow. The streets become quieter around here and there are elegant terraces, notably the broad white sweep of Royal Crescent.

5–6

Cross over, then turn right up Kelvin Way past bowling greens and tennis courts. Just before you reach the large, red sandstone **Kelvingrove Museum & Art Gallery** (▶ 78), the route takes you over the River Kelvin and gives good views of the Gothic-style **Glasgow University buildings**. Go over the bridge, turning right at the roundabout into Gibson Street. Follow this road. Then, at a small roundabout, turn right and drive uphill into Park Avenue, just by Glasgow **Caledonian University** buildings. Turn left at the top into Park Drive, then right up Cliff Road.

6–7

Turn left and keep walking round to the three towers of **Trinity College**. Go left into Lynedoch Street and right at the end into Woodlands Road. At traffic lights turn right and walk over the footbridge. The peace of the West End is left on the other side of the motorway as you walk up the rather scruffy-looking Renfrew Street. But soon you come to the **Glasgow School of Art** (▶ 92), Charles Rennie Mackintosh's most famous, and some would argue most important, work. Simple and elegant, the building exemplifies Art Nouveau at its most striking.

Go into Dalhousie Street, turn right, then left into Sauchiehall Street. Turn right along Hope Street, then left along St Vincent Street. Follow the road back into **George Square** to complete your circuit of Glasgow's architectural treasures.

Built in 1889, the ornate, brightly decorated Templeton's Carpet Factory was inspired by the Doge's Palace in Venice

THE GREAT GLEN TOUR

Drive

DISTANCE 83mi (134km) along steep and narrow roads in places
TIME Half a day   **START POINT** Fort William ✚ 209 E3
END POINT Inverness ✚ 210 A4

The Great Glen was formed more than 300 million years ago, and for centuries it has linked the east and west coasts between Inverness and Fort William. Along its rugged 62mi (100km) is the Caledonian Canal, Thomas Telford's 19th-century engineering masterpiece, which linked the four lochs of the glen – Ness, Lochy, Oich and Linnhe – with a series of channels, enabling ships sailing from east to west to avoid the treacherous seas to the north. Its 29 locks raised large sea-going vessels to a height of 105ft (32m) above sea level at Loch Oich. This leisurely drive along the canal's 22mi (36km)-length has options for the final stretch along Loch Ness from Fort Augustus to Inverness. Alternatively, make the journey by boat, or try the Great Glen Walk along towpaths and forest trails, with optional hill climbs to the most impressive views. There's also the Great Glen Cycle Route.

The eight locks on the Caledonian Canal near Banavie are known as Neptune's Staircase

❶–❷

In Fort William spend some time at the **West Highland Museum**, which has some excellent Jacobite relics. The Great Glen was Bonnie Prince Charlie's escape route into the Highlands after Culloden. If you have time, take a look at **Neptune's Staircase**, the great flight of locks on the Caledonian Canal at Banavie, just west of Fort William on the A830 (▶ 155).

Leave Fort William on the A82 and head 10mi (16km) northeast to Spean Bridge. Stay on the A82

for about 1.1mi (5km) to the junction with the B8004 to the **Commando Memorial** – massive bronze soldiers commemorating commandos who trained here and died in World War II. If you continue on the B8004 and turn right on to the B8005 you'll find **Achnacarry House**, the wartime heart of the Commando Basic Training Centre. It's now home to

There are fine views of Loch Ness from Urquhart Castle near Drumnadrochit

Cameron of Lochiel. Learn more about the Commandos and the Camerons at the **Clan Cameron Museum**, up a long private drive on the left. This is a 30-minute detour.

2–**3**
Return to the A82 and head north-east via Laggan to Invergarry. Turn left on to the A87; after 10mi (16km) go right on to the A887.

In a further 14mi (22km) turn right at Invermoriston, along the A82, hugging the western shore of **Loch Ness**, to Fort Augustus. This circuit takes in Loch Garry, brushes

LEGENDS & HIDDEN GEMS
Pass the Clan Cameron Museum, and just before Loch Arkaig, stop at the little humpbacked bridge for a view of the **Chia-aig waterfall** with the Witch's Cauldron pool at its foot. The legend is that when some of Cameron's cattle became sick, an old woman living near the loch was blamed. The men sent to apprehend her found nothing at her house but a cat that they put in a sack, weighted and threw in the water. Of course the cat immediately changed into the old woman, who drowned and the curse on the cattle was lifted.

If you clamber up through the trees here you may find the cave that Bonnie Prince Charlie hid in for two weeks after he escaped from Culloden.

past Loch Loyne and passes along Glen Moriston. At **Invermoriston** take the woodland walk to the **Telford Bridge** and **waterfalls**.

If you're short of time miss this stage and stay on the A82 from Invergarry to Fort Augustus, continuing along Loch Ness via Urquhart Castle and Drumnadrochit to reach Inverness.

The Great Glen Tour

magician Aleister Crowley, the self-styled "Great Beast". The secluded house and surroundings were, it was believed, afflicted by evil spirits, which Crowley tried, unsuccessfully, to remove using supernatural rites. Subsequently, Boleskin House has been associated with strange (although probably explicable) phenomena. The house is privately owned and is not open to the public.

4–5

Continue along the B852 to reach Dores, then along the B862 to **Inverness**.

WADE ROADS

The B862 follows the line of General George Wade's old military road of 1742. The English soldier Wade was posted to the Highlands to build roads and bridges to help control the Jacobite clans after the 1715 rebellion. For some serious walking, the most famous stretch of Wade Road runs from Fort Augustus over the Corrieyairack Pass. In its time, this was the highest road in Britain, and, at 12mi (19km) long, it's the longest surviving stretch of his original road. Before Wade's arrival, it was a drovers' route.

3– 4

Take the B862 along the quieter eastern side of Loch Ness. After about 14km (mi) turn left on to the B852 to shortly reach **Foyers** and a short woodland walk to the waterfall. From Foyers continue on the B852 for about 1.5km (1 mile). On your left is a cemetery, and opposite, partially obscured by trees, is **Boleskin House,** once owned by the

West Highland Museum
✉ Cameron Square, Fort William ☎ 01397 702 169; www.westhighlandmuseum.org.uk
🕐 Mon–Sat 10–5 March, Nov, Dec 10 –4; April–Oct 10–5 💷 Free

Clan Cameron Museum
✉ Achnacarry ☎ 01397 7124 80; www.clan-cameron.org
🕐 Easter to mid-Oct daily 1:30–4:30; Jul–Aug 11–4:30 💷 £3.50

Caledonian Canal
The canal links the several lochs that run though the Great Glen, and thus the east with the west coast of Scotland enabling boats to pass through from Inverness to Fort William. The Great Glen Way footpath/cycle route (www.greatglenway.com) runs parallel to the towpath.

5 ULLAPOOL, LOCH BROOM AND THE DROVE ROADS
Hike

DISTANCE 8mi (13km), gradual ascent over surfaced paths and hillside **TIME** 3–4 hours **START/END POINT** Somerfield supermarket car park, Ullapool ✚ 213 E3

A herd of cattle being driven through a mountain pass is a familiar scene in countless Hollywood westerns. But instead of blue sky and buckskinned cowboys on horseback, picture grey drizzle and cowboys on foot, wrapped in lengths of woollen plaid cloth. This was the wild west of Scotland, and the cowhands were Highlanders on a drove road herding their cattle to the markets of the South. This walk follows in their tracks.

0–2
From the car park next to the Somerfield supermarket, exit to Latheron Lane and turn left into Quay Street. At the Riverside Hotel, where the road curves right, turn left into Castle Terrace. Go down the steps to the Ullapool River on the right and cross a bridge. Although the road along the river is now surfaced, the surrounding hills and lochs are unchanged and the drove would have crossed the rivers by the many fords shown on old maps.

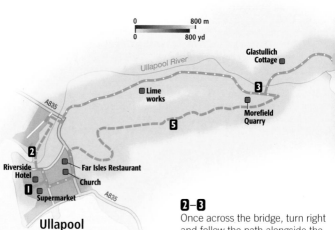

2–3
Once across the bridge, turn right and follow the path alongside the river to a wooden bridge and go up some steps. The ford is quite clear at the second bridge, and in summer you could cross by the ford to experience it as a drover would, or just to avoid the rickety bridge later. Turn right on to the main A835 road. Turn right and

Ullapool lies on a spit of land at by Loch Broom

cross the river by another footbridge, then turn left up the minor road towards **Morefield Quarry** and continue on this road past the **lime works** on your right. After about 1.1mi (5km), pass the quarry and continue through a small parking area and over a cattle grid.

🔳–🔳

Just past the quarry, keeping left all the way, step on to the banking for a superb view along **Glen Achall** towards nearby Loch Achall to the east. When the road forks, take the left fork and continue downhill. Cross the river by the bridge and walk past **Glastullich Cottage** on your left until you reach **Loch Achall**. Cattle from the Isle of Lewis were regularly ferried across the Minch to Ullapool and were then driven through Glen Achall, making for the sales at Ardgay – a journey of more than 149mi (240km), excluding the

trip across the water. From Loch Achall the drove road continues for a fair distance.

🔳–🔳

At the loch, you can turn left or right to walk a short distance along its shore. A bridge across the neck of the loch has collapsed, so retrace your steps to the junction and turn left downhill to a cattle grid, where

TAKING A BREAK

Call in for a meal at the informal **Ceilidh Place** (14 West Argyle Street, Ullapool; tel: 01854 612 103) owned by Jean Urquhart, widow of the actor Robert Urquhart. The venue is home to a bar, bookshop and art gallery. During the summer, there is also live entertainment in the form of traditional music and dancing in the evenings.

During the summer you can explore Loch Broom and its islands by boat

a path heads up along a line of trees on your right. The path is not obvious at this point, but in about 90m you'll see a deer fence with a kissing gate. Go through the gate and follow the well-defined path along the side of the hill, and through another kissing gate and deer fence. When the path forks, choose the left-hand route up the side of the hill.

5–6

Follow one of the rough, winding paths down the side of the hill, through a kissing gate and out to the main road (A835). Turn left and follow the road, passing the **Far Isles Restaurant** on the right-hand side, to the **church** in Ullapool. Turn right here and make your way back to the supermarket car park.

ANCIENT TRACKS

Droving in Scotland goes back at least to the 14th century. Meat did not form a substantial part of the Scottish diet, and with no means of sustaining cattle through the harsh winter, they had to be driven south and sold. The drove roads followed the line of least resistance through straths (broad river valleys) and glens. While some of these ancient tracks are now buried under the tarmac of modern highways, many remain as rights of way (www.oldroads ofscotland.com).

UNROMANTIC TRYSTS

Moving 10mi (16km) a day, drovers would sleep beside their animals and rise at dawn for another weary day on the road to the great cattle trysts (fairs) at Ardgay, Muir of Ord, Crieff and Falkirk. The trysts were colourful affairs, with musicians, beggars, pickpockets and pedlars mingling with the drovers and buyers. Drinking dens in makeshift tents helped disperse the men's worries, while huge bubbling cauldrons of broth provided them with a warm meal.

Practicalities

Practicalities

WHAT YOU NEED

	UK	USA	Canada	Australia	Ireland	Netherlands
● Required · Some countries require a passport						
○ Suggested · to remain valid for a minimum period						
▲ Not required · (usually at least six months) beyond						
△ Not applicable · the date of entry – check beforehand.						
Passport/National Identity Card	●	●	●	●	●	●
Visa (regulations can change – check before booking)	▲	▲	▲	▲	▲	▲
Onward or Return Ticket	▲	▲	▲	▲	▲	▲
Health Inoculations (tetanus and polio)	▲	▲	▲	▲	▲	▲
Health Documentation (► 198, Health)	▲	○	○	○	○	○
Travel Insurance	○	○	○	○	○	○
Driving Licence (national) for car hire	●	●	●	●	●	●
Car Insurance Certificate	●	△	△	△	●	●
Car Registration Document	●	△	△	△	●	●

WHEN TO GO

Edinburgh

High season Low season

JAN	FEB	MAR	APR	MAY	JUN	JUL	AUG	SEP	OCT	NOV	DEC
5°C	5°C	8°C	11°C	14°C	16°C	18°C	18°C	15°C	11°C	9°C	7°C
41°F	41°F	46°F	51°F	57°F	61°F	64°F	64°F	59°F	51°F	48°F	44°F

Sunshine and showers Very wet

Temperatures are the **average daily maximum** for each month. The best times of the year for fine and temperate weather are in the spring and early summer (April and June) when the countryside looks its best. In high summer (July and August) the weather is changeable and can be cloudy and wet. Generally autumn (Sep & Oct) is more settled and there's a better chance of good weather, but nothing is guaranteed. The winter months, from November to March, can be dark, wet and dreich (dreary), but clear sunny days are great, even when cold. Winter can also bring severe conditions to the Highlands and high ground. But no one comes to Scotland for the weather – consider it a bonus if it's fine, but be prepared for rain. The cities are great to visit any time, regardless of the weather.

WEBSITES

VisitScotland
www.visitscotland.com
Edinburgh
☎ 0845 225 5121

GETTING THERE

By air Glasgow and Edinburgh are well connected with London and most other cities in the UK and Ireland. From Heathrow, the main carriers are British Airways (0844 493 0787; www.ba.com) and bmibaby (tel: 0905 828 2828; www.bmibaby.com); from Gatwick, BA; from London City, ScotAirways with Air France (tel: 0870 142 4343; www.scotairways.com) and BA; and from Luton, easyJet (tel: 0871 244 2366; www.easyjet.com). Flybe (tel: 0871 700 2000; www.flybe.com) also runs direct flights to Aberdeen from London, Birmingham, Bristol and Manchester and also fly to Dundee from Birmingham. ScotAirways with Air France operate the London City–Dundee flight. You can fly to Inverness from Heathrow, Gatwick and several regional airports. Ryanair (tel: 0871 246 0000; www.ryanair.com) flies to Prestwick from Stansted. There are non-stop flights from many European cities to Edinburgh, Glasgow, Aberdeen and Prestwick. **From the US** Continental Airlines (www.continental.com) flies to Glasgow and Edinburgh regularly from New York (Newark) as does American Airlines (www.aa.com). Delta Airlines (www.delta.com) operates between New York (JFK) and Edinburgh. Schedule and charter flights operate from Canada to Edinburgh, Glasgow and Aberdeen. Australia and New Zealand flights connect in London.

By rail The main links from England to Scotland are on Virgin Trains (08457 222 333; www. virgintrains.co.uk) and the East Coast operator (tel: 08457 225 333; www.virgin traineastcoast.co.uk), which both serve Edinburgh and Glasgow, with extensions to Dundee and Aberdeen; Virgin Trains East Coast also runs trains to Inverness. First Scotrail (tel: 0344 811 0141; www.scotrail.co.uk) run overnight trains from London to Edinburgh, Glasgow, Aberdeen, Inverness and Fort William.

TIME

In common with the rest of Britain, Scotland follows **Greenwich Mean Time (GMT)** in winter, but British Summer Time (BST), or daylight saving time (GMT plus one hour) operates from late March until late October.

CURRENCY AND FOREIGN EXCHANGE

Currency The basic unit of currency in the UK is the pound sterling (£), divided into 100 pence (p). Bank notes come in denominations of £5, £10, £20 and £50. Notes are produced by Scottish banks and therefore feature different designs to those originating in England. Note that although Scottish bank notes are generally accepted elsewhere in Britain, some places may be reluctant to accept them. You can change them at any bank. Sterling and all major credit cards are recognised.

Exchange All banks offer exchange facilities, and bureaux de change are common in Glasgow and Edinburgh, at airports and larger rail stations. They often operate longer hours than banks but offer poorer rates of exchange. Most banks have cashpoints for cash withdrawals, and you'll also find them at airports, railway stations and in larger supermarkets and filling stations.

BRITISH TOURIST AUTHORITY: www.visitbritain.com

In the US	In Canada	In Australia
New York	Toronto	Sydney
☎ 1 800 462 2748	☎ 1 416 646 6674	☎ 1 300 85 85 89

Practicalities

WHEN YOU ARE THERE

NATIONAL HOLIDAYS

1 Jan	New Year's Day
2 Jan	New Year's Holiday
Mar/Apr	Good Friday, Easter Monday
First Mon May	May Day
Last Mon May or First Mon Aug	Bank Holiday
25 Dec	Christmas Day
26 Dec	Boxing Day

When a national holiday falls on a weekend, the following Monday is observed as the holiday. The 2 Jan holiday is movable depending on when the New Year's Day holiday is taken.

ELECTRICITY

In common with the rest of the UK, the power supply is 240 volts (50Hz) AC. Sockets take square three-pin plugs for 3, 5 and 13 amp fused appliances. All visitors from other countries will need an adaptor – these are widely available.

OPENING HOURS

- ○ Shops
- ● Offices
- ● Banks
- ● Main Post Offices
- ● Museums/Monuments
- ● Pharmacies

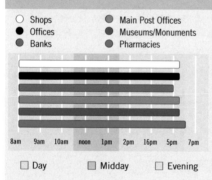

8am 9am 10am noon 1pm 2pm 16pm 5pm 7pm

- ☐ Day
- ☐ Midday
- ☐ Evening

In larger towns and resorts, shops usually open all day every day. Supermarkets open daily and close between 7pm and 10pm; some are open 24 hours. In rural areas, shops may close at lunchtime, for one afternoon a week and on Sun. All shops close on Sun in the Highlands and Islands, and attractions may not be open on Sun, even in summer.

TIPS/GRATUITIES

As a general guide:

Restaurants (if service not included)	10%
Cafés / Bar meals	10%
Tour guides	£1
Hairdressers	£1–2
Taxis	10%
Chambermaids	£2 a day
Porters	£1 per bag

LICENSING LAWS

Bargain offers are forbidden in bars and clubs. It is illegal for under 18s to buy alcohol or to purchase it for anyone under the age of 18. Alcohol can only be bought and sold in shops between 10am and 10pm.

TIME DIFFERENCES

Scotland (GMT)
12 noon

London (GMT)
12 noon

New York (EST)
7am

Los Angeles (PST)
4am

Sydney (AEST)
10pm

STAYING IN TOUCH

Post Towns and many large villages have at least one post office. Opening hours are Mon–Fri 9–5:30, Sat 9–12:30. Small branches close for lunch. You can also buy stamps in supermarkets, filling stations, newsagents and shops selling postcards.

Public telephones Public telephones are found on streets and in bars, hotels and restaurants. Some accept only 10p, 20p, 50p, £1 and £2 coins (these types of phones are slowly disappearing), while others can be used only with prepaid phone cards, available from newsagents, post offices and supermarkets. Many phones also take credit cards. In rural areas you'll come across the occasional old red telephone box, but they are now few and far between. Mobile phones have also affected availability.

International Dialling Codes Dial 00 followed by

USA:	1	Germany:	49
Ireland:	353	Netherlands:	31
Australia:	61	Spain:	34

Mobile providers and services Vodaphone, O2, Orange, T-Mobile, Virgin and 3 are the main mobile phone providers in Scotland. Pay-as-you go phones with SIM cards and SIM cards that can be used in phones that are not locked to a specific network can be purchased in high street stores and supermarkets.

Wi-Fi and Internet Many hotels and other accommodations may also have a computer where guests can go online. Wi-Fi is increasingly available in hotels, cafés and other public spaces for those travelling with their own computers. These services may be provided free, or pre-payment may be required for internet usage via a Wi-Fi hotspot. Pay-per-use internet access is typically sold in denominations ranging from one hour to 24 hours.

PERSONAL SAFETY

Theft from cars is common in Scottish cities, as are bag-snatching and pickpocketing. Report any crime to the police, and ask for a written report for an insurance claim. Otherwise, take reasonable precautions:

- Never leave anything of value in your car.
- Keep passports, tickets and valuables in the hotel safe.
- Don't carry money, credit cards or valuables in a bumbag – this marks you out as a tourist and is a magnet for pickpockets.
- Don't walk alone in dimly lit areas at night.
- Carry shoulder bags diagonally across your chest, making them hard to snatch. Also keep any clasps or openings facing inwards towards you. Remember, if someone grabs your bag, it is safer to let them take it.
- If you are travelling on an empty bus, sit close to the driver.

Police assistance:
☎ 999 from any phone

	POLICE	999
	FIRE	999
	AMBULANCE	999
	EMERGENCY	999

Practicalities

HEALTH

 Insurance European Union nationals (EU) and certain other countries are entitled to free emergency medical treatment in the UK; private medical insurance is still advised and is essential for all other visitors.

 Dental Services Dental treatment is very limited under the National Health Service (NHS) scheme and even EU nationals will probably have to pay. However, your private medical insurance should cover dental treatment. There are dentists in most small towns.

Weather Even in a country with a reputation for so much rain it's still possible to get sunburn and sunstroke.

Medication Prescription and non-prescription drugs and treatments are available from pharmacies. Over-the-counter items are also widely available in supermarkets, filling stations and other shops, such as newsagents. Pharmacies tend to keep shop hours but operate a rota system to ensure there is usually late opening somewhere nearby.

Drinking Water Tap water is safe to drink, including all rural areas and the Highlands. Mineral water is readily available.

CONCESSIONS

Students Holders of an International Student Identity Card (ISIC) are often entitled to a discount at museums and galleries. Some places also accept a matriculation or NUS card (university/college ID), if it has a photo. The *Young Person's Railcard*, available from railway stations to those under 26, gives a 34% discount on many rail fares, the *National Express Discount Card* allows 30 per cent off coach fares.
Senior Citizens get reductions on services and at museums on proof of age. The *Senior's Railcard* provides a discount similar to that for young people, and the National Express card is also available for coach travel.

TRAVELLING WITH A DISABILITY

Increasing numbers of accommodation and other public buildings are being adapted or purpose-built to cater for travellers with disabilities, but much remains to be done, so make sure you establish what facilities are available when booking.

CHILDREN

Pubs and bars operate individual admission policies and may admit children during the day and early evening. Special attractions for kids are marked out with the logo shown above.

RESTROOMS

Public toilets are mainly clean and safe, especially in shopping malls, large supermarkets, department stores etc. Some are coin entry, while others are free.

LOST PROPERTY

You should report the loss of property to the nearest police station and get a signed and dated copy of the paperwork for insurance claims. Items lost on public transport should be reported to the operator.

CONSULATES & HIGH COMMISSIONS

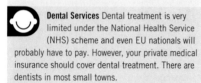

USA
(Edinburgh)
☎ 0131 556 8315

Canada
(Edinburgh)
☎ 0770 2359 916

Ireland
(Edinburgh)
☎ 0131 226 7711

Australia
(London)
☎ 0207 887 5816

New Zealand
(Edinburgh)
☎ 0131 222 8109

Road Atlas

For chapters: See inside front cover

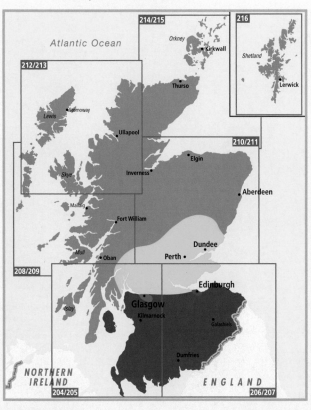

214/215

Atlantic Ocean

Orkney

● Kirkwall

216

Shetland

● Lerwick

212/213

Thurso

Lewis

● Stornoway

● Ullapool

210/211

Elgin ●

Skye

Inverness ●

Aberdeen ●

Mallaig ●

Fort William ●

Mull

Dundee ●

● Oban

Perth ●

208/209

Islay

Edinburgh ●

Glasgow ●

Kilmarnock ●

Galashiels ●

NORTHERN IRELAND

Dumfries ●

ENGLAND

204/205

206/207

214/215
216
212/213
210/211
208/209
204/205
206/207

Key to Road Atlas

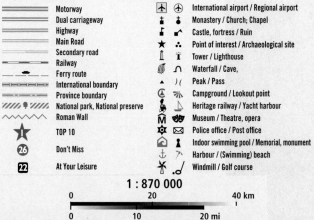

═══════ Motorway	✈ ⊕ International airport / Regional airport
═══════ Dual carriageway	♨ ♦ Monastery / Church; Chapel
─────── Highway	♟ ↙ Castle, fortress / Ruin
─────── Main Road	★ ∴ Point of interest / Archaeological site
─────── Secondary road	⌂ ☖ Tower / Lighthouse
─┴─┴─ Railway	⋔ ∩ Waterfall / Cave,
─●─●─ Ferry route	▲)(Peak / Pass
─┼─┼─ International boundary	⊙ ☈ Campground / Lookout point
─·─·─ Province boundary	♞ ⚓ Heritage railway / Yacht harbour
///// ♠ ///// National park, National preserve	Ⓜ 🎭 Museum / Theatre, opera
∿∿∿∿∿ Roman Wall	⊠ ✉ Police office / Post office
★ TOP 10	⌂ ♦ Indoor swimming pool / Memorial, monument
㉖ Don't Miss	⚓ ⚲ Harbour / (Swimming) beach
㉒ At Your Leisure	✗ ♦ Windmill / Golf course

1 : 870 000

0	20	40 km

0	10	20 mi

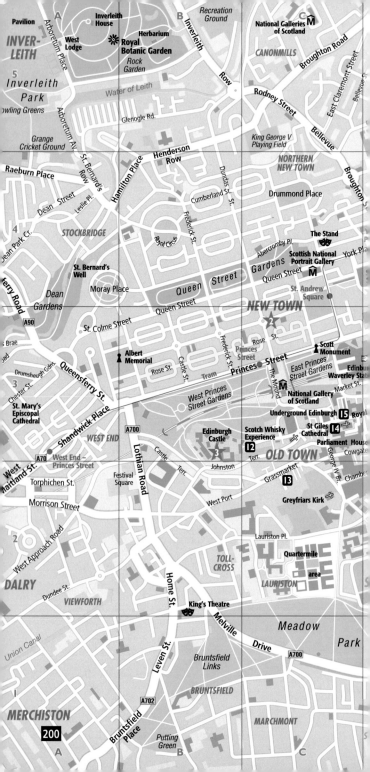

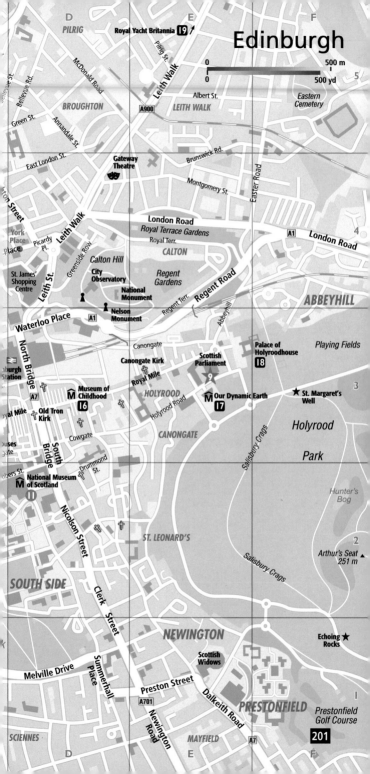

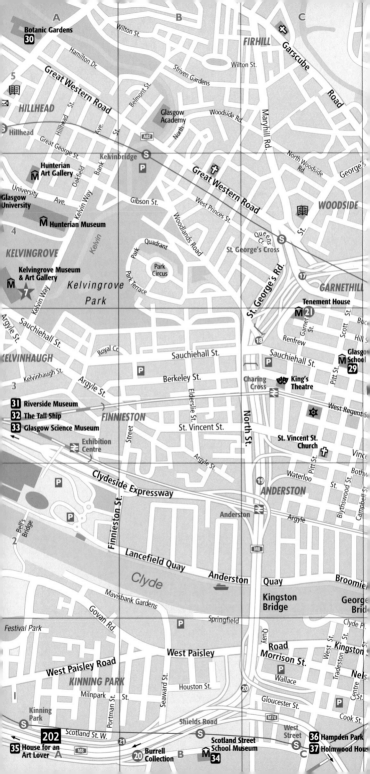

Botanic Gardens
30

FIRHILL

Garscube

Road

Wilton St.

Striven Gardens

Wilton St.

Woodside Rd

Maryhill Rd.

George's

5

Hamilton Dr.

Great Western Road

HILLHEAD

Hillhead

Glasgow
Academy

North

Woodside Rd

North Woodside Rd.

WOODSIDE

Hunterian
Art Gallery

Kelvinbridge

Great Western Road

Hunterian
Art Gallery

Oakfield

Bank

Hillhead St.

Kelvin Way

Glasgow
University

University

Ave.

Gibson St.

West Princes St.

Queens

St.

Hunterian Museum

Kelvin

Woodlands Road

St. George's Cross

4

KELVINGROVE

Quadrant

Park

St. George's Rd.

17

GARNETHILL

Kelvingrove Museum
& Art Gallery

7

Kelvingrove
Park

Park
Circus

Park Terrace

Park Circus

Tenement House

21

Garnet St.

Scott St.

Hill St.

Buc

SAUCHIEHALL ST.

Kelvinhaugh St.

Sauchiehall St.

Royal Cr

Sauchiehall St.

Renfrew

18

Sauchiehall St.

Pitt St.

Glasgow
School
29

KELVINHAUGH

Argyle St.

Berkeley St.

Charing
Cross

King's
Theatre

31 Riverside Museum

32 The Tall Ship

33 Glasgow Science Museum

FINNIESTON

Street

Elderslie St.

St. Vincent St.

North St.

West Regent St.

St. Vincent St.
Church

Vince

Exhibition
Centre

Argyle St.

Clydeside Expressway

Waterloo

Pitt St.

Blythswood St.

Bothw

St.

19

ANDERSTON

Campbell St.

Finnieston St.

Anderston

Argyle

Bell's
Bridge

Lancefield Quay

M8

2

Clyde

Mavisbank Gardens

Govan Rd.

Anderston

Quay

Kingston
Bridge

Broomie

George
Bridge

Festival Park

Springfield

Road
Morrison St.

Clyde P.

Kingston

WEST PAISLEY

West St.

Tradeston St.

Nels

Centre

KINNING PARK

West Paisley Road

Milnpark

Portman St.

St.

Houston St.

Wallace

Gloucester St.

Cook St.

Kinning
Park

Seaward St.

Scotland St. W.

M8

21

Shields Road

M74

West
Street

202

35 House for an
Art Lover

A

20 Burrell
Collection

B

Scotland Street
School Museum

34

C

36 Hampden Park

37 Holmwood House

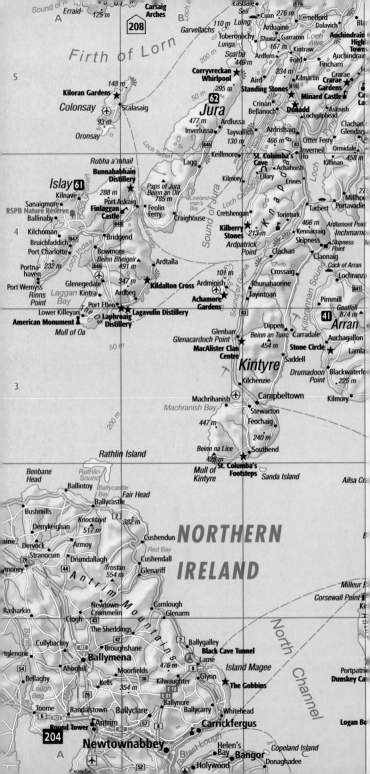

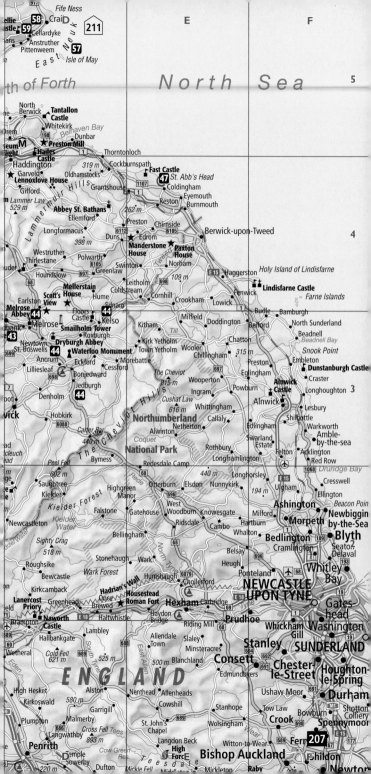

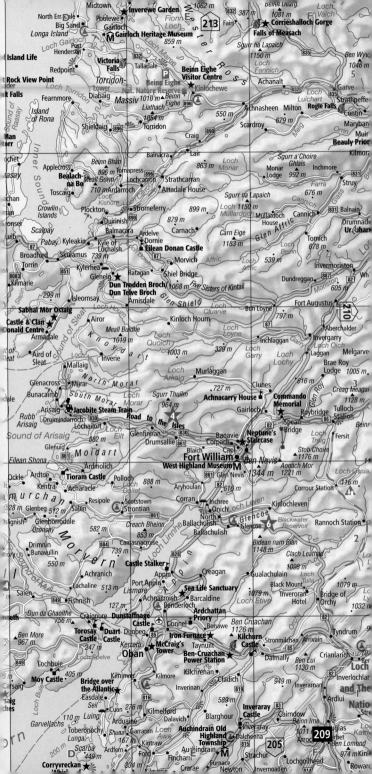

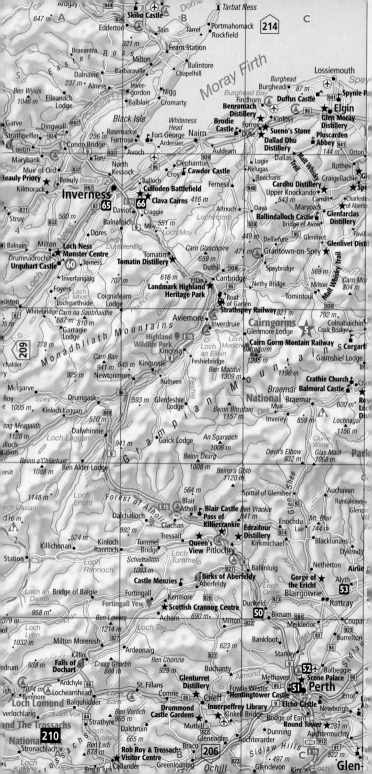

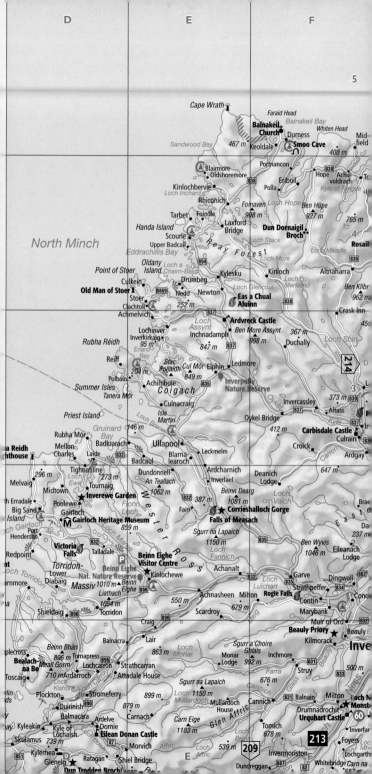

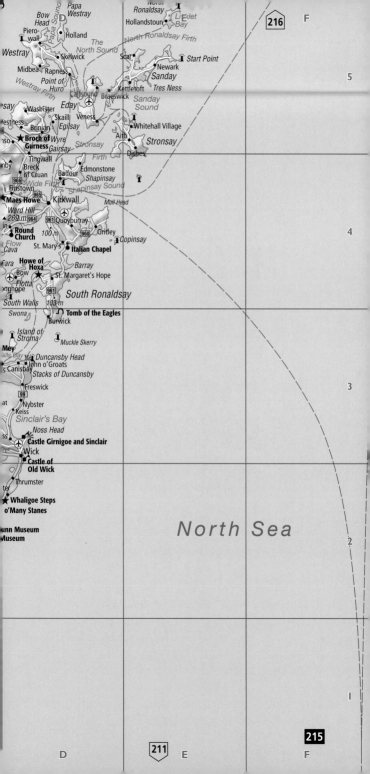

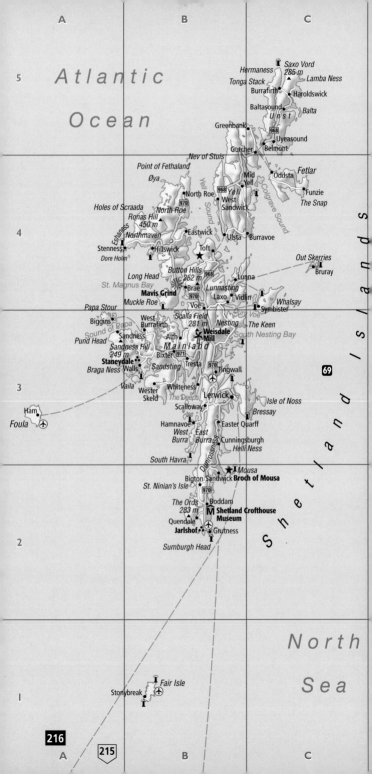

Atlantic Ocean

A5 Atlantic Ocean

Hermaness Saxo Vord 285 m
Tonga Stack Lamba Ness
Burrafirth
Baltasound Haroldswick
Balta
Unst
Greenbank
Uyeasound
Gutcher Belmont
Nev of Stuis
Point of Fethaland
Øya Mid *Fetlar*
North Roe Yell Oddsta Funzie
[968] West *The Snap*
Holes of Scraada North Roe Sandwick
Ronas Hill [970] Ulsta Burravoe
450 m
Eshaness Northmaven Eastwick
Stenness Hillswick Toft
Dore Holm
Long Head Button Hills [968] Out Skerries
262 m Lunna Bruray
St. Magnus Bay
Mavis Grind Brae Lunnasting
Muckle Roe [970] Laxo Vidlin
Voe Symbister Whalsay
Papa Stour Scalla Field *The Keen*
Biggins 281 m Nesting
West Aith **Weisdale** South Nesting Bay
Burrafirth **Mill**
Pund Head Sandness *Mainland*
Sandness Hill Bixter Tresta [69]
249 m
Staneydale [971]
Braga Ness Walls Sandsting Tingwall
Vaila [970]
Wester Whiteness
Skeld *The Deeps* **Lerwick**
Ham Scalloway *Isle of Noss*
Foula Hamnavoe Bressay
West Easter Quarff
Burra East Cunningsburgh
Burra *Helli Ness*
South Havra
Bigton Sandwick *Mousa*
St. Ninian's Isle **Broch of Mousa**
[970]
The Ords Boddam
283 m M **Shetland Crofthouse**
Quendale **Museum**
Jarlshof Grutness
Sumburgh Head

North Sea

Fair Isle
Stonybreak

St. Magnus Bay
Sound of Papa
Yell Sound
Colgrave Sound
Dales Voe
Durrossness
Shetland Islands

Index

Index

Index

Picture Credits

AA: 10 (left), 26, 29, 51, 89, M Alexander 90, 92 (bottom), 103 (top), 104, 117, S Anderson 109, 111, 132, 133 (top), 163, 181, J Beazley 50, 191, K Blackwell 60, L Campbell 10 (right), J Carnie 155, D Corrance 66, S Day 125, 126, 131, 133 (bottom), 145, 147, 156, 187, E Ellington 32/33, 170, 178, 180, R Elliot 166, S Gibson 14, 87, 88, 91, 113, 185, M Hamblin 11, 158/159, J Henderson 152, 157, 162, K Paterson 27, 64, 105, 127 (bottom), 197, D W Robertson 124, 128, J Smith 32, 55, 56, 57, 65, 127 (top), 136, 139, 159, 160, 160/161, 165, 188, R Weir 134, 149, 168, S Whitehorne 15, 76, 78, 83, 85, 92 (top), 94, 110, 146, 150, 164, 167, 171, 184, 186, H Williams 130

akg-images/VIEW Pictures Ltd.: 63

Bildagentur Huber/Justin Foulkes: 153

Corbis: 18, Bettmann 19, Demotix/Ken Jack 31, TWPhoto 34 (left), Reuters/Dylan Martinez 34 (centre), Bettmann 34 (right), Demotix/Tony Clerkson 81, In Pictures/Barry Lewis 86

DuMont Bildarchiv: Jörg Modrow 17 (top), Axel M Mosler 48, 103 (bottom), 151, 154, 169, 179, 182

Getty Images: John Finney Photography 4, Lonely Planet 13 (left), William Shaw 13 (right), VisitBritain/Britain on View 17 (bottom), Redferns/Ross Gilmore 21 (bottom), Culture Club 23, AFP/Paul Ellis 30, VisitBritain/Britain on View 54, Sean Caffrey 59, VisitBritain/Britain on View 80, Andy Linden 106/107, Epics/RDImages 108, DEA/J Ciganovic 116

laif: hemis.fr/Bertrand Rieger 7, hemis.fr/Sylvain Cordier 8, Gerald Hänel 21 (top) 77, Dagmar Schwelle 49, 52, Arcaid/Nicholas Kane 61, Thomas Linkel 79, hemis.fr/Giuglio Gil 82, Loop Images/Cath Evans 115

mauritius images: age 53, 84, Prisma 112, Alamy 17 (centre)

picture-alliance: empics/Andrew Milligan 24, dpa 25, Arco Images 192

On the cover: huber-images.de/Spila Riccardo (top), laif/Gerald Haenel (bottom), Getty Images (background)

Credits

1st Edition 2017

Worldwide Distribution: Marco Polo Travel Publishing Ltd
Pinewood, Chineham Business Park
Crockford Lane, Chineham
Basingstoke, Hampshire RG24 8AL, United Kingdom.
© MAIRDUMONT GmbH & Co. KG, Ostfildern

Authors: Hugh Taylor, Moira McCrossan, Elizabeth Carter,
Jenny McKelvie, Robin McKelvie, Martin Müller
Editor: b2 Text- und Redaktionsbüro (Gabriele Gaßmann)
Revised editing and translation: Sarah Trenker, Munich
Program supervisor: Birgit Borowski
Chief editor: Rainer Eisenschmid

Cartography: © MAIRDUMONT GmbH & Co. KG, Ostfildern
3D-illustrations: jangled nerves, Stuttgart

Printed in China

Despite all of our authors' thorough research, errors can creep in.
The publishers do not accept any liability for this. Whether you
want to praise us, alert us to errors or give us a personal tip –
please don't hesitate to email or post to:

MARCO POLO Travel Publishing Ltd
Pinewood, Chineham Business Park
Crockford Lane, Chineham
Basingstoke, Hampshire RG24 8AL
United Kingdom
Email: sales@marcopolouk.com

FSC
www.fsc.org
MIX
Paper from
responsible sources
FSC® C124385

10 REASONS
TO COME BACK AGAIN

1. **The wind and clouds** continually create fascinating formations in the Scottish sky.

2. No other country offers so many wonderful **golf courses**.

3. **Fish & Chips** are generally so fresh and piping hot here that you could eat them every day.

4. There are tons of beautiful **old pubs** waiting to be discovered on your country walks.

5. **Scottish whisky** is the "water of life", and it tastes best at its source.

6. **My home is a castle** – and in Scotland you can visit a different laird every day.

7. **Excellent beaches** are the norm here – and nobody minds their solitary nature.

8. Even though it's the umpteenth visit to Scotland, you still haven't managed to see the **Shetlands**.

9. The bewitching **aroma of peat fires** will soon have you back in the Highlands.

10. Some time or other you are bound to run into **Harry Potter** or **Sean Connery**!